G000129207

For Richard

Examining British Politics

A.J. Baker

Senior History Master/Head of Sixth Form,
The Hulme Grammar School for Boys, Oldham

Hutchinson
London Melbourne Sydney Auckland Johannesburg

Hutchinson Education

An imprint of Century Hutchinson Ltd

62–65 Chandos Place, London WC2N 4NW
and 51 Washington Street, Dover, New Hampshire 03820, USA

Century Hutchinson Publishing Group (Australia) Pty Ltd
16–22 Church Street, Hawthorn, Melbourne, Victoria 3122

Century Hutchinson Group (NZ) Ltd
32–34 View Road, PO Box 40–086, Glenfield, Auckland 10

Century Hutchinson Group (SA) (Pty) Ltd
PO Box 337, Bergvlei 2012, South Africa

First published 1980
Reprinted 1982
Reprinted with minor alterations, 1983
Second edition 1984
Reprinted 1985
Third edition 1986

Set in Century Schoolbook

Printed and bound in Great Britain by
Anchor Brendon Ltd, Tiptree, Essex

British Library Cataloguing in Publication Data
Baker, A.J. (Andrew John)
  Examining British politics.—2nd ed.
  1. Great Britain—Politics and
  government—1979–
  I. Title
  320.941   JN231
Library of Congress Cataloging in Publication Data
Baker, A.J. (Andrew J.)
  Examining British politics
  Includes index.
  1. Great Britain—Politics and government.
  I. Title.
  JN231.B29 1986   320.941   86–2859

ISBN 0 09 165551 X

Contents

Figures

Preface

The study of government and politics in schools has grown considerably in recent years. Ten years ago the subject was looked upon with distrust; it was too value-laden, too contentious and too easily abused for the purpose of political indoctrination. Today, the emphasis has changed. While political education has its critics, it has many more friends. Its value both as an academic discipline and as a preparation for citizenship has been widely accepted. In many schools it now forms an integral part of the curriculum.

This book was conceived and written in response to a need I have felt in teaching government at public examination level. Many textbooks describe the main institutions of government but convey nothing of the life of politics. In this book I have tried to redress the balance. I have not rejected an institutional approach altogether for I believe that little sense can be made of politics in Britain today without an institutional foundation. But what I have also tried to do is to place British politics in a rather broader context and to introduce the student to the debate about the subject. I hope that some will be sufficiently interested and provoked to do further reading of their own.

I have also chosen to include some source material and questions; the former to elaborate upon issues raised in the text, the latter to encourage students to think — and at times write — about these issues. Many questions may usefully serve as the basis for class discussion. I have directed myself primarily towards the needs of GCSE candidates for all the main examining boards, but I hope that the book will also serve as an introduction to more advanced study and be of interest to the general reader.

Preface to the third edition

It is little over two years since the second edition of this book appeared, but the need for a revised edition is clear.

In many respects the agenda of British politics has changed more fundamentally in the 1980s than at any other time in the post-war period. It is difficult now to speak of Britain having a two-party system or to point to an underlying consensus between the major parties. It is also questionable whether class is any longer the basis of party politics. There has been renewed talk of Prime Ministerial government – or even Presidential government — and the Civil Service has become 'politicized' in a way which few would have anticipated eight years ago. The balance of power between local government and central government has been quite fundamentally affected by recent legislation and the frontiers of the state have been 'rolled back' through the sale of council houses, the privatization of many industries and a general enthusiasm for more 'laissez-faire' economics. The powers of the police have been reviewed and increased but the 'crime wave' has continued. The power of the trade unions, on the other hand, has declined, and with it union militancy.

Whatever else can be said of British politics in the eighties they have not been without incident. This edition, which has involved substantial rewriting, has been prepared in response to those developments and to the emergence of the GCSE examinations. Many syllabuses are now concerned not only with ideas and institutions, but with issues as well. Many are covered in this book. I have also removed some tables, revised many others and added a dozen new ones. The questions too have been extended and revised.

I hope the end product is a book which will be useful to those taking the new examinations. Other teachers and students should continue to find it suitable as an introductory text for advanced level study.

1 The nature of politics and Government in Britain

The purpose of Government

Man is a social animal. Throughout history people have lived in groups and in communities. Part of the reason for this may be an instinctive feeling that their happiness is more likely to be realized within a community than alone. But people are also drawn together for economic and political reasons. Especially in complex societies, no one individual could possibly provide by himself all the goods and facilities he might need for a full life; nor could he satisfy by himself the basic desire for security.

But if people are going to live in communities, then they cannot simply do as they please. They must renounce the law of the jungle and accept their responsibilities towards others. They will need to develop rules to determine how their community is to be organized and governed. Today we can see this at a very simple level in the rules adopted by, for example, golf clubs, film societies or youth groups for the control and convenience of their members, but we can see it also in the organization of states.

States are communities organized for the purpose of Government under a recognized **sovereign**. The sovereign may be an individual, a group or an elected body, but what is distinctive about him (or it) is his (or its) entitlement to require the obedience of the governed. We often speak of sovereigns or rulers exercising **power**, and this is true in the sense that what they want to happen, they are often (but not always) able to make happen. But sovereigns also wield **authority** in that their powers are defined by, and exercised within, established rules or customs.

The term **Government** refers to something generally much less permanent than the state or the sovereign. Government represents, quite simply, the group of people who, at a particular moment, have responsibility for controlling the state. Governments can and do change very frequently (except in dictatorships, where one group of people may try to hold power indefinitely). Governments make rules or laws relating to, for example, murder, theft, taxation, property or motoring, for the supposed good of the whole society. The particular laws and customs which determine how the Government shall be chosen and changed, which persons or bodies shall be empowered to carry out the various duties of government, and what the extent of those powers shall be, are known as a **constitution**.

Government then is necessary because, as the seventeenth-century political philosopher, Thomas Hobbes, put it rather dramatically, without it man would live in a state of nature in which there would be 'no Arts, no Letters, no society; and, which is worst of all, continual fear, and danger of violent death; and the life of man, solitary, poor, nasty, brutish and short'. Hobbes recognized that without government there would be chaos and disorder, but that with government it was possible to provide the minimum possible conditions for human **liberty** and **security**. And that, of course, is what government is about. Most human beings want to feel free to organize their lives as seems good to themselves without excessive interference from government. They want liberty. But people also want to be able to go about their daily business free from the threat of intimidation or violence. They want security. Not all Governments satisfy these needs. For over a decade the people of Northern Ireland, for example, have been denied security by terrorism, and as the number of dictatorships in existence today (in, for example, Russia, Chile and Cuba) reminds us, Governments can just as easily destroy liberty as promote it. The challenge for Britain and other similar countries is to make the Government strong enough to enable it to carry out its duties effectively and to provide security for its citizens, while preventing it from becoming so powerful that it can destroy liberty. It is true that there can be no liberty without law, but the eternal problem in such countries such as Britain (often referred to as 'free societies') is to find the right balance between the two, to reconcile the claims of efficiency and security, on the one hand, with the claims of human freedom, on the other. In free societies politics is the means by which such questions are settled.

Questions
1 Distinguish between (a) state and Government, (b) power and authority.
2 What is a constitution?
3 Why is Government necessary?
4 Why can there be no liberty without law? Why can too much law destroy liberty?

The nature of politics

At its simplest — and in common usage — **politics** is about the pursuit and exercise of power. Those who dislike it and regard it as something distasteful assume too easily that people pursue power for its own sake. In reality many are driven by personal ambition, but they also pursue power for a purpose. Some abuse their power and use it for completely inhumane purposes. Hitler, Stalin and General Amin all fall into that category. But most people seek power to do good as they see it, to give further expression to deeply felt personal principles, to pursue justice or freedom or equality. It is an honourable calling.

But politics is about much more than the pursuit of power. Politics is a process. It is one approach, but not the only approach, to the problem of Government. Many are the occasions in the twentieth century when politics has been pushed aside in favour of, for example, the rule of one man or one party seeking to exercise total authority over all aspects of a nation's life. The word we use to describe such forms of Government is **totalitarian**. The political and totalitarian approaches to the problem of Government are quite distinct. Moreover, politics is quite distinct from democracy. **Democracy** is a form of Government in which sovereignty resides in the people and is exercised either directly or indirectly by them. Although it may be an important part of politics, politics can exist without it. For example, many of the characteristics of genuinely political systems (see pages 11–14) existed in Britain in the 1820s, but Britain was not then democratic, for only a small proportion of adult men (and no women) were entitled to vote. Democracy matters in that without it the wishes of the people could be easily set aside. But by itself it tells us little about how a country is governed. Politics, in contrast, denotes a specific approach to the problem of Government. Its characteristics may be summarized as follows:

A belief in Government by consent
The philosopher John Locke was responsible for developing this idea in the seventeenth century. Locke criticized the idea of kingship known as Divine Right (the belief that kings were God's appointees on earth and that to challenge their absolute power was blasphemous) by arguing that authority was something received not from God but from the people. Government, Locke suggested, ought to be based on the consent of the governed and that consent could always be withdrawn. It is one of the most important differences between political and totalitarian forms of government that in the former people may not only criticize the Government without being regarded as enemies of the state, but also cause the Government to be changed without violence. In Britain, France, West Germany or America, for example, the rulers are ultimately accountable to the people and can be removed by the people. In this sense, democracy appears as an element within politics. But democracy is present in other systems too. Russia, for example, holds elections and

claims to be democratic, but the elections are not meaningful, first, because there is only one party and one candidate to vote for; second, because the body which the Russian people elect, the Supreme Soviet, is not itself the real centre of power.

In conclusion, it is difficult to think of politics today without democracy. But politics is greater than democracy for it is concerned with much more than the periodic counting of heads.

The recognition and acceptance of diversity

In any society there are various individuals and groups having different interests and holding different beliefs and attitudes. Within totalitarian systems conflict and debate are regarded as wasteful. Within political systems, in contrast, the conflict between ideas is seen as creative and it is recognized that because no one person has all the answers, it must be possible for us to give different answers. The political approach to government involves an acceptance of the fact that different people will wish to make different choices about how they are to lead their lives and that, provided that they do not infringe the liberty of others, they should be allowed to do so within a framework of understanding and tolerance. And politics involves patience. It is an attempt to resolve the inevitable conflicts within society through discussion, persuasion and compromise rather than through violence. This is why countries such as Britain and West Germany have difficulty in dealing with those who seek violent solutions rather than political solutions to the problems which confront them. The problems presented to Britain by the IRA in Northern Ireland, or by the extremists of the right and the left are clear reminders of this. The idea that the end justifies the means, so frequently given practical expression by terrorists (as well as by dictators), is fundamentally anti-political.

The recognition that the field with which Government may concern itself is limited

This is the exact opposite of the totalitarian view that everything is the concern of Government and that the function of even art, music and literature is to strengthen the state. Inseparable from politics is uncertainty. Because dictators often seek to control all aspects of life in their countries, the pattern is in many ways more predictable than in political societies, where, precisely because Government concerns itself with only a part of national life and because so many things lie beyond its control, there must always be a degree of uncertainty. In political societies different interests and ideas compete. Some might want higher wages, others a reduction in the rate of inflation. Some might want lower taxes, others better welfare or educational services. Some might want further nationalization, others a strengthening of private enterprise. Politics is the means by which conflicts of this kind are reconciled, but the outcome is never certain. Very frequently a Government following a particular course of policy is defeated at a general election, whereupon many of its policies are reversed by the new Government. In dictatorships the direction of policy seldom changes (unless through deliberate choice) because the Government never changes. (It should be remembered, however, that in some dictatorships, such as that in Poland, the Government has been forced to make concessions to public opinion. In other countries — for example Iran — the Government was overthrown by popular revolution.) Politics might not offer certainty, but it makes violent change less likely by providing channels for the peaceful settlement of differences.

A belief in more open Government

Whereas in Russia the two daily newspapers, *Pravda* and *Isvestia*, are controlled by the state and serve its purpose (carefully shielding the Russian people from information the state would prefer them not to have), in Britain and other countries in the free world, the policies of the Government are openly debated and criticized in the press, on radio and television, in Parliament, at public meetings, in public houses and in private homes. There is a constant flow of information and comment, a permanent dialogue between the Government and the governed. Moreover, whereas dictatorships tend to concentrate power in the hands of a leader and an elite with the intention of controlling society, the Government and the legal system, within political systems power is diffused to prevent one person, party, group or institution from having a monopoly. This idea is generally referred to as the **separation of powers** (see also page 18), and its most famous advocate was the eighteenth-century French philosopher, Montesquieu. He identified three important sources of power: legislative power (making law), executive power (ruling according to the law) and judicial power (judging violation of the law). Montesquieu argued that freedom was best promoted by keeping these separate, and his ideas influenced those who drafted the American Constitution. Thus the President and Congress are elected separately. Moreover, the President, as head of the executive and head of state, is not a member of, and is not directly responsible to, the legislature (Congress). He has no power to dissolve Congress, and neither he nor Congress is able to control the judiciary.

The American experience is very different from that in Russia where the separation of powers is not recognized at all. All candidates for the legislature (the Supreme Soviet) are chosen by the party, and the function of the Supreme Soviet is to ratify legislation proposed by the Politburo of the Communist Party. This body consists of about twelve people and is the real centre of both legislative and executive power. Since 1937 all decisions in the Supreme Soviet on matters submitted to it have been unanimous. Moreover, the judiciary is not independent. The judges are elected by the Supreme Soviet whose choice, in turn, is determined by the Politburo. Even the Procurator-General, who receives appeals against arrests by the Committee of State Security (KGB), is himself appointed by the Supreme Soviet. In the USSR power is not spread out. It is concentrated in the hands of the leaders of the one political party allowed to exist. Russia is a very good illustration of what politics as a process is not about. This is not, of course, to say there is no politics in Russia, merely that it is of a different kind.

In Britain and other similar societies, politics involves a process of continuous dialogue not only within the Government but between the Government and others. It is a public activity. In Russia and other totalitarian systems, politics is a more private activity; it is confined mainly to the political elite, and it lacks that openness, vigour and unpredictability which is such a distinctive feature of open and free societies. But politics has not been eliminated altogether. The growth of the 'dissident' movement in Russia led by men such as Sakharov, Bukovsky, Ginzburg and Solzhenitsyn is evidence of a dialogue, however strained and repressed, between Russia's rulers and a segment of her people. Only when 'dissidents' and other critics come to be seen as a welcome expression of the diversity in Russian society, rather than as an intolerable threat to the state, will politics as an open and public activity have come to life.

The rule of law
This is one of the most important characteristics of political societies. It is considered separately below (see page 19).

Questions
5 Divide a page into two columns and use these to identify the main differences between political and totalitarian forms of government.
6 It is often said that certain issues (for example, education, health, defence, industrial relations) should be 'taken out of politics'. What does this mean and is it desirable? Refer in particular to page 12.
7 Politics has been described as 'a great and civilizing human activity' and as an 'evil smelling bog'. Consider the meaning behind both these phrases and try to decide which is the more accurate description.

The main features of the British Constitution

Before embarking on a detailed study of British Government, it will be helpful to understand some of the main features of the Constitution and the ways in which it differs from systems adopted in other countries. Many features, as we shall see, are rooted in history.

Unwritten

Britain is an island and this geographical fact has tended to insulate her from the major political currents on the continent of Europe. She has also been free from major constitutional upheavals since the seventeenth century. She has not had a modern revolution as have, for example, America, France, Russia and Germany. The British approach to politics has been **gradualist and evolutionary** rather than revolutionary. Our Constitution consists not only of laws and documents but also of customs and conventions stretching back in many instances over centuries. This makes Britain strikingly different from, for example, the USA, France and most of the Commonwealth countries, which have written constitutions defining clearly the powers of the main institutions of the state and guaranteeing to citizens certain basic rights and freedoms. To say that Britain has an unwritten Constitution does not mean that none of our rules and practices are set out in writing but that they have never been brought together in a single statement.

Flexible

It is a characteristic of states with written constitutions that a particular category of law (that relating to the Constitution) is superior to all other law and made more difficult to change. This tends to give the constitutions a high degree of rigidity and inflexibility. Thus in America the agreement of at least two-thirds of both Houses of Congress, followed by at least three-quarters of the states is necessary before any article in the Constitution can be changed. In Australia amendments to the Constitution must be approved by both Houses of Parliament and then submitted to the judgement of the people in a referendum. In South Africa changes must be approved by a two-thirds majority in both chambers. In Britain no such distinction between ordinary law and constitutional law is made, and the Constitution is therefore much more flexible and easily changed. If Parliament wanted to extend its own life, there is no constitutional reason why it could not do so. But, of course, to recognize that Parliament is sovereign is not to say that there are no constraints upon its freedom of action. There are but they are of a different kind (see page 16).

Unitary

States may be of two kinds, federal and unitary. In a **federal** state (of which Canada and the USA are good examples) a number of smaller states are permanently linked together to form a federation. The Federal Government deals with questions of concern to all states, such as foreign policy and defence, while the individual states have very wide powers over other areas of policy such as education or justice. In America the school-leaving age varies between states, and while some states retain the death penalty for murder, others do not. Federalism entails a quite definite sacrifice of sovereignty by the Federal Government on some questions and by the individual states on others.

Britain, on the other hand, is at the moment a **unitary** state in the sense that authority rests in a single legislative body, Parliament. Of course Parliament delegates some of its powers to ministers and local authorities, and before her own Parliament (Stormont) was suspended in 1972, Northern Ireland had enjoyed a substantial measure of home rule since the Government of Ireland Act in 1920. Moreover, Scotland and Wales have their own Secretaries of State, and Scotland has its own education system and legal system, together with wide powers over the environment. Nevertheless despite this delegation of responsibility, Britain remains a unitary state because of the legislative supremacy of the Westminster Parliament.

It was because many people saw in them a threat to the unitary basis of government in Britain that they opposed the Labour Government's devolution proposals in 1977–8 (see Chapter 9).

Parliamentary sovereignty

In America neither Congress (consisting of the Senate and the House of Representatives) nor the President is the final source of authority, for the Supreme Court has the power (which it has exercised over eighty times since the Civil War) to declare an Act of Congress unconstitutional and therefore void.

In Britain, however, there is no legal limitation to the sovereignty of Parliament, for parliamentary law is the highest form of law except insofar as it is in conflict with legislation of the European Economic Community (see page 199), some of which is 'directly applicable' in Britain without being made the subject of an Act of Parliament. But if EEC membership has imposed some limitation on the sovereignty of Parliament, there are other constraints on Parliament as well. For example, no Parliament can bind a future Parliament. Legislation passed by one Government can be, and very frequently is, changed by its successor. And there are more practical considerations. It would be extremely unlikely, for example, that a Government would break one of the conventions of the Constitution or pursue policies so at variance with the interests of the people as to threaten its electoral popularity. Governments are also restricted at times by the parliamentary situation. If they are without a majority in Parliament their freedom of action is severely impeded. Finally, all Governments now recognize the importance of consultation with interest groups before framing policy (see Chapter 12).

Bicameral legislature

Most constitutions (including Russia's) have bicameral legislatures. This means quite simply that there are two chambers (or in Britain, houses) through which Bills must pass before they can become law. However, whereas in America the Senate and the House of Representatives have equal legislative power, in Britain the House of Commons is far more powerful than the House of Lords. Indeed it is the very weakness of the Lords (as well as its composition) which has caused many people recently to give urgent consideration to the question of the reform of the second chamber (see Chapter 6).

Constitutional monarchy

Britain is one of the few countries in which an hereditary monarchy has survived. But the political importance of monarchy has declined steadily since the seventeenth century, and today it would be much truer to say that the Sovereign exercised influence than that she exercised power (see Chapter 6).

Question

8 Using pages 15–17, pick out the main differences between the British and American systems of government.

Two-party system

The British political system is commonly referred to as a two-party system. This does not mean that only two parties are allowed to exist for there is no limit to the number of parties allowed to fight elections. What it does mean is that, largely because of the electoral system (see Chapter 2), power has, in the past, tended to alternate between two parties, Labour and Conservative. How far this will continue to be the case in view of the recent marked decline in support for Labour (see page 50) and of the emergence of the Liberal/SDP Alliance as a major political force is considered in Chapter 3.

Political freedom

Most countries with written constitutions guarantee basic freedoms such as freedom of speech and association, although in Russia these may only be exercised 'with the aim of strengthening the socialist order'. In Britain these freedoms, together with the right of organized opposition to the Government, are recognized by convention although other political liberties, such as the right to vote, are established in law. They have a **statutory** foundation. Moreover, the idea of the 'rule of law', one of the foundations of freedom, is very much part of the English political tradition.

An impartial Civil Service and an independent judiciary

The Civil Service is independent of parties in Britain. Its function is to serve the Government of the day, and it has a long tradition of impartiality, which is protected by laws preventing senior civil servants from becoming involved in party political work and by the doctrine of ministerial responsibility (see page 137). The judiciary too enjoys a great tradition of independence, and because it cannot question the consitutionality of legislation, it is free from direct involvement in party politics.

Checks and balances and the separation of powers

We have seen how one way of judging whether a form of Government is genuinely political rather than totalitarian is to examine the extent to which the doctrine of the separation of powers applies. In Britain other means are used for preventing an abuse of power, as strict separation is far from complete. Thus the head of the executive, the Prime Minister, and his or her Cabinet and Government, are drawn from Parliament (the legislature) and sit in Parliament. Some judicial functions are exercised by the Home Secretary, such as the advice he tenders to the Sovereign concerning the Royal Prerogative of Mercy (see page 114). Moreover, the leading members of the judiciary are appointed by the Prime Minister and the eleven Law Lords, who constitute the final court of appeal in Britain (see page 193), are also, as members of the House of Lords, part of the legislature. The position of the Lord Chancellor is unique. He is at once a member of the executive in that he has a seat in the Cabinet, a member of the legislature because of his position in the House of Lords, and head of the judiciary with wide responsibilities over judicial appointments (see page 196). The very office of Lord Chancellor is a powerful reminder of how, in many ways, it is more correct to speak of the fusion of, rather than the separation of, powers in Britain. Finally, on breaches of parliamentary privilege (see page 70), Parliament is judge in its own cause.

Yet this does not mean that the British Constitution may be compared to that of Russia, in which, as we have seen, there is a concentration of power in the Politburo of the Communist Party. For in Britain, in place of total separation, we have devised a system of restraints or checks and balances which is intended, like the doctrine of separation, to prevent the abuse of power. For example, before the proposals of the Cabinet and Government can become law, they must be approved by a majority in both Houses of Parliament and receive the Royal Assent. Also the Government does not have the power to control all parliamentary time. MPs have the freedom to question ministers and to force them to explain their policies, and on nineteen days each year the main opposition party has the right to initiate a debate, usually on a matter calculated to cause the Government embarrassment. Furthermore, although judges are appointed by the executive, the choice is exercised from members of the Bar, which has a great tradition of independence (see page 192). And once appointed, they may only be dismissed by the passing of resolutions in both Houses of Parliament. A final example of a restraint, and probably one of the most important, is the tradition which exists at Westminster of accepting constitutional conventions and the importance of the rule of law. It is unlikely that any party in Government would deliberately seek to abuse its power because it would thereby set a precedent which the opposition party might be tempted to follow when it returned to power.

It would be wrong, however, to suggest that the system of checks and balances is working perfectly at the moment. Its weaknesses are given further consideration in Chapter 5.

Question
9 Consider why each of the checks and balances mentioned above matters.

The rule of law
Most people would agree that there can be no liberty without the rule of law. Yet, as an idea the rule of law is easier to sense than to define. The great constitutional theorist, Professor Dicey, writing at the end of the nineteenth century, thought that the rule of law meant, first, that no man can be punished or made to suffer in body or goods except for a distinct breach of the law established before the ordinary courts, second, that no man is above the law and that all are subject to the law and, third, that rights in Britain depend not upon any written declaration, but upon the ordinary law of the land upheld in the courts.

Dicey's analysis was written in 1885 and today it is not entirely satisfactory. For example, contrary to Dicey's first principle, individuals can and do 'suffer' without having broken the law. Because of the growing involvement of government in many areas of our national life, such as welfare and planning, ministers have certain powers which they may exercise at their discretion. They may, for example, compulsorily purchase land or property for the purpose of redevelopment. Moreover, in any dispute between a minister and a citizen on such issues, the matter is not settled in the normal courts but before a wide range of tribunals (see page 214) where the procedure is different and from which there is very frequently no right of appeal.

Dicey's second principle is also one not universally applied today in that, despite legal aid (see page 208), not all have equal access to the law simply because of the cost of litigation (going to law). Moreover, not all are subject to the law on all occasions. Members of the armed forces, the church and the legal and medical professions, for example, have their own disciplinary procedures. Finally, Dicey's third principle has been criticized by those who suggest that because the law passed by Parliament is superior to all other law, the sovereignty of Parliament is the key to the Constitution rather than the rule of law.

If Dicey's famous definition is perhaps no longer adequate, then what meaning ought to be given to the rule of law today? We may say that it has two main elements. First, the procedures of law themselves must be honest, and justice should be regarded as something worthwhile in itself rather than something to be twisted to suit government policy. This means that the courts should operate independently, that the laws should be clear, known and fairly applied, and that those accused should be given a fair hearing and the opportunity to demonstrate their innocence. Second, it means that the freedom of an individual may be restrained only under the law, and that when politicians or officials exercise authority, they must be able to demonstrate that it has a lawful foundation. It is no real threat to the rule of law that ministers are able to exercise discretionary powers, for those powers are not **arbitrary** (exercised without reference to the law) but founded upon an Act of Parliament. A minister must, however, in exercising his discretionary powers, give full consideration to whatever individual rights may be affected, and it should be possible for an individual to be fairly compensated for any loss (of, for example, property rights) he may suffer. The rule of law cannot by itself explain what it is to live in a free society, but it is both a restraint upon the power of government and an assurance to the individual that there can be certainty about the law and its application.

Question
10 Why is the idea of the rule of law of importance for every citizen?

Sources of British constitutional law

Constitutional government has a very long history in Britain, and the law relating to it comes from many sources. In Figure 1 some of the main sources are set out. These should not be confused with the sources of English law in general, which are discussed on page 198.

Civil rights and freedoms

There is a great difference between the ways in which the rights and freedoms of citizens are protected in America and Britain. In America liberties are defined quite precisely in a Bill of Rights, but in Britain there is no comparable statement of general principle. Here citizens are free to do what there is no law against, although, as we shall see, we are only free to enjoy our rights to the extent that we do not prevent others from enjoying theirs. Much that is implicit in the idea of rights is defended by the rule of law, which we have already discussed, and by the knowledge that for every wrongful encroachment on liberty, the citizen has the right of redress in the courts. Here we shall consider three broad categories of liberty, although readers will be aware that there is a considerable overlap among the three.

Personal freedom

This is a many-sided question and we can refer here only to some of the more important meanings of the term. We are free, for example, to choose where we shall live — subject to our being able to afford to buy or rent the house we desire. We are free to own property — although for some articles we may require a licence and some of our property (money) is taken from us by the state in taxation. We are free to decide our religion or to subscribe to no religion, to work — subject to employment being available — and to travel both within the country and abroad — subject to our having the means to do so. Finally, we are free to vote at elections — but only if we are able to satisfy the terms of the franchise acts.

But personal freedom does not consist purely of being able to do certain things. It requires also that others shall be prevented from denying freedom to us without good cause. The police have no general power to detain a citizen for questioning or to require him to offer his name and address. To make an arrest, the police normally require a warrant from a magistrate specifying the individual concerned. Moreover, to lay hands on another person without his consent and without lawful authority constitutes an assault, and a person who believes himself to be unlawfully arrested is entitled to use reasonable force to free himself. Also

Figure 1   *Sources of British constitutional law*

Source	Examples
Acts of Parliament	*Concerning Parliament* The Bill of Rights 1689. The Act of Settlement 1701. The Act of Union with Scotland 1707. The Acts of 1832, 1867, 1884, 1918, 1928 and 1969 dealing with the Reform of Parliament The Parliament Acts of 1911 and 1949 (see page 119) The Life Peerage Act 1958 and the Peerage Act 1963 (see pages 120–21) *Concerning civil liberties* The Habeas Corpus Act 1679 (see page 23) The Public Order Act 1936 (see page 24) The Race Relations Acts 1965 and 1976 (see page 24)
Common law	With the exception mentioned above, a good deal of the law relating to civil liberties in Britain is made by judges (see page 198)
Conventions and customs of Parliament	That the leader of the party commanding a majority in the House of Commons shall be invited by the Sovereign to form a Government (see page 34) That the Sovereign shall appoint as ministers those recommended to her by the Prime Minister (see page 113) That the Sovereign shall give her assent to every bill which has been accepted by both Houses of Parliament (see page 114) That the Prime Minister shall sit in the House of Commons That a Government shall resign without meeting Parliament if it has been clearly defeated at a general election That a backbench member of the opposition party shall be appointed chairman of the Public Accounts Committee (see page 80) That the Speaker of the House of Commons shall be impartial (see page 71)
Community Law	Some laws of the European Community (of which Britain became a member in 1973) are 'directly applicable' in Britain without being made the subject of a separate Act of Parliament (see page 199)
Authoritative books	Great importance is attached at times to the opinions expressed in classic writings on the Constitution, such as Walter Bagehot's *The English Constitution*, Dicey's *The Law and Custom of the Constitution* and Erskine May's *Treatise on the Law, Privileges, Proceedings and Usage of Parliament*

during any arrest reasonable efforts must be made to tell the accused why he is being arrested, and if someone is detained illegally, he or a representative may ask a High Court judge to issue a writ of *habeas corpus* requiring the person detaining the prisoner to present his case before the court. If the court finds the imprisonment to be unlawful, it will order the release of the detainee, who may then sue his gaoler for false imprisonment. The right of *habeas corpus* is a very precious one, but it is one which presumes that it will be possible for court hearings to take place normally without intimidation. When, as in Northern Ireland recently, the possibility of witnesses being intimidated prevented the normal course of justice from being followed, internment was introduced, *habeas corpus* suspended and suspects imprisoned without the right of appearance before the courts.

In what we have said so far, the emphasis has been on the safeguards for personal liberty, but of course a balance needs to be struck between that and offering the public security from unlawful behaviour, not all of which could be prevented or dealt with should the police first have to obtain a warrant for arrest. In fact any policeman or member of the public may arrest without warrant either anyone who is committing a breach of the peace (for example, at a football match) or anyone committing an arrestable offence (one for which the punishment would be at least five years in prison). Moreover, although to enter another person's land or house without permission constitutes trespass, the police may enter private premises without permission in order to suppress a breach of the peace or to search (with or without a warrant) for someone they believe to have committed a criminal offence. They may also hold a person's property if they have reason to believe that it would be important evidence in court proceedings.

Anyone taken into custody on criminal charges must be brought before a magistrate as soon as possible, after which he may be remanded in custody or offered bail before his trial. For a person with no previous convictions, bail is normally granted. Having guaranteed a sum of money to assure his attendance at trial, the accused is released. If, however, the magistrate judges the risk to the public to be unacceptable, bail may be refused.

Freedom of expression

The general position in Britain relating to freedom of expression is that a person may say, write or have published whatever he pleases (including criticisms of the Government), subject to a number of controls, the general purpose of which is to protect others and to prevent offence being given to them. For example, the law of defamation outlaws untruthful statements tending to expose another person to hatred, ridicule or contempt. Libel is written defamation and slander spoken defamation. Libel can represent a very considerable restraint upon press freedom, for damages awarded by the courts to injured parties can be high. In a High Court case in 1977, a jury awarded the television personality, Telly Savalas, £34,000 damages concerning an article about him which appeared in the *Daily Mail*. The press is also affected by laws relating to contempt of court and contempt of the Houses of Parliament. It is an offence for a newspaper to publish any comments or reports during a trial which might tend to interfere with the course of justice. Equally, premature disclosure of the report of a parliamentary committee is a contempt of the House of Commons.

A further source of restraint is the law of sedition, which makes it an offence to write or to speak with the intention of inciting others to use unlawful means to bring about changes in the Government and Constitution, the Houses of Parliament or the judiciary. And there are further limitations on freedom of political expression. The Public Order Act of 1936 makes it an offence to use threatening, abusive or insulting words or behaviour likely to cause a breach of the peace, while the Race Relations Acts of 1965 and 1976 make similar behaviour likely to stir up racial hatred unlawful. Under the terms of the 1976 Act, it is no longer necessary for the prosecution to demonstrate intent.

There are also restrictions on freedom of expression in the interests of good taste. Local authorities have the power to prevent films they consider undesirable from being shown in their area, and under the Obscene Publications Act of 1959 it is an offence to publish anything which may be read, seen or heard which, taken as a whole, would tend to 'deprave or corrupt' the person exposed to it. The difficulty of defining these terms precisely is very obvious.

A final and very important example comes from the Official Secrets Act 1911, to which further consideration is given in Chapter 7.

Freedom of association and assembly

Individuals have a right to join groups or associations of people having a common interest and to take part in public meetings or processions. This is not because these rights are established in law but because there is no general act of prohibition. There are, however, certain restrictions under the Public Order Act 1936. A chief officer of police has the power to direct the route of a march or even to apply to a local council for an order prohibiting processions for a period for up to three months. The council is entitled to make such an order with the consent of the Home Secretary. In London an order may be made by the Commissioner of the Metropolitan Police himself. In 1978 the Chief Commissioner, Mr McNee, exercised these powers to prevent the National Front from staging certain public demonstrations because of the possibility of a breach of the peace. The police also have a further general power to prevent gatherings in any public places which they have reason to believe might provoke a breach of the peace. Civil liberties are such an integral part of the political process in Britain that we shall have occasion to refer to them again at many points in this book.

Question

11 Using this section on civil rights and freedoms make a list, using two columns, of (a) the freedoms we enjoy in Britain, and (b) the constraints which are placed on the use of those freedoms. In your view are the constraints upon personal freedom which are mentioned here always justifiable?

12 In recent years a number of influential people have suggested that rights in Britain should be more clearly defined and set out in a Bill of Rights as in, for example, America. Consider the arguments which might be used for and against this proposal.

13 In this chapter a number of important words and phrases appear in bold type. Make a list of the words and, alongside each, write a short definition. This you will be able to find in the text.

2 The electoral system

Elections are about choice. General elections in Britain are about the ability of parties to govern on a broad range of issues, and they are the means by which authority is given to a particular party to provide Government for a defined period of time. They confer **legitimacy** on Government. Through affording the opportunity for removing one party and installing another, they demonstrate clearly the principle of **accountability** — that the authority of Government derives from the consent of the governed. The knowledge that within five years the Government will have to place itself before the electorate is the most decisive restraint upon its freedom of action in office.

Yet an electoral system is more than an instrument for affording choice. The particular kind of system we have influences both the choices the electorate makes and the kind of Government it gets. It might well be true that both voting habits and the style of Government would be different under a different electoral system.

Recently a good deal of disquiet has been expressed about the British electoral system. This has many causes, which are discussed below. What we shall first be concerned to do in this chapter is to see how the British system operates. We shall then consider its strengths and weaknesses and examine possible alternatives. In Chapter 11 we shall examine the question of why people vote as they do, but here our concern is with the mechanics of the system and the results it produces.

Question
1 What is meant by (a) legitimacy, (b) accountability?

The main features of the British electoral system

The franchise
The right to vote in elections in Britain is given to British citizens (or citizens of the Commonwealth and the Republic of Ireland living in Britain) who are over the age of eighteen at the time of the election. A small group of people are excluded from the franchise: peers, bankrupts, felons, the mentally disturbed and those who have committed

serious criminal offences or corrupt and illegal practices at elections during the preceding five years.

Universal adult suffrage is relatively new to Britain. Before 1832, fewer than half a million people were entitled to vote, and these were all men who held property over a certain value. Moreover, voting took place in public, and corruption, for example the buying and selling of votes, was common. Reform Acts passed in 1832, 1867 and 1884 gradually extended the franchise, but it was not until 1918 that all men over twenty-one (and women over thirty) could vote. In 1928 the right of women over the age of twenty-one to vote was granted. Steps were also taken, through the Secret Ballot Act of 1872 and the Corrupt and Illegal Practices Act of 1883, to remove the opportunity for exercising unfair influence on voters. In 1948, all forms of plural voting were abolished, and in 1969 the right to vote was extended to all adults over the age of eighteen.

But there is one important condition. Each voter has the responsibility for ensuring that his or her name is on the electoral register. This is available for inspection in the town hall or local library. The register is renewed each autumn, and October 16 is the qualifying date for inclusion on it. New registers, however, do not come into force until February 16 of the following year, by which time they are already four months out of date. When a register is about to be replaced, it is effectively sixteen months out of date. This need not deny the franchise to those who attain the age of eighteen during the life of a register, for they may be included on it, in anticipation of their eighteenth birthday, as 'Y' voters and are entitled to vote as soon as they come of age.

The register is divided into polling districts of between about 500 and 3000 voters, and each district has its own centre for polling — usually a school or some other public building. Voting takes place between 7 a.m. and 10 p.m. and is conducted secretly. Each elector is first checked against the register in order to establish his right to vote, and is then given a slip containing the names of all candidates contesting the constituency and the parties they represent. The voter marks with a cross the candidate of his choice and places his folded slip into the ballot box.

Constituencies

At general elections voters are expressing a broad preference for the party they wish to govern the country for the next five years, but they are also electing at the same time a Member of Parliament for their constituency. At present there are 650 constituencies. The two main parties generally fight all constituencies except the seventeen constituencies in Ireland. The number of seats contested by the Liberals has fluctuated greatly. In 1979 they fielded 577 candidates and in 1983, in Alliance with the Social Democrats, 633. The boundaries between constituencies are redrawn by the boundary commissions for England, Wales, Scotland and Northern Ireland every ten to fifteen years. This is necessary because of the number of factors, of which the most important are the sometimes rapid depopulation of city centres caused by redevelopment and the growth of new towns and housing estates. Boundary commissioners are influenced by many considerations in determining electoral areas. It is clearly desirable that constituencies should contain approximately the same number of electors, but this is not always achieved because the commissioners are mindful too of considerations such as matching constituency boundaries with local government boundaries and not creating, in an area of sparse population, a constituency lacking cohesion because of its geographical size. New constituency boundaries, involving major changes in the political map of Britain, came into force in 1983 and were used in the General Election of that year. Of the 650 constituencies represented in the Commons, 584 had had at least some change in their boundaries. The average constituency electorate was 65,700. The largest constituency was the Isle of Wight, with an electorate of 95,357, while the smallest was the Western Isles with an electorate of 23,020.

Candidates
Any citizen in Britain, the Commonwealth or the Republic of Ireland who is over the age of twenty-one is entitled to stand as a parliamentary candidate provided that he is not disqualified for reasons which would also disqualify a potential elector. In addition clergymen of the Established and Roman Catholic Churches, holders of judicial office, civil servants, some local government officers and members of the armed forces and the police are not able to become Members of Parliament. There is no residential qualification. In the event of a disqualified person standing successfully for election, his defeated opponent may apply to the High Court to have the election declared null and void.

Candidates (the vast majority of whom represent the major parties) are obliged by law to give their names, supported by ten other electors, in writing to the returning officer by nomination day. They must also leave a deposit of £500, which is returned in the event of their obtaining at least 5 per cent of the total vote in their constituency. The purpose of the deposit is to discourage frivolous candidates and it was raised from £150 in 1984 (where it had remained unchanged since 1918) because the trend in by-elections, in particular, had been towards having many candidates representing such non-parties as the 'Monster Raving Loony Party'. Whether raising the deposit will discourage such candidates in future remains to be seen.

Control of selection procedures in the major parties in Britain rests with the local organizations. The Conservative Party Central Office keeps a list of approved candidates which local associations are expected to consult before making their choice. The Labour Party keeps two lists; list 'A' contains the names of those candidates sponsored by trade unions affiliated to the party and list 'B' the names of other individuals. Local parties may choose from outside either list if they wish, but any other candidate must be nominated by a body attached to the constituency Labour Party. In the Liberal Party and the SDP, again, Headquarters maintains a list of approved candidates, but selection is conducted locally. In all parties, the usual practice is for a short list to be drawn up and for the candidates to be asked to make a brief speech and then to answer questions. The system gives considerable power to local activists — usually a small group of between 50 and 200 — for in many constituencies the right to choose the candidates becomes, in effect, the right to choose the MP. In the SDP, however, it is the members of the local party who finally determine, by postal ballot, the candidature, while in the Labour and Conservative parties the national organization has the right to confirm selections.

The influence of a candidate on a campaign appears to be very small and most estimates suggest that a 'good candidate' may be worth at the most 500 votes to his party. But it would be dangerous to make firm generalizations. Some MPs, such as Mr Powell when he was the member for Wolverhampton South-West, or Mr Foot, the member for Blaenau Gwent, do clearly acquire a personal following which gives them a natural advantage over any opponent.

Questions
Look closely at Figure 2.
2 Do candidates represent a cross-section of the community? Work out some figures to support your answer.
3 What are the main differences between the occupational backgrounds of Conservative and Labour candidates?

Election date
General elections in Britain must be held at least every five years in accordance with the Parliament Act of 1911. Provided that he or she gives the country at least three weeks' notice of intention to hold an election (which usually takes place on a Thursday), a Prime Minister may ask the Sovereign for a dissolution of Parliament at any time within that five-year period. It is an important aspect of the power of Prime Ministers for it enables them to choose a moment calculated to allow their party the best possible circumstances in which to fight the campaign. But the Prime

Figure 2 *Occupation of candidates in the General Election of 1983*

	Conservative		Labour		Liberal		SDP	
	E	D	E	D	E	D	E	D
Professions								
Barrister	56	21	9	15	3	13	1	24
Solicitor	26	15	8	10	1	23	–	15
Chartered Secretary/Accountant	19	12	3	6	1	9	–	10
Civil Servant/Local Govt	16	3	10	25	–	29	1	15
Armed Services	18	3	–	1	1	–	–	3
Teachers	24	34	52	153	3	76	–	95
Other	18	12	5	11	2	20	1	8
Total	177	100	87	221	11	170	3	170
	(45%)	(42%)	(42%)	(52%)	(65%)	(55%)	(50%)	(56%)
Business								
Company Director/Executive	100	47	5	4	–	39	–	34
Commerce/Insurance	31	19	4	9	–	13	–	6
General Business/Clerical	11	19	10	27	1	17	–	21
Total	142	85	19	40	1	69	–	61
	(36%)	(36%)	(9%)	(10%)	(5%)	(22%)		(20%)
Miscellaneous								
Publisher/Journalist	31	15	9	13	3	13	2	30
Farmer	19	8	1	–	1	6	–	4
Other miscellaneous white collar	24	17	23	88	1	43	1	29
Total	74	40	33	101	5	62	3	63
	(19%)	(17%)	(16%)	(24%)	(30%)	(21%)	(50%)	(21%)
Manual								
Miner	–	1	20	–	–	–	–	2
Skilled worker	4	9	35	48	–	4	–	8
Semi/Unskilled worker	–	1	15	14	–	–	–	–
Total	4	11	70	62	–	4	–	10
	(1%)	(5%)	(33%)	(14%)	–	(1%)	–	(3%)
Grand Total	397	236	209	424	17	305	6	305

E – Elected   **D** – Defeated

Source: Adapted from D. Butler and D. Kavanagh, *The British General Election of 1983* (Macmillan 1984), pp. 236–7

Ministers' freedom of choice is not absolute. In making their judgement they will be influenced by a wide range of factors such as the economic situation, the strength of their majority in Parliament and the popularity of their Government as reflected in local election and by-election results as well as in public opinion polls. They will also not wish to be seen to be hanging on to power until the last moment (possibly a mistake made by the Conservative Prime Minister, Sir Alec Douglas-Home, in 1964) or to go to the country well before their five-year period has expired. Furthermore, Prime Ministers will be reluctant to face the country in the winter months when weather conditions are likely to be adverse or in the summer months of July and August when the holiday season is at its peak. In practice the most popular months are March and October. In certain circumstances Prime Ministers may find their freedom even more restricted. When a Government is in a minority position in the House of Commons, as was Mr Wilson's Government from March to October 1974, it is clear that a general election is likely to be held at any time. An even better example concerns the position of the Labour Government from March 1977. At the time, the Government concluded a pact with the Liberal Party by which the Liberals agreed to support the Labour Government in office, thus averting a general election, which neither party wanted at that time. It was widely assumed that the conclusion of the pact gave Mr Steel, the Liberal leader, the right to determine the date of the next election, should he wish to exercise it, simply by withdrawing Liberal support from the Government. Although in this instance the Labour Party remained in Government after the ending of the pact in the summer of 1978, it is clear that the famous 'right of dissolution' is not entirely the prerogative of the Prime Minister. Indeed the General Election of May 1979 came not because the Prime Minister, Mr Callaghan, wanted an election at that time, but because the Labour Government was defeated in March on a 'no confidence' motion in the House of Commons.

Campaign

Before the Second Reform Act of 1867, election campaigns were conducted mostly on a local basis. Members returned to their constituencies for the duration of the campaign and hoped through personal effort to influence the result. The first political leader to tour the country in an attempt to influence national opinion was Mr Gladstone in 1879 in his famous Midlothian campaign. Today the local campaign still matters but not as an explanation of the result. Its importance is that it tends to bring the constituency parties to life. Party members, habitually inactive, find themselves drawn into the work of campaigning. There are many time-consuming duties to perform. Each party is allowed to send one communication free of charge to each elector. These generally contain the candidate's own 'election address', and party workers spend much time preparing envelopes. Canvassing is another essential duty, but its purpose is not, as is often thought, to change opinion on the doorstep, but to locate party support. This enables the party organizers to arrange for transport on polling day where necessary. Party officials may also help the candidate in a tour of the constituency using a loudspeaker, and the candidate himself will usually address at least one public meeting in his constituency, perhaps, if his seat happens to be **marginal**, being joined by a senior member of the party visiting the constituency as guest speaker.

The real election campaign is national and is conducted by the party leaders who tour the country making major speeches in important centres. Since the 1959 election the party leaders have developed the practice of giving daily press conferences. The importance of both the speeches and the press conferences is that they reach a far wider audience through television. Modern electioneering is done on television, and today it is inconceivable that a party leader could be successful without developing a powerful media image. For many, and especially for those with little interest in public affairs, television, and to a much smaller extent radio, constitute the main source of political information (see also Chapter 11). Parties also use television for their own political broadcasts which are screened free of charge by the BBC and the Independent Broadcasting Authority.

Although there is no limit on the amount of money a candidate or party may spend prior to nomination day, election expenses after that day are strictly controlled by law. In 1983 each candidate was allowed to spend no more than £2700, together with 2.3p for each elector in a borough constituency and 3.1p for each elector in a county constituency. The candidate's election agent is responsible for keeping expenditure within the prescribed limits. Most candidates find little difficulty in doing this. In 1983, Conservative candidates spent on average £3320, Labour candidates £2927, SDP candidates £2777 and Liberal candidates £2282. The main item of expenditure is printing and stationery.

In addition to the campaigns conducted within each constituency, parties also conduct a national campaign for their headquarters in London. In the General Election of 1983, the cost of the national campaigns of the Labour and Conservative Parties was in excess of the joint cost of all local campaigns. The main items of national expenditure are set out in Figure 3.

But despite the effort and urgency which all parties bring to their campaigns, there was until recently little evidence to suggest that campaigns influenced opinions decisively. This may now be changing. Since the emergence of the Liberal/SDP Alliance the number of voters who are 'undecided' has increased markedly and many more may now be influenced by the campaigns. Campaigns are also important in a number of other senses too.

Figure 3 *Cost of national campaigns 1983*[1]

	Conservative	Labour
Posters	843,000 ⎱	878,000
Press advertising	1,725,000 ⎰	
Party political broadcasts	306,000	182,000
Opinion research	96,000	145,000
Publications	212,000	140,000
Staff and administration	262,000	319,000
Grants to constituencies	62,000	305,000
Leader's tour	52,000*	58,000
Total	3,558,000	2,057,000

[1] The total central election spending of the Alliance was £1,934,000.
* In addition a plane was loaned, without charge, by a party supporter.

Source: *Parliamentary Affairs*, Vol. 38, No. 3, pp. 328–47

First, smaller parties very often benefit from the increased publicity they receive. Second, campaigns increase awareness of the election and probably increase the 'turnout' which is usually around 72–78 per cent although, in 1983, as low as 51.8 per cent in the City of London and Westminster South and as high as 88.6 per cent in Fermanagh and South Tyrone. Third, a good local organization can increase the postal vote. In all, there were 624,000 postal votes in 1983. Fourth, the simple activity of being involved in a hectic campaign helps to keep up the morale and enthusiasm of party members and supporters. Without the prospect of a general election campaign, many local party organizations would probably crumble. Fifth, campaigns can help to spread political knowlege. It is difficult for even the most politically indifferent elector to ignore a modern television campaign, or to fail to glean something of the policies and approaches of the respective parties and of the main issues being debated. Last, elections bring political leaders into direct contact with the people and involve them in an exercise of persuasion. Thus they demonstrate the central principle of government in a free society, the accountability of political leaders to those who elect them.

The result
At 10 p.m. on the day of polling the ballot boxes are closed and taken to a public hall where counting usually begins immediately. The result in each constituency is announced individually by the returning officer in the

presence of the candidates. The first declarations are usually about midnight. Although some results are not known until the following afternoon, it used to be possible to make a very accurate prediction of the final outcome from the first few results. With the rise of a stronger third force in British politics, that is no longer so easy, because the impact of the Alliance is different in different constituencies, and because the 'swing' (the movement of opinion) is no longer between two parties but three, and very often fluctuates in different regions of the country. When the result of the election is clear, the leader of the party with the most MPs in the House of Commons is generally invited by the Sovereign to form a Government. Should the election lead to a change of Government, the Sovereign delays the invitation until the defeated Prime Minister has tendered his or her resignation. The new Prime Minister moves into No. 10 Downing Street immediately and announces his or her Government shortly afterwards.

Because of the electoral system, general elections usually, but not always, lead to the formation of single-party Governments. To win a constituency a candidate needs one more vote than any other candidate. He does not need to have the support of the majority of voters in his constituency. The system makes no attempt to allocate seats in the House of Commons in proportion to votes, but in the past it has generally allowed what every Prime Minister wants — a clear working majority for his or her party. The merits and demerits of this system are considered below.

By-elections

What has been said so far about campaigns and electoral behaviour is much less true of by-elections, which are held in constituencies in which the MP dies or resigns in the course of a Parliament. Because the electors are being asked between general elections to choose a new MP rather than a new Government, the possibility of the electorate behaving in a more volatile manner is far greater, and the personality of the candidate is probably more important. Between 1981 and 1983 there was a series of spectacular by-election results in which the Liberal/SDP Alliance made gains at the expense of both the other major parties. Although the Alliance was unable to maintain this level of support in the 1983 General Election, and lost the gains of Crosby and Croydon North-West, it did hold on to Glasgow Hillhead and Bermondsey. The pattern of by-election volatility — stretching back to the 1960s — will probably continue.

The case against the present electoral system

Recently the British electoral system has come under strong attack from those who think it is unfair and that the kind of Government it produces is not that favoured by the majority of people in the country. Some of the weaknesses identified could be corrected without drastic reappraisal of the method of election; others are directly related to the way in which those choices are then assessed to produce the result.

Examples of the first kind of weakness are the power of the Prime Minister to call an election at the moment most favourable to his or her party (as Mrs Thatcher did in 1983), the continued enfranchisement of the 1,000,000 citizens of the Irish Republic who are resident in Britain, and the power of the local constituency organization to choose the candidate (and in safe constituencies, effectively, the power to choose the MP). There has also been criticism in the past about inequalities in the size of constituencies (although this problem has been relieved through the adoption of new constituency boundaries in 1983), and about the register (which deteriorates in accuracy by about ½ per cent for each of the sixteen months of its life because, for example, no provision is made for the removal of the deceased or those who have moved or even for the addition of those who have come into the constituency). It is also widely acknowledged that certain groups, such as the unemployed and non-whites, are under-represented on the register through their failure to complete the formal procedures.

Most critics of the electoral system, however, concentrate their attack around the second category of weaknesses — those connected with the actual method of voting and producing the result. First, there is no direct relationship between the number of votes cast for a particular party and the strength of representation at Westminster.

Questions
Look at Figure 4.
4 What injustices concerning the relationship of seats to votes do the elections of 1951 and February 1974 reveal?
5 Why did the results of the two General Elections in 1974 and 1983 cause first the Liberal Party and then the Alliance to criticize the 'unfairness of the system'?
6 Compare the fortunes of the Liberal Party in 1974 with those of the other smaller parties.

The reason for the inconsistencies to which attention is drawn in questions 5 and 6 above is that the electoral system tends to reward parties which are regionally concentrated, such as the Scottish National Party, and discriminates heavily against parties whose vote is thinly spread over the whole country, such as the Liberal Party and the SDP. In 1983 these two parties fielded 633 candidates, gained 7.8 million votes, won only twenty-three seats and yet lost only eleven deposits; whereas the Labour Party, whose support tends to be more concentrated, gained 8.5 million

Figure 4 *British general election statistics 1945–83*

Year	Turnout %	Conservative %	(seats)	Labour (%)	(seats)	Liberal %	(seats)	Welsh and Scottish Nationalists (%)	seats	Others (%)	(seats)	(Total seats)
1945	73.3	39.8	199	48.3	393	9.1	12	0.2	0	2.5	36	640
1950	84.0	43.5	298	46.1	315	9.1	9	0.1	0	1.2	3	625
1951	82.5	48.0	321	48.8	295	2.5	6	0.1	0	0.6	3	625
1955	76.8	49.7	345	46.4	277	2.7	6	0.2	0	0.9	2	630
1959	78.7	49.4	365	43.8	258	5.9	6	0.4	0	0.6	1	630
1964	77.1	43.4	304	44.1	317	11.2	9	0.5	0	0.8	0	630
1966	75.8	41.9	253	47.9	364	8.5	12	0.7	0	0.9	1	630
1970	72.0	46.4	330	43.0	288	7.5	6	1.3	1	1.8	5	630
Feb. 1974	78.1	37.8	297	37.1	301	19.3	14	2.6	9	3.2	14	635
Oct. 1974	72.8	35.8	277	39.2	319	18.3	13	3.5	14	3.2	12	635
1979	76.0	43.9	339	36.9	268	13.8	11	2.0	4	3.4	13	635
1983	72.7	42.4	397	27.6	209	25.4*	23*	1.5	4	3.1	17	650

*Figures relate to the performance of the Liberal/SDP Alliance. Of the MPs elected, 17 were Liberals and 6 Social Democrats.

Source: Adapted from D. Butler and D. Kavanagh, *The British General Election of 1979* (Macmillan 1980), and Factsheet No. 22, Public Information Office.

votes, won 209 seats and lost 119 deposits. The system is also unfair at times to major parties in areas where their support, while significant, is insufficiently concentrated to bring success. For example, in 1983 in the South-West, Labour gained 370,000 votes but won only one seat.

Second, there are other important statistical anomalies in the present system. About 75 per cent of constituencies are 'safe' in the sense that they do not change hands from one election to another. The result of the election is decided in the remaining constituencies. Those who happen to reside in these 'marginals' are more likely to be able to exert political influence than those who live in constituencies where the result of the contest may be confidently predicted. Moreover, not since 1935 has a single party had a majority mandate to govern. Labour became the party of Government in October 1974, with an overall majority in the House of Commons, having won only 39.3 of all votes cast. There are those who doubt whether it is proper that a party should be able to carry its programme through Parliament, after having been rejected by over 60 per cent of the electorate. It has also been pointed out that the percentage of the vote going to the two main parties fell from 96.8 per cent in 1951 to around 75 per cent in the elections of 1974. This figure increased to 80.8 per cent in 1979 but fell again, sharply, to 70 per cent in 1983. The British electoral system may well be adequate when the electorate is choosing essentially, between only two parties, but when a significant third force emerges, it produces freakish results which, for example, in 1983 minimized the significance of the very substantial growth in support for the Alliance, while translating a 1.5 per cent fall in support for the Conservative Party from 1979 into a net gain of fifty-eight parliamentary seats. Thus the electoral system often distorts the patterns of electoral support in the country.

It is also said that our system greatly exaggerates the importance of small shifts in the opinions of the electorate. A rough estimate is that a swing of 1 per cent between the two main parties will cause thirteen seats to change hands. A swing of 3.1 per cent between 1959 and 1964 changed a Conservative majority over Labour of 107 to a Labour majority over the Conservatives of four.

A third criticism is that in a single-member constituency it is impossible to represent more than one shade of opinion, and all votes going to unsuccessful candidates are 'wasted'. This is generally around 45 per cent of the total. A good example of this occurred at Carmarthen in 1983 where the Labour candidate was elected with 16,459 votes (31.6 per cent), although 35,669 votes (68.4 per cent) were cast for other candidates. In 1979, 203 constituencies were won on a minority vote and in 1983, the number increased to 334. Moreover, in many constituencies, tactical voting is common. Voters do not express their 'true allegiance' but vote to keep a particular candidate out. Thus, a Labour voter may, in a constituency where his candidate usually runs third, give his vote to the Liberal to keep the Conservative out. The results in Yeovil perhaps illustrate this very clearly:

	Oct. 1974	*1979*	*1983*
Conservative	24,709	31,321	23,202
Labour	17,330	14,098	2,928
Liberal	17,298	19,939	26,608

The fourth main line of criticism directed at the British system concerns its impact on the party system and on national policy. By discouraging minority parties, as we have seen, it tends to perpetuate the two-party struggle, presenting the country with a choice of extremes both of which are removed from the natural inclination of the electorate, which is towards the centre. Moreover, it makes the parties into broader coalitions than they need to be, thus diminishing electoral choice and encouraging the grouping within one party of individuals who have little in common. This problem has been discussed recently with reference to the Labour Party in particular. It is argued that from left to right at least two different parties exist within the Labour Party and that a different electoral system would allow and encourage them to seek a separate identity. The electoral system is also said to work against the national interest by installing first one group of politicians and then another, both of which, rather than building on the work of their predecessors, have devoted much parliamentary time to reversing the other's policies. The laws relating to housing and rents have changed with each Government since 1951, and over the past twenty years education has been subjected to many changes with little prospect as yet of a consensus emerging. This produces uncertainty and instability, at times for decades, over important areas of our national life.

Fifth, the advocates of change have defended proportional representation – a system by which seats are awarded in proportion to votes gained — against the criticisms made of it. They counter the view that proportional representation would lead to a multi-party system, by pointing out that we already have such a system which is obscured by the electoral system itself. They oppose the view that proportional representation would lead to instability, arguing that this has not been the case in West Germany and the Irish Republic; nor, until recently, was it true of Sweden and Norway. Moreover, there is no reason why majority Governments should not come to power under proportional representation, as this has already happened in the four countries mentioned above. The difference between such majorities and the majorities obtained by British Governments under the present system is that the former emerge through electoral choice, whereas the latter are artificially created by the system.

The case for the electoral system

The main defence offered by friends of our present electoral system concerns the effect which change would have on the stability and strength of Governments. It is argued that our system generally has the virtue of returning Governments with a sound parliamentary majority, which enables them to see their programme through and thereby honour the commitments of the previous election. Only on rare occasions, such as in February 1974, is the outcome indecisive.

Second, the present system gives the electorate a clear choice between distinct alternatives, each of which is usually capable of forming a Government without the help of other parties. Proportional representation, on the other hand, would give small parties power out of all proportion to their electoral strength, and such influence would not always be exercised in the interests of moderation, as is usually supposed by the advocates of change. If, for example, proportional representation helped to bring about a new extremist party of the left or encouraged the growth of the National Front, then any coalition agreement involving those parties would probably drag British politics further from the centre, contrary to the expectations of the advocates of change.

Third, as well as handing over considerable power to small parties, reform may transfer power from the electorate to the party politicians. If no party had a clear majority following an election, then politicians would be free to deal with each other behind the backs of the electorate to produce a majority in the House of Commons. Although he was unsuccessful, Mr Heath, having been defeated in February 1974, did try to make an agreement with Mr Thorpe, then the Liberal leader, which would have brought into existence a Conservative–Liberal coalition. This would not have been what the electorate had voted for, but they would have been powerless to stop it. Perhaps an even better example of what might become common practice under proportional representation occurred in March 1977. The Labour Government found itself in a minority in the House of Commons, and Mr Callaghan therefore concluded a 'pact' with the Liberals which enabled the Government to remain in office. Again, a Labour–Liberal alliance had not been a possibility presented to the electorate in October 1974. Such agreements of political convenience may well become more frequent under proportional representation.

Fourth, our present system, while discouraging extremism, does nothing to prevent the rise of a third party if that party has a sufficiently wide body of support. Earlier in this century, the Labour Party replaced the Liberal Party as the principal alternative to conservatism. Indeed once a party has managed to capture about 30 per cent of the poll, its support begins to grow appreciably. Similarly once support for a party falls below that figure, its decline, as with the Liberals, can be rapid.

Fifthly, the British electoral system makes possible something which may, from time to time, be very desirable; the opportunity to break with the past and set out on a new course. In 1945, for example, the return of Labour to power perhaps symbolized the electorate's desire to see a new 'Welfare State' created, while Mrs Thatcher's success in 1979 may equally have symbolized the electorate's wish to break with the policies of the 'post-war consensus' — policies to which both parties had, for many years, been committed. If Governments in Britain, because of proportional representation, were to be coalition Governments, that kind of political reorientation would be more difficult.

Critics of change are also concerned about its effect on the close link afforded by the present system between an MP and his or her constituents. Under certain proposed changes this link would be destroyed by the creation of multi-member constituencies. But last and perhaps most importantly it is argued that the results of change would be so unpredictable (in that one does not know how far voting habits are determined by the electoral system itself) that it is better to preserve a system which, whatever its imperfections, is familiar, well understood, widely accepted and which has been able to provide constitutional Government in this country for a very long period. Until great popular demand for change becomes apparent (and it is absent at the moment) there are many who feel that the system we have (the one we know, the one which has worked) is that which we ought to keep. The burden of proof, they say, is on those who would change the system, and the case has not been made out.

Proposals for reform

Over the past decade many proposals for reforming the electoral system have been put forward by, for example, the Hansard Society, the Liberal/ SDP Alliance and by a minority of politicians in the Labour and Conservative Parties. Three systems are considered below — the single transferable vote (which is used in the Irish Republic and Malta), the additional member system (which is similar, in many respects, to the West German system) and the alternative vote which was considered seriously in 1931, but which has fewer supporters today.

Single transferable vote (STV)

Under this system constituencies are much larger than at present, each containing perhaps five members. Each party nominates candidates — usually as many as there are vacant seats — and voters number the candidates on the ballot paper in order of preference. Thus it is possible to cast five votes for one party or to spread choices between parties. To decide which candidates have been elected, the necessary quota of votes is calculated according to the formula:

$$\text{Quota} = \frac{\text{total votes cast}}{\text{number of seats to be filled} + 1} + 1$$

First preferences are counted, and if a candidate achieves more than the quota, he is elected and his surplus votes (the difference between the quota and the votes he received) are distributed according to second preference. If no candidate reaches the quota, the votes of the least popular candidate are distributed according to second preference. The two processes are repeated until five candidates achieve the required quota.

The system is complicated and time-consuming, but it does have certain specific advantages. It allows the elector to choose between a variety of candidates offered by the same party. The importance of the candidate himself is therefore increased and the power of the local party organization diminished. Moreover, as the single transferable vote allows the voter more freedom to vote for more than one party, it allows him to support candidates who favour the same policies. For example, a voter may feel so strongly about the European Economic Community that he would like to give his votes to candidates from different parties who share his views. The single transferable vote would make this possible.

Additional member system (AMS)
This system has been supported by the Hansard Society which has proposed the following version of it. The House of Commons would have 640 MPs of whom 480 would be elected, as at present in single-member constituencies. This would involve an increase in the average size of constituency from 65,000 to about 85,000. The remaining 160 seats would be for 'additional members' to represent Scotland, Wales, Northern Ireland and the English regions. To qualify for an additional member in a particular region, a party would have to obtain at least 5 per cent of the total votes cast in the region. Candidates not directly elected would be placed in order according to the percentage of the vote they had obtained in their constituencies, and seats would be awarded to the highest placed candidates.

The Hansard Society felt that either STV or AMS would greatly increase proportionality (while retaining a bias towards single party government), allow adequate minority representation, give parties representation in areas where they had strong but not majority support and greatly increase the value of each individual vote. It did emphasize however, the virtues of the additional member system: that it was simple, that it preserved the link between an MP and his or her constituents, that it involved fewer changes from the present system and that it provided for the representation of regional as well as local interests in the House of Commons.

The alternative vote
This system is closest in nature to the present electoral system. Constituencies would continue to return single members but, instead of simply voting for one candidate, the voter would number candidates in order of preference. To be elected a candidate must obtain over half the total vote. If no candidate obtains this on counting first preferences, then the last candidate is eliminated, and his second choices are distributed amongst all other candidates. The process is repeated until one candidate

obtains the minimum requirement. This particular form of voting has never been widely supported. As Winston Churchill once said, it means that elections are decided by the most worthless votes given to the most worthless candidates.

Conclusion

Any judgement on whether the electoral system is in need of major reform depends upon what the system is supposed to do. If its major purpose is to ensure that the representation of interests at Westminster is in direct proportion to the strength of those interests in the country, then only electoral reform will suffice. If its purpose is to prevent a situation in which one party is able to force its programme through the House of Commons with only minority public support, then arguably that purpose might equally well be served by taking steps to strengthen the control of the House of Commons over the executive, by reforming and increasing the authority of the House of Lords, or even by a Bill of Rights. It should also be remembered that many improvements could be made to the present system without changing its essential character.

Finally, the future of the electoral system is uncertain for a number of reasons. If, for example, proportional representation should ever be adopted for elections to the European Parliament, then the case for similar reform at Westminster might be strengthened. Equally, the forces for change may become irresistible if the erosion of support for the two main parties and the growth in popularity of the minority parties continue. But perhaps most important of all, reform will not come unless and until the two main parties are persuaded of the case for it. At the moment neither the Labour Party nor the Conservative Party shows much enthusiasm for a proposal which could destroy their shared pre-eminence in British politics.

Questions

7 Consider the criticisms of the present electoral system made on pages 34–8. Which of the criticisms would be made less obvious through the introduction of (a) STV, (b) AMS?

8 What virtues of our present system might be lost through the introduction of (a) STV, (b) AMS?

9 Having considered the whole of this chapter make a list of the many different functions of an electoral system. For example, one might be to try to create a close relationship between votes cast for a particular party and seats obtained by it. Which do you think are the most important functions? Why do you think this? Does our present electoral system satisfy the functions you consider important?

3 Political parties

Left, right and centre: socialism, conservatism and liberalism

Nobody can understand much about political debate in Britain today without recognizing the terms 'left', 'right' and 'centre'. They are frequently used to characterize attitudes of individuals and parties as well as to describe specific policies, and very often they become terms of abuse. Some people would wish to dispense with them altogether, believing that they are unhelpful and as likely to confuse issues and ideas as to clarify them. And yet they are still meaningful.

A person who is left-wing in his views is, broadly speaking, one who believes in change and in challenging conventional attitudes and practices. Tradition means little to him. But he also has more specific beliefs in, for example, equality, the redistribution of wealth and the importance of high levels of Government expenditure to provide services and benefits for citizens. He wishes to protect and further the interests of the 'working class' rather than those of the rich, of managers in industry or of members of the professional classes. To this end many on the left favour the public ownership of industry and are hostile to private enterprise and profit. Some but not all left-wingers look forward to the development of a totally classless society, in which all inequalities of wealth and status will have been eradicated.

The person of right-wing views, in contrast, prefers stability to change, the familiar to the unknown. He is strongly in favour of 'law and order'. He respects and wishes to preserve old habits and customs. He sees the claims of liberty as being stronger than those of equality (although those on the extreme right in the figure on page 44 would probably destroy liberty as we understand it altogether). He is anxious to encourage and reward individual effort and initiative, to reduce the role of the Government in providing services and to encourage individuals to provide for themselves. He also believes that individuals are most likely to achieve happiness if they are given the freedom to conduct their lives without excessive state interference or regulation. He believes in less government rather than more government. In social terms his sympathies lie more with the middle and upper classes, and their life styles, than with the working class. Last, far from looking forward to the creation of a classless society, the right-winger sees differences in status and wealth among people as natural and desirable and finds diversity preferable to uniformity.

Generally speaking, the terms 'left' and 'right' as defined here correspond to the positions of the Labour Party and the Conservative Party respectively. The Liberal Party is seen as being a party of the 'centre', although one of the major difficulties it faces is in establishing an image and sense of identity. The formation of the Social Democratic Party (SDP) in March 1981 created the possibility of strengthening the centre in British politics. The SDP quickly established an electoral alliance with the Liberal Party and enjoyed remarkable public support in 1981. The party has presented itself as a radical left-of-centre alternative to conservatism, rejecting all shades of political extremism. Social Democrats and Liberals speak with one voice on issues such as individual liberty, the mixed economy, membership of the European Community and, in many respects, the welfare state. They are also united on a number of important institutional questions — the need for proportional representation, the reform of the House of Lords and decentralization of Government.

The positions of Britain's political parties are set out below.

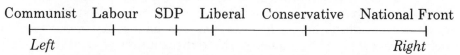

Communist   Labour   SDP   Liberal   Conservative   National Front

Left   *Right*

To see political differences in linear terms, as in this diagram, is certainly helpful. The differences between socialism and conservatism are very clear. Moreover, in many respects communism is a version of socialism which is further to the left in terms of the greater emphasis it gives to equality and its total hostility to private ownership. Equally, fascism, a political doctrine first developed in Italy in the 1920s under Mussolini and in Germany in the 1930s under Hitler, is an exaggerated and more authoritarian version of conservatism in terms of its insistence on order, discipline, inequality, elites, competition and individual effort.

However, the linear diagram is in many ways an inaccurate and unsatisfactory representation of political differences. First, viewpoints overlap. Some members of the Labour Party may be very sympathetic to communism and others virtually indistinguishable from many Liberals or Social Democrats. Equally, although some Conservatives would fit easily into the Liberal Party or even the right of the Labour Party, others hold attitudes which would place them close to the extreme right — in British terms, the National Front. It is perhaps fair to point out, however, that the Conservative Party has been more successful in resisting infiltration from the extreme right in recent years than the Labour Party has been in resisting infiltration from the extreme left.

Second, it is not the case that supporters accept every principle and policy for which their party stands. As we shall see later the supporters of the two main parties are in agreement on many issues. Third, there is a sense in which the Labour, Liberal and Conservative Parties are nearer to each other than to either of the two extremes. They are all parties with a time-honoured commitment to political democracy. They do not believe in revolution; they do believe that Government must be founded upon popular consent. They have all won and lost elections, but each, having lost, has accepted the verdict of the electorate and resigned itself to a period in opposition. The SDP fits easily into this tradition.

Fourth, the linear diagram is inaccurate because it suggests that the parties between which there is least agreement are the Communists and the National Front. They are of course different, mainly in their attitudes to class, property, wealth and equality, but in many ways they are very similar. One of the difficulties we face is in assessing what British Communist or National Front Governments would be like *in practice*, for, very simply, Britain has never had such Governments. We know that a Communist Government would redistribute wealth on a larger scale than the Labour Party has done and that it would abolish private ownership in industry. We know that a National Front Government would implement racialist policies, try to take Britain out of the European Economic Community and weaken the welfare state. But we know little about what attitudes their parties might take towards questions such as future elections, the rights of opposition parties or civil liberties in general if they were ever in power. What we do know is what such Governments have done in other countries, and the lessons are instructive. Fascist Governments (such as those in Italy and Germany during the inter-war period) have behaved in very similar ways to Communist Governments such as those in Russia, China, Cuba and Czechoslovakia. Under both systems the rights of individuals have been systematically violated; there has been imprisonment without trial, degrading punishment, torture, the persecution of dissidents and minorities, the destruction of all other political parties and of independent trade union movements, withdrawal of the right to leave the country freely, and the use of the press, the media and the education system for propaganda purposes. Moreover, neither Fascists nor Communists have, in power, found any use for democracy, except as a device for bolstering their own power. With the single exception of Dr Allende's Government in Chile in 1970, no Communist Government has ever come to power through free elections. The general pattern has been that of revolution, followed by the destruction of the opposition. Although Fascist Governments can claim to have come to power constitutionally, their interest in political democracy quickly disappeared once they held the reins of power.

For these reasons the terms 'left' and 'right' should be used with care. We need them and yet they can be deceptive. By themselves they tell us little about who are the friends of constitutional and democratic Government.

Question
1 In this section 'left', 'centre' and 'right' political *attitudes* are described.
   Divide your page into three columns and, over a period, build up a list
   of *policies* associated with the Labour, Liberal/SDP and Conservative
   Parties which reflect the attitudes described here.

The nature and role of parties

What are political parties? Some writers have tended to define them as
groups of people believing in the same general principles. Others, such as
the late Professor Robert McKenzie, recognizing that within all parties
there are at times fundamental differences of principle, have argued that
what is distinctive about a political party is not its principles, but the
common desire of its members to pursue and achieve power in order to be
able to do certain things. Indeed what is often striking is the extent to
which parties in pursuit of power have to modify and adapt their
principles in response to outside pressures. One simple and accurate
definition of a political party in a free society is, then, a group of people in
broad agreement on general principles, seeking to acquire political power
through parliamentary elections. But this definition can be sharpened
and the idea of party made clearer if we discuss what role parties are
supposed to play.

Most obviously, parties help to give stability and purpose to
Parliament. They select and organize into broad groups the candidates
among whom the electorate chooses. Without parties there could
certainly be Members of Parliament, but there would be no means of
translating the choices of the electorate in 650 constituencies into a
coherent Government. Elections would settle little. Thus parties help to
make Parliament more accountable to the country. The electorate
expresses a broad preference, knowing in general terms what its vote may
produce in actual policy. In a sense political parties help to make elections
more honest.

Furthermore parties help to organize public opinion. The views of the
public are often vague, disjointed and incoherent. Parties draw on the
many different threads of opinion and shape them into a policy. They help
to educate the electorate and to generate political interest. They also
encourage (but not on every occasion) an understanding of the
importance of reason, tolerance and persuasion in public discussion.

Finally, political parties make possible a change in the Government
without violence. If the electorate is dissatisfied with the broad choice it
made at the previous election, political parties enable it to transfer its
allegiance and change the Government at the next election. Without
organized parties, this simple but necessary process would be impossible.

The two-party system in Britain

Party systems can be of many kinds. In some African states and Communist countries there is only one party, while in countries such as France, West Germany and Italy, there are many fairly strong parties, which means that coalition Governments have to be formed from two or more of them.

Britain, in contrast, has had a two-party system in which power has tended to alternate between the Labour and Conservative Parties. Why this should be so is not a simple question to answer. In part, it is a product of the electoral system, as we saw in Chapter 2. It is also related to the importance of class as a basis of party support (which is discussed in Chapter 11) and, as a number of writers have pointed out, to the British political tradition. Voters, it is often argued, see parties not only as representatives of particular interests but as instruments of Government. They like a clear choice between two distinct alternatives and distrust coalitions. Thus before the First World War, the choice was between the Liberal and Conservative Parties. In the 1920s Labour replaced the Liberals as the second party in the two-party system, and has alternated in power with the Conservatives since. The survival of the two-party system in Britain after 1945 can probably be explained partly in terms of its own success. Between 1945 and the early 1960s the economy was expanding and most people in Britain, as Harold Macmillan remarked, had 'never had it so good'. There was a broad consensus between the Labour and Conservative Parties on issues such as the mixed economy, maintaining a high level of employment and advancing welfare services. The word 'Butskellism' was coined at the time (from the names of the Conservative Chancellor of the Exchequer R.A. Butler and the Labour leader Hugh Gaitskell) symbolizing the considerable area of common ground which existed between the two parties. There was no need to look outside the two major parties. Both were capable of Government, both had contributed to our post-war prosperity, and each was in broad agreement with the other over the direction policy should follow. If you tired of one you tried the other. The choice was simple.

The effects of the system

What has been the effect of the two-party system on the parties and on the electorate? First, it has made both major parties very broad coalitions. Labour, for example, contains people with widely divergent views. The 'left' of the party believes in unilateral nuclear disarmament, nationalization for its own sake and a radical redistribution of wealth, the right wishes to make a success of the mixed economy, defends capitalism, is doubtful of the value of further nationalization and accepts limits on wealth redistribution. It is mainly the recognition that disunity would destroy its electoral prospects that keeps the Labour Party together. Whether it will remain together is an open question. The formation of the SDP may well come to be seen as the first major step towards the break-up of the Labour Party as it was once known.

The second effect of the two-party system has been to reinforce the area of common ground between them. On many issues the differences between the two parties have been of emphasis rather than of principle. This has to be so for neither party can win an election by appealing only to its most fervent supporters (although Labour may have made the mistake of making its appeal too narrow in 1983).

The third effect has been to make the loyalty and discipline of party members of the highest importance. Members of Parliament owe their seats not to their own qualities (although these may be influential on some occasions) but to their party label. In return they are expected to give loyal support to their party. Most MPs feel a natural sense of loyalty to their party, but this is reinforced at Westminster by the fear of rejection by constituency parties, the hope of promotion and the pressure of the 'Whips' (see page 73).

Fourthly, despite the 'common ground' between the two major parties referred to above, the actual party system has become 'adversarial' in nature; that is, the argument between them tends to be conducted in terms of conflicting and mutually exclusive alternatives. Many writers, such as Nevil Johnson, have argued that the adversarial system creates conflict where none need exist and that it destroys any sense of there being a 'common good'. In a sense, parties often disagree with each other for the sake of disagreeing rather than because there are deep and genuine divisions between them.

A fifth effect of the two-party system has been to make the choice for the voter a very broad one. If he is at all conscious of his party's programme, he will undoubtedly disagree with some aspects of it, while still finding the party preferable to any other. What he is not free to do is to endorse part of the programme while rejecting the rest. This is as true of MPs as of the ordinary elector. Sometimes the party in Government will produce a majority in Parliament for a particular policy when, had the House of Commons been able to exercise its judgement free from party pressures, the policy would have been supported by only a minority in the House. Equally, some potential majorities in the House of Commons are never mobilized because they cut across party boundaries. Only on matters of personal conscience, such as abortion, homosexuality and capital punishment, is the House of Commons able to express its own view, free from the pressure of the Whips. The party system then has tended to strengthen the executive, enabling it to get its programme through the Commons, while undermining the power of the House as a whole (see also pages 110–11).

Sixth, the party system has made it virtually impossible for anybody to hold a seat in the Commons as an Independent. In 1973 the Labour MP for Lincoln, Dick Taverne, resigned his seat after conflict with his local party and won the ensuing by-election as an Independent (Democratic Labour) candidate. He held the constituency again in the General Election of February 1974 but lost it in the October election of that year. Mr Taverne's defeat was due less to any personal shortcomings than to the party system.

Last, the party system has helped to perpetuate class division. The roots of this division lie deep in our history but, it is often argued, are unnecessarily and artificially perpetuated by the party system today. This indeed has been one of the central arguments of the Social Democrats since 1981. They have argued the need to 'break the mould' of British politics to get away from the politics of class confrontation.

Question
2 On balance, do you consider the effects of the old two-party system to have been desirable or undesirable?

The challenge to the two-party system
What is quite clear today is that the two-party system is no longer as rigid as it used to be. In the General Election of 1951, for example, the two main parties gained 96.8 per cent of votes cast but in 1983 they gained only 70 per cent. Third and fourth parties have been gaining ground. In the seventies the two-party system was eroded through a growth in support for the Liberals and the Nationalist Parties and in the eighties a further and perhaps more significant challenge to the pre-eminence of the two old parties emerged in the Liberal/SDP Alliance (see page 59). In 1983, Labour and Conservative candidates came either first or second in 284 constituencies. In the same election, Conservative or Liberal/SDP Alliance candidates shared first or second place in 283 constituencies. In effect there are now two separate two-party systems. Further evidence of the decline of the two-party system can be seen in the decline in membership (see page 60) and in the fact that Governments have been defeated much more frequently in Parliament in recent years (see page 111).

But why has there been a challenge to domination of the two older parties? There are many explanations. In the first place, just as the strength of the Labour and Conservative Parties in the early sixties derived from their relative success in managing the economy, so since the 1960s they have been punished for their relative failure. Living standards have not risen and the economy has not expanded as had been expected. In many respects, Britain has slumped behind her international competitors. The years have been characterized by inflation and unemployment. Public disillusion has set in and is reflected in the fact that the proportion of the electorate approving the performance of one or other of the party leaders has declined from about 100 per cent (in total) in 1964–6 to only 72 per cent (in total) during the years 1979–83.

Secondly, it is argued, disillusion has grown because the electorate has been taught to expect more from Government than it can actually produce. Government has been 'overloaded' with demands and expectations at a time when its ability to meet those demands has been in decline. In part, the expectations have been encouraged by the very promises Governments have made to attract support, but if the policies have been irresponsible and the hopes exaggerated, the frustration of the electorate is all the greater when the expectations are unfulfilled.

Thirdly, the two-party system has been weakened because of the emergence of many issues which cut across traditional party divisions. The EEC, devolution, electoral reform, the environment and participation, for example, have all been major issues over the past decade and have often been issues with which third or fourth parties, rather than Labour or the Conservatives, were more closely identified.

Fourthly, there has been a considerable amount of social change in the past twenty years which has eroded the old traditional class pattern of voting (see pages 225–7). Many 'working-class' people have been able to adopt a more 'middle-class' life-style which has diminished their commitment to Labour. Worryingly for the party, an increasingly large proportion of Labour supporters no longer identifies with traditional Labour policies such as sympathy with trade unionists, belief in further public ownership and high spending on the social services. Indeed, after the 1983 General Election, a number of leading figures in the Labour Party acknowledged that there was too wide a gap between many attitudes of the electorate and many policies of the party.

Fifthly, it is argued, the two major parties in Britain have, over the past decade, become increasingly polarized. The broad consensus which used to exist between them has gone. The Conservatives under Mrs Thatcher have moved to the right and the Labour Party under Mr Foot's leadership between 1980 and 1983 drifted to the left. Both parties were felt to have become more 'extreme', creating a new opportunity for parties representing the political centre — the Liberal/SDP Alliance.

Finally, because both the major parties have moved from the centre ground, the degree of friction, tension and bitterness within each party has increased and this has often been only too clear to the electorate. Within the Labour Party, for example, there was considerable bitterness in the wrangles between left and right over the changes in the party's constitution in the early eighties (see pages 52–4) and also over the programme upon which Labour fought the 1983 election. Mr Kinnock, who became leader in 1983, has tried to unite the party and also to pull it back towards the centre ground. Whether Labour's 'unity' will survive the heat of the next general election campaign remains to be seen.

Divisions have also been apparent within the Conservative Party. Mrs Thatcher's brand of Conservatism is regarded with distrust by many Conservatives such as Sir Ian Gilmour, Francis Pym, Norman St John Stevas and James Prior, all of whom have either been dismissed from her administration or have resigned. Peter Walker has remained in Mrs Thatcher's Government but very frequently makes clear the extent of his own disagreement with Mrs Thatcher's economic policy. A party whose leaders appear divided to the public is likely to divide its own supporters in the country as well.

Question
3 Follow carefully the extent of public support for political parties in Britain through for example, opinion polls, by-election results and local election results. Is Britain developing a genuinely three-party system or are the Labour and Conservative Parties managing to regain ground which they had lost?

Party organization

There are a number of important differences in the organization of the Conservative and Labour Parties. To a great extent, these are historical. The Conservative Party was firmly established in Parliament before its mass organization developed after the Second Reform Act in 1867, whereas the Labour Party had a national organization before it became a strong parliamentary party. These differences have affected the structure of both parties. In the Conservative Party, policies tend to be initiated at the top and to be accepted by rank-and-file members. The Labour Party, in contrast, is internally more democratic, and, as we shall see, its members are more actively involved in policy formation. This is one factor which makes the Labour Party more difficult to lead, although it would be dangerous to exaggerate the extent to which the leader's power is *in practice* undermined by the democratic structure. We shall review briefly the main differences in the organization of both parties and then draw attention to a number of common characteristics.

The Conservative Party
The leader of the Conservative Party is elected by Conservative Members of Parliament. His (or her) power is considerable. Responsible for the formulation of party policy and for the party's election manifesto,

he or she also chooses the Cabinet when in Government and Shadow Cabinet when in Opposition. The party headquarters, Central Office, is under the direction and control of the leader, although day-to-day responsibility for this is usually delegated to the party chairman, appointed by the leader. The leader also appoints all other principal officers working at headquarters.

The strength of the leader is also reflected in the role of Annual Conference, which is convened by the National Union of Conservative and Unionist Associations, a body representing all constituency associations. Each constituency party is allowed to send up to seven delegates, and usually about 3000–4000 delegates attend. But Annual Conference is more like a rally than a genuine forum for debate and decision. In conferences between 1966 and 1977, only nine of 192 motions debated were rejected. Voting is rare and Conference cannot bind or direct the party leader in any of its resolutions. Its function is to endorse rather than to challenge.

Thus the organization of the Conservative Party places the leader in a powerful position. But she is not all powerful. A wise leader will not distance himself too much from his followers and will consider the general feeling in the party as expressed through the Cabinet or Shadow Cabinet, Annual Conference, Central Office and the 1922 Committee. This last is the weekly meeting of Conservative back-bench MPs. The 1922 Committee does not vote and therefore seldom causes embarrassment to party leaders, but it does effectively have the power not only to appoint leaders but also to remove them. Mr Heath's removal and replacement by Mrs Thatcher in 1975 is a forceful reminder to Conservative leaders of their own vulnerability to election defeats. The Conservative Party instinctively feels a strong sense of loyalty to its leader, but it has no respect for those who are unsuccessful.

The Labour Party

The structure of the Labour Party is different. As a result of changes in 1981 the leader is not now elected by the parliamentary party but by an electoral college consisting of constituency parties (30 per cent), the parliamentary party (30 per cent), and the trade unions (40 per cent). When the party is in Government, the leader, as Prime Minister, is free to choose his own Cabinet, but in Opposition his position is less strong. For example, he has to be re-elected annually to the leadership and may be challenged. Furthermore, fifteen members of his Shadow Cabinet (the Parliamentary Committee) are elected annually by the parliamentary Labour Party as a whole.

The leader's position is also weakened by his relationship to the party's bureaucracy. The party's headquarters is responsible to the party's

National Executive Committee (NEC) and is controlled by the NEC rather than the leader (although the party's leader and his deputy are automatically members of the NEC). The NEC appoints the party's General Secretary, speaks for the mass of party members between conferences and directs the work of party officials in Transport House. It is in turn elected by Annual Conference and consists of twenty-nine members, eighteen of whom are effectively chosen by the trade unions who control about 90 per cent of the votes at conference.

The main organizational difference between the two major parties concerns the respective roles of their Annual Conference. In the Labour Party it is Annual Conference, and not the party leader, which is responsible for policy. No proposal may be included in the party's programme unless it has been adopted by Annual Conference by a majority of two-thirds. This takes place through a 'card-vote' in which leaders of delegations cast their vote as a 'block' on behalf of the total membership. Thus it is quite possible for a handful of large unions to secure a majority for any particular policy. In 1981 the combined votes of the 5 largest unions exceeded the votes of 49 other unions, 548 constituency parties and 9 socialist and co-operative societies. (For details of the block vote, see page 251).

But although Labour's leader is less powerful constitutionally than the leader of the Conservative Party, in practice the differences are less obvious and less acute. For example, to be re-elected annually when the party is in Opposition has not proved a great threat to the leader. The last time there was a contest came in 1960 when Mr Wilson unsuccessfully challenged Mr Gaitskell. Indeed Labour leaders in general have been far more secure than Conservative leaders. Moreover, although fifteen members of the Shadow Cabinet are chosen by the Parliamentary Labour Party, the choice has very frequently been similar to that which the party leader would have made himself. The leader is also entitled to give responsibility for a particular area of policy to someone not elected by the parliamentary party. The leader need not become a slave to Annual Conference, for although Annual Conference is the main policy-making body, hitherto the Shadow Cabinet (or the Cabinet when in Government) together with the NEC have always selected items to be included in the party's election manifesto. Last, although the Parliamentary Labour Party has weekly meetings at which resolutions critical of the party leadership may be passed, when in office a Labour leader is unlikely to experience too much trouble from back-benchers. Whatever they think of him, they will prefer him to the Conservative alternative. The leaders of both parties are often sustained by the natural loyalty of back-benchers to themselves and their party.

The major difficulty for Labour leaders recently has come from the NEC. At times there has been unease and tension between the NEC and the parliamentary leadership, and this will probably continue, for the 'left' in the party has a far stronger base in the NEC than it has ever had in a Labour Cabinet. Moreover, at the party conference in 1979, responsibility for the party's manifesto was made the exclusive concern of the NEC. That decision was reversed by the 1980 Labour Conference but should the NEC ever gain exclusive control of the manifesto it would represent a major shift in the balance of power within the party from the leader and the parliamentary party to the NEC.

Like all party leaders, the Labour leader has to be responsive to the organization of his party. To an unusual degree the leader must adjust conflicting ideas, attitudes and interests. He must know when to conciliate his followers and when to confront them. It is a position which calls for tact, delicacy and sensitivity, but it is not an impossible one.

Other features of party organization

But although there are differences in the organizational structure of both parties there are also a number of important similarities.

Labour's Annual Conference is clearly different from that of the Conservatives, and yet for both parties the conference serves the simple but necessary function of keeping the leadership informed of the mood in the constituencies (and in the Labour Party in the trade unions as well). Equally, in both parties, headquarters are responsible for publishing pamphlets, leaflets and posters, for preparing notes on specific topics to assist party speakers, for researching policies and generating new ideas, for helping in the preparation of party political broadcasts, for organizing speaking tours for party leaders and generally for making the party bureaucracy function as efficiently as possible. One of their main responsibilities is to help organize, motivate and co-ordinate the work of the local constituency parties, where again the two parties have much in common.

The Conservative Party is organized nationally into twelve areas, each headed by an area organizer and each serving about fifty constituencies. In the Labour Party the structure is similar, but there are only eleven regional or area divisions. In both parties area organizations supervise the work and activities of the constituencies in their region, but considerable responsibility falls upon the local party. Conservative constituency parties elect an Executive Council (and Labour parties a General Management Committee) to handle constituency affairs. The majority of Conservative local parties and a minority of Labour parties also employ a full-time agent. Together, agents and elected bodies are responsible for maintaining the local organization in a state of readiness for local and national elections. They are also involved in fund raising, in trying to develop support in the constituency for the party's policies, in maintaining the morale of members, and, very importantly, they are responsible for nominating party candidates and for fighting campaigns (see page 32).

Party finance

The ways in which political parties in Britain are financed are complex and totally accurate statistics are difficult to produce. The central income of the Conservative and Labour Parties is set out in Figure 5 but, in addition, the parties have local funds and companies or organizations

Figure 5   *Central income of the Conservative and Labour Parties 1973–84*

(a) *Conservative Party*

	Donations (mainly companies)		Constituency associations		State aid		Total	
	£m	%	£m	%	£m	%	£m	%
1973–4*	2.4	86	0.4	14			2.8	100
1976–7	1.3	62	0.6	28	0.2	10	2.1	100
1979–80*	4.5	80	0.9	16			5.6	100
1981–2	2.9	71	1.0	24			4.1	100
1983–4*	8.7	89	1.1	11			9.8	100

(b) *Labour Party*

	Trade union affiliation fees		Constituencies		State aid		Other **		Total	
	£m	%	£m	%	£m	%	£m	%	£m	%
1974*	0.7	39	0.1	6			1.0	55	1.8	100
1977	1.3	87	0.1	7			0.1	6	1.5	100
1979*	1.8	58	0.2	7	0.1	3	1.0	32	3.1	100
1981	2.5	68	0.6	16	0.3	8	0.3	8	3.7	100
1983*	3.0	48	0.6	10	0.3	5	2.4	39	6.2	100

* General election year.
** In general election years this is mainly trade union contributions to the party's general election fund.

Source: Parliamentary Affairs, Vol. 38, No. 3, pp. 328–47.

sympathetic to the Conservative Party often finance anti-nationalization campaigns in the months immediately preceding general elections. Similarly, the trade unions also contribute to the Labour Party by 'sponsoring' parliamentary candidates. This is very often welcomed by constituency parties because it involves the trade union in a substantial contribution of up to 80 per cent of the candidate's election expenses. In 1983, 26 trade unions sponsored a total of 171 candidates of whom 123 were elected to Parliament. As these figures suggest, sponsorship tends to take place mainly in the safer Labour constituencies where the unions have a greater chance of getting a return on their investment — an MP favourable to themselves.

Figure 5 shows clearly the very heavy dependence of the Conservative Party on business donations and the equally heavy dependence of the Labour Party on trade union affiliation fees. This dependence is particularly marked in general election years. Each member of trade unions 'affiliated' to the Labour Party pays, unless he 'contracts out', a 'political levy' to the party. These arrangements have often been criticized by those who consider that it is unhealthy for one party to be financed by one side of industry and the other party by the other. Whether any alternative method of financing parties would be more desirable is considered below (see pages 60–61).

Questions

4 Prepare, in two columns, lists of the main organizational differences between the Conservative and Labour Parties. Are their differences more important than their similarities?
5 What effect could the manner in which political parties are financed have on the policies they pursue?

Political parties today

The Labour and Conservative Parties

In the 1960s, it was often argued that there was really very little difference between the parties in attitude, ideas or policy. In 1969, a former Labour minister, Christopher Mayhew, wrote, 'Their words have a deadly similarity, the debates between them are sterile and absurd.' If this ever was true — and Mr Mayhew probably overstated his case — it is certainly not true today. Of course on many issues the parties are now in agreement. Their attitudes to foreign affairs are broadly similar, and each party has given support to the other in its handling of the Irish problem in recent years. Furthermore, both parties are now 'welfare' parties in the sense that they believe it is the duty of the state to make provision for education, health, social security and pensions available to all citizens. Indeed it could be argued that the debate between the two parties today starts from a position left of centre because both parties now accept as common ground policies which were previously seen as to the left. One of the most notable achievements of the Labour Party since the Second World War has been to define the ground on which party debate shall take place and thus to shift the political centre of gravity in Britain to the left. The central purpose of Mrs Thatcher's two administrations after 1979 was to try to shift the centre of gravity in British politics back to the right by, for example, reducing the power of the unions, pursuing a policy of 'privatizing' industries which had previously been nationalized, selling council houses and, generally, 'rolling back the state' to encourage people to take greater responsibility for the direction of their lives rather than to look to Government for support. In pursuit of some of her objectives Mrs Thatcher has been successful. Industries have been privatized (see pages 185–7) and between 1979 and 1983 half a million tenants bought their own council houses. The power of the unions has, by a policy of gradual reform (see page 255), been considerably reduced and a year-long strike by the National Union of Mineworkers in 1984–5 over the issue of pit closures ended in a costly defeat for the union. Equally, the size of the Civil Service has been cut substantially (see page 131) and there has been a renewed emphasis upon managerial efficiency.

But in other respects Mrs Thatcher has been less successful. She has failed to satisfy the expectations she herself generated on, for example, law and order (see page 210). The level of crime in Britain has continued to rise since 1979 and in 1981 there was serious rioting in Liverpool, Brixton and Manchester. This was followed by a further wave in Handsworth and Tottenham in 1985. Mrs Thatcher has been equally unsuccessful in cutting taxation and public expenditure, both of which have risen during her two administrations. Similarly, her efforts to regenerate the economy through the pursuit of 'monetarist' policies have contributed to a substantial increase in the level of unemployment in Britain without, as yet, producing clear evidence that Britain's industrial base has been strengthened and her economic future assured.

It is largely because they have questioned the wisdom of her economic policies that some 'wets' in the Conservative Party have been critical of Mrs Thatcher. They have argued that Mrs Thatcher, while a courageous and formidable leader (as her role during the Falklands War of 1982 showed), has placed too much dogmatic emphasis on 'monetarism' and conquering inflation and has been too little concerned with trying to reduce the level of unemployment. The wets have also argued that the 'tone' of the Government has often sounded harsh, unattractive and unsympathetic and that, while many of the basic economic policies may have been correct, they have often been applied in too inflexible a manner. They have been concerned about the development of major social divisions in Britain (of which the riots are an example) and feel that it is the duty of Government not to divide the nation but to try and bind it together. The wets are distrustful of ideologies and theories. In Francis Pym's words, they feel 'that the habit of viewing life, politics and personalities in black and white terms is both false and dangerous'. They much prefer to think in terms of finding practical solutions to given problems. They distrust blue-prints and all-embracing explanations. They feel the truth is often complex and many-sided, that no theory can be right in all circumstances, and that they represent the heart of the British Conservative tradition.

The Labour tradition is different. Whereas the Conservatives have, generally speaking, been a united party — united in general attitudes and sharing a common desire to hold power — Labour's history is one of often heated internal division between 'left' and 'right'. In 1960 the left favoured unilateral nuclear disarmament; the right did not. The right wanted to abolish clause four of the party's constitution (committing the party to public ownership as a general principle) and was opposed by the left. More recently the left has been opposed to British membership of the European Economic Community and to the idea of having an 'incomes policy', in favour of cuts in defence and an extension of public ownership, and anxious to develop closer understandings with Communist parties in many European countries. The right has taken the opposite view on each of these questions. There are differences too on the role the party ought to play. Some have seen it essentially as a party of protest; others, following the former Labour leader Sir Harold Wilson, have wanted to make the party the natural party of Government. Mr Kinnock follows Sir Harold closely in this and, after becoming party leader in 1983, gave considerable emphasis to his own view that the essential challenge for Labour, to which all else was secondary, was to achieve power. This, he has argued, could only be achieved if Labour remained united and if it attached more importance to fighting other parties than to fighting within itself. Labour's prospects of future electoral success will depend to a great extent upon how far it is able to appear to the electorate as a united and cohesive political force.

Questions
6 Summarize the main differences between Mrs Thatcher and her critics in the Conservative Party.
7 Using the evidence in this chapter make a list of ways in which leading the Labour Party is, in many respects, more difficult than leading the Conservative Party.

The Liberal/SDP Alliance

One of the most remarkable features of British politics in recent years has been the emergence of the Liberal/SDP Alliance as a major political force. For much of the post-war period, and certainly up to 1974, the Liberal Party had been notable more for the ideas it generated than for the political support it attracted or the seats at Westminster it won. The Liberal Party supported British entry into the EEC before either of the other two major parties, they were early and forceful advocates of industrial democracy, and long-standing, if unsuccessful, advocates of proportional representation. Their political influence, however, remained negligible.

In 1974 the party's fortunes changed and the Liberals obtained over 19 per cent of the popular vote in the election of February 1974 — appearing to draw support from both the older parties. In March 1977, the Liberal leader David Steel took the party closer to power than it had been for fifty years when he negotiated with the Labour Prime Minister James Callaghan the Lib-Lab Pact — a loose arrangement whereby the Liberals agreed to support a minority Labour Government in exchange for which Labour would drop its 'socialist' policies and address itself to conquering the problems of inflation. In July 1978 the pact ended and the Liberals entered the 1979 election hoping once more to be able to hold the balance of power.

That hope was frustrated but a new opportunity arose in March 1981 when initially eleven and later nearly thirty Labour MPs (together with one Conservative) helped to create the Social Democratic Party (SDP). The new party and the Liberals quickly established an electoral Alliance and achieved a number of remarkable by-election victories (see page 34). Support for the Alliance in public opinion polls rose to over 40 per cent. In 1982, helped by the Falklands War, the Conservatives began to recover their electoral support, but Labour's support remained low and raised the question of whether Labour or the Alliance constituted the main opposition. In the election of 1983, the Alliance obtained over 25 per cent of the popular vote (6 per cent more than the Liberals had ever achieved in the post-war years) but they fell short of the degree of support needed to win an appreciable number of seats. The Alliance could, however, legitimately point to the evenness of their support throughout the country, to the fact that their popular vote was very close to that of the Labour Party and to the considerable weakening of traditional party loyalties. The 1983 election may prove to be a major step on the road to political realignment in Britain. Certainly, for 'third forces' in British politics the prospects are more hopeful than at any other time in the post-war years.

Some issues today

Three important contemporary issues affecting all parties in different ways
are those of membership, finance, and the growing demand, especially in the
Labour Party, for greater participation — for greater party democracy.

Reliable figures on membership are difficult to get hold of but it
appears the Conservative Party has an individual membership of about
1,200,000, the Labour Party about 290,000, the Liberals about 100,000,
and the Social Democrats about 50,000. The membership of political
parties has declined substantially since the 1950s. This has had two
important side effects. First, it has increased the financial dependence of
the Labour Party on the trade unions and, to a lesser extent, of the
Conservative Party on business and industry. It has also made it
increasingly difficult for both parties, but especially for the Labour Party,
to maintain a national organization commensurate with the party's
importance. The problem is even more acute in the Alliance parties
which, enjoying neither industrial nor trade union support, are very
heavily dependent on the voluntary contributions of their members.

For these reasons a Parliamentary Committee under Lord Houghton
reported in 1976 in favour of a state grant to political parties based on the
volume of support for them at the preceding election. Houghton
recommended a sum of about £2,250,000 each year. Supporters of the
idea have argued that this is a very small price to pay for helping to
maintain in a proper state of efficiency bodies which make such an
important contribution to British democracy. Opponents have pointed
out that subsidies are already provided in a way through the provision of a
free postal service for election addresses (costing nearly £8,000,000), free
broadcasting time and through the provision of modest financial aid to
Opposition parties in Parliament. They have also argued that few
candidates experience difficulty in raising the £2500 which generally
covers a constituency campaign. By far the most decisive argument
against subsidy, though, has been that it would tend to decrease the
activity of party members in the constituencies and probably party
membership as well. Very often it is precisely the need to raise the money
for campaigns which provides the stimulus to organization and involvement. If this were removed, party organization in the constituencies could
tend to atrophy even more than it has done already.

A further report on party finance in 1981, 'Paying for Politics' by the
Hansard Society, sought to meet this point. They suggested that for every
£2 contributed by individuals to a political party, a matching payment
should be made by the Exchequer, provided that the party had, for
example, saved a minimum of six deposits at the previous election or had
two MPs returned. The effect of these proposals would be both to
encourage parties to broaden their membership *and* to give them greater

financial assistance. The Hansard Society also suggested changes in the law to reduce Labour's financial dependence on the trade unions and the dependence of the Conservative Party on business. No action has so far resulted from the report.

The final problem is that with the decline in the size of party membership and the fact that about only one-third of party members play any kind of active role in the parties at local level, it has become very easy, especially in the Labour Party, for the constituency party to come under the influence and control of minorities whose opinions are not representative of the average Labour voter. Recent changes in the Labour Party's constitution have magnified the importance of this issue. From 1979, Labour MPs have been required to submit themselves for reselection during the course of a Parliament. Clearly, if MPs were to become the servants of their local party organization, then they could not be free to carry out their traditional role of exercising their judgement on matters of importance on behalf of all their constituents (see also pages 83–5).

Some people have suggested that primary elections, as in America, would be useful in that they would enable voters to choose not only the MP but the candidate as well. As we saw in Chapter 2, the advocates of proportional representation by the single transferable vote have been quick to point out that this reform would also give the electorate a much wider choice among candidates than is offered at the moment.

But the pressure for 'democracy' is coming to be more widely felt than in the constituencies alone. When Mr Steel replace Mr Thorpe as leader of the Liberal Party in 1976, and when Mr Jenkins became leader of the SDP in 1982, they did so after elections in which the memberships of their respective parties were directly involved. The choice was not made by the parliamentary party alone. Similar tendencies are apparent in the other parties, particularly Labour. The success of those who have sought to increase the power of the activists over the MP, to give more power to Annual Conference and to involve the whole party in elections to the leadership, has already been noted. Pressure is also building up to restrict the freedom of Labour Prime Ministers in choosing their Cabinets. In the Conservative Party, democratic tendencies are less likely to assert themselves because of the deference the party habitually shows to a successful and popular leader and because, internally, it has never had a democratic tradition. But in the Labour Party, which grew out of popular feeling and unrest, the force of democracy is, in different forms, beginning to grow. It could have a radical effect on British politics in the next decade.

Question

8 What should 'making a party more democratic' mean? Would the Labour Party be made less or more democratic by the changes in the

Party's organization discussed in this chapter concerning (a) the transfer of responsibility for the manifesto from the NEC and Cabinet to the NEC alone, (b) the compulsory reselection of MPs?

Below are three extracts from recent political writings. The first two are on conservatism; the third is on socialism. They do not represent all shades of opinion within the two major parties, but they do introduce some of the main elements in conservative and socialist thought. Read them carefully and then answer the questions below.

Documents: conservatism and socialism

1 *Sir Ian Gilmour,* Inside Right *(Hutchinson 1977), pp. 109–17*

So far then as philosophy or doctrine is concerned, the wise Conservative travels light. Conservative principles cannot be precisely tabulated.... Yet certain themes are apparent... a preference for things that have grown over things that have been made... the idea that it is the duty of the Tory Party to be national and ... that the preservation of the national institutions and the improvement of the condition of the people are the overriding objectives of the party.... The rule of law is of overriding importance.... Conservative thinking is, or should be, always grounded in practice... it is based in facts and human nature.... Conservatives do not favour the imposition of economic equality but they can easily imagine a distribution of income that would be intolerable and would require adjustment. ... Conservatives agree that competition is indispensable to a free society. But they do not make a god of it. ...

2 *From Sir Keith Joseph,* Observer, *28 May 1978*

For Conservatives there are neither past Golden Ages nor future Utopias, only prospects of improvements — slow and provisional — and dangers of deterioration, which can become cumulative and can destroy assets that cannot be replaced. ...

Democracy is the best way we have of selecting the Government of a free society, but democracy is no guarantee against tyranny. Only a combination of democracy, the rule of law and adherence to the concept of limited government, can preserve us as a free society. ...

When we advocate organising economic life by competition we are not advocating a free-for-all. Nor are we advocating unlimited power for those with more drive. Nor do we claim that free enterprise will produce all good things. But we do say that free enterprise and competition make possible a dispersion of ownership and decision-making that is the necessary, though not sufficient, condition for freedom. And we believe that competition enables all the people to benefit from what is achieved by those with more drive. ...

Equality before the law and equality of opportunity do ensure freedom and are compatible with prosperity. But a devotion to equality of reward . . . is the way to despotism and impoverishment.

3 *From C.A.R. Crosland,* Observer, *23 November 1975*

The word 'Socialism' is not in any way an exact descriptive term. . . . Rather it describes a set of values, of aspirations, of principles which socialists wish to see embodied in the organisation of society. What are these values?

First, an overriding concern for the poor, the deprived and generally the underdog, so that when considering the claims on our resources we give an exceptionally high priority to the relief of poverty, distress and social squalor.

Secondly, a belief in equality. By equality we mean more than a meritocratic society of equal opportunities, in which unequal rewards would be distributed to those most fortunate in their genetic endowment or family background. We also mean more than a simple redistribution of income. We want a wider social equality embracing the distribution of property, the educational system, social-class relationships, power and privilege in industry — indeed all that is enshrined in the age-old socialist dream of a 'class-less' society. To us, the fundamental divide between Left and Right, socialists and non-socialists, has always been about the distribution of wealth, power and class status.

Thirdly, strict social control over the environment — to enable us to cope with the exploding problems of urban life, to plan the use of our land in the interests of the community.

Questions

5 Which elements of conservatism are emphasized by both Sir Ian Gilmour and Sir Keith Joseph?

6 What are the main differences between the views of Gilmour and Joseph and those of Crosland?

7 Can you give any current examples of policy differences between the two major parties which reflect these different principles?

4 The House of Commons

At the heart of the British Constitution is the doctrine of the sovereignty of Parliament — of Commons, Lords and Monarch together. Parliament has the authority to make new laws, to repeal old laws and even to extend its own life. With the exception of the right of the courts to interpret its laws, the authority of Parliament cannot be challenged. The major constraints upon its freedom of action are political rather than legal. Parliament derives its authority from the people and is answerable to them.

The function of Parliament

It is not the function of Parliament to govern the country. That responsibility rests with the Government. Parliament's duties are several. It is, in the words of Lord Stockton, a former Conservative Prime Minister, a 'great inquest of the nation'. It provides a forum where Government can explain its policies to the electorate and where those policies can be not only questioned and debated, but also amended, approved or rejected. Parliament also restrains and influences Government through controlling the raising and spending of money. Finally, it is an important channel of communication through which grievances are articulated on behalf of the electorate.

Today the ability of Parliament to carry out all these duties satisfactorily is often questioned, for Parliament has fallen increasingly under the control of the executive. This will be more easily understood when we have considered the authority of the Government in Britain, and a full discussion will therefore be left until Chapter 5 (see page 110).

Life in the House of Commons

Structure

The structure of the House of Commons is shown in Figure 6. The chamber is rectangular in shape, and the benches of the Government and Opposition face each other. Although there are today 650 members of Parliament, there is seating in the Commons for fewer than 450. The relatively small size of the chamber is a result of deliberate policy. During World War 2 German bombing destroyed the old chamber and gave the

Figure 6 *The chamber of the House of Commons*

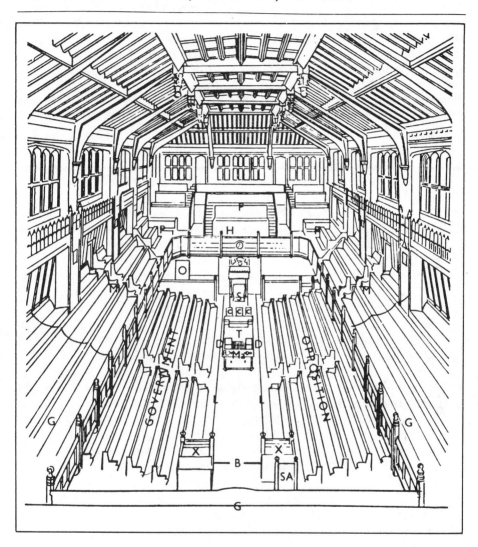

KEY: S — Mr Speaker P — Press galleries H — *Hansard* reporters O — Government officials' box C — Clerks of the House (when the House goes into committee, Mr Speaker leaves the chair, and the chairman sits in the chair of the Clerk of the House, which is the one on the left) T — Table of the House D — Dispatch boxes Ma — Mace (when the House goes into committee, the Mace is put 'below the Table' on hooks) L — lines over which members may not step when speaking from the front benches B — Bar of the House X — Cross benches SA — Serjeant-at-Arms M — Members' galleries G — Public galleries.

Source: A Guide for Visitors to the House of Commons, HMSO.

Commons the opportunity to discuss the nature of its replacement. Winston Churchill in a famous speech, argued for a small chamber because, 'If the House is big enough to contain all its members, nine-tenths of the debates will be conducted in the depressing atmosphere of an almost empty or half-empty chamber.' Churchill also argued, 'There should be on great occasions a sense of crowd and urgency', and that this could only be generated within a small place. His arguments prevailed. The size and intimacy of the House make it well suited to the conversational style of debate which is one of its main characteristics.

The parliamentary timetable

The life of a Parliament (the period between two general elections) cannot in normal circumstances exceed five years, although during both World Wars in this century, the Parliament was extended until the end of the war. The Prime Minister has, subject to the consent of the Sovereign, the right to dissolve Parliament and call a general election at any time within the five-year period.

The life of each Parliament is divided into sessions. Each session is opened, usually in October or November, by the Royal Speech from the throne in the House of Lords. This is prepared by the Cabinet, and it sets out the Government's legislative programme for the session. The duration of each session is normally about 160 days, and Parliament adjourns for recesses at Christmas, Easter, Whitsun and in summer. The latter is the longest recess of all. Any business which is incomplete at the end of one session (when Parliament is 'prorogued') cannot be carried over into the next, but automatically lapses.

The House normally meets from Mondays to Thursdays from 2.30 p.m. to 10.30 p.m. and on Fridays from 9.30 a.m. to 3 p.m., the earlier finish enabling MPs to leave London in good time for weekend engagements. While these are the official hours, it is not unusual for sittings to go on well beyond 10.30 p.m. and at times all through the night. In the session of 1980–81 the Commons sat after midnight on seventy occasions.

The business for each day is set out on the Order Paper. A typical parliamentary day might take the following form:

2.30   Prayers.

2.35   Question time. A minister answers questions relating to his department. Each MP is entitled to table two questions a day. Forty-eight hours notice must be given, and the MP must indicate if he requires an oral rather than a written answer. Of about 40,000 parliamentary questions tabled each year less than a quarter receive an oral answer. Although the minister will have been thoroughly briefed by his civil servants for the questions set out on the Order Paper, the Speaker may allow a supplementary question which affords greater opportunity to expose the minister.

3.15–3.30 (on Tuesdays and Thursdays ony) Questions to the Prime Minister.

3.30 General matters such as ministerial statements, requests to raise matters of great public importance, the introduction of new MPs and occasionally 'ten minute rule' Bills (see page 74).

3.45 The major debate of the day. Government and Opposition spokesmen each address the House for about forty-five minutes. They are usually followed by Privy Councillors (see page 114) who occupy the House until about 7 p.m. Then back-benchers are called until (at about 9 p.m.) front-bench spokesmen for both the Government and the Opposition wind up the debate. Although the House will probably be well attended for the ministerial speeches at the beginning and the end of the debate, very few MPs will be found in the chamber between about 5 p.m. and 9 p.m.

10.00 If a vote is to be taken at the end of the debate, 'tellers' are appointed and MPs file out behind the Speaker's chair into the 'ayes' and 'noes' lobbies to be counted. The Speaker announces the result to the House when it has reassembled.

10.00–10.30 Debate on adjournment in which back-benchers raise issues, grievances or matters of concern to their constituents. Every fortnight a ballot is held to determine which MPs will have the right to speak, but on one day each week the Speaker chooses the subject for debate from a list submitted by MPs. The custom is for a junior minister to reply to the speech.

10.30 Adjournment.

The parliamentary timetable is arranged by the Leader of the House in consultation with the Opposition. The greater part of the time is at the disposal of the Government for its legislative programme, but opportunity to criticize governmental policy is provided for in major debates and adjournment debates, at question time, in the nineteen days reserved for Opposition business, and in the three days set aside to discuss the Estimates. The particular Departmental estimates to be debated on the three days available are chosen by the Liaison Committee — a new select committee consisting of the Chairmen of the other select committees. In addition, ten Fridays per session are set aside for Private Members' Bills (see page 73).

Traditions of the Commons

The long history of the House of Commons has established traditions and customs relating to procedure which, although criticized as archaic by some MPs, are still revered by the majority. In the chamber MPs are referred to not by name but as the honourable member for a named constituency. An MP usually refers to another MP from his party as 'my honourable friend' and to a Privy Councillor from his party as 'my right honourable friend'. Queen's Counsel are referred to as 'honourable and learned' and former officers in the armed forces as 'honourable and gallant'. The House of Lords is always referred to as 'another place'.

Of the many customs and traditions which govern the conduct of the House, constitutionally the most important is the doctrine of parliamentary privilege, denoting the special privileges to which MPs are entitled. To offer a bribe to an MP or to disrupt the proceedings of the House, for example, are breaches of privilege and contempts of Parliament. It is the responsibility of the Speaker to decide if there might have been a breach of privilege and to refer a case for decision to the Commons Committee of Privileges.

The most significant aspect of parliamentary privilege provides MPs with immunity from court action in respect of anything said in the Commons. It is a privilege which needs to be exercised with care. In June 1980, for example, one MP, Mr Rooker, suggested that an executive at Rolls Royce had, in the course of his work, accepted bribes. The executive denied the allegation and challenged Mr Rooker to repeat his remarks outside the Commons. This Mr Rooker declined to do. A fortnight later Mr Rooker withdrew the allegations and apologized. The case illustrated very clearly the way in which privilege can be abused and yet, without it, an MP's role would be diminished as Mr Powell makes clear below.

Document: Parliamentary privilege

The ability of Parliament and its members to represent and to defend those who elect them is obviously dependent on freedom of speech. Their only masters ought to be their electors; and the only punishment to which they ought to be liable, even at their electors' hands, for anything they do or say in Parliament is the penalty of not being elected again. . . . If members were liable to threats or bribes . . . designed to stop their mouths or pervert their actions, there would be an end to their usefulness. If members were not able to name and denounce, as they thought fit, the most influential and wealthy persons or corporations in the land without fear of civil action or prosecution, the citizen would have lost a safeguard and a champion which nothing else could replace.

Parliament is either supreme over all other courts and outside their jurisdiction, or it is nothing. Thus, in his capacity as a citizen, the member of Parliament is tried and punished like anybody else, for exceeding a speed limit or for committing murder, and his fellow citizens can sue him for damages or wrongs that he may do to them. In what he does, including what he says, in his capacity as Member of Parliament, he enjoys, because he must, complete immunity.

(From an article by J. Enoch Powell MP, *Spectator* 11 December 1976.)

Question

1 Why must MPs have privileged status and how might their privileges be abused?

Officials of the House of Commons

The Speaker

The Speaker is effectively the chairman of the House of Commons and plays a very important part in its proceedings. He is a Member of Parliament, usually of considerable experience, and is elected by his fellow MPs, generally unopposed. Although a Speaker may in his earlier career have been strongly identified with a particular political party (Mr Speaker Lloyd, for example, who held the office from 1970 to 1976, was a former Conservative Chancellor of the Exchequer), he is expected to act with impartiality once he has assumed the chair. Because of his impartiality, the Speaker does not necessarily change when the Government changes. Very often his constituency is not contested at general elections.

Much ritual is attached to the office. The Speaker wears a wig, a black robe and knee breeches. Before taking office he pretends a reluctance to accept the chair and MPs gently drag him to it. He leads the procession to the chamber each day, preceded by the Serjeant-at-Arms carrying the Mace, the symbol of the House's authority. The Speaker, following a principle established during the Speakership of Abercrombie between 1835 and 1839 and unlike the Lord Chancellor in the Upper House, takes no active part in the debates of the Commons.

His duties are many. He calls all speakers in the House, generally giving precedence, as we have seen, to Privy Councillors, but considering also the interests of particular MPs and factors such as the interval since an MP last addressed the House. Frequently MPs write to the Speaker in advance, informing him of their desire to take part in a debate. The

Speaker also tries to ensure that parties receive a fair share of debating time and that opinions within parties are fairly represented. He may, if many members wish to contribute to a debate, restrict speeches to no more than ten minutes. He disciplines MPs and rules on points of procedure. He can oblige them to apologize for unparliamentary language, and even suspend or eject them. If he wishes to eject an MP he 'names' him or her, whereupon the Leader of the House moves the suspension of the MP, who then leaves the chamber. If he fails to do so the Serjeant-at-Arms comes to eject him.

The Speaker announces the results of divisions in the House and has the casting vote in the event of a tie. (Traditionally, he uses this to preserve the status quo.) He decides whether to accept a closure motion or to accede to a request from the House for a debate on a matter of great urgency. He issues writs for by-elections, is the sole judge of a money Bill, appoints all chairmen of standing committees and acts as the intermediary between the Commons and the Crown and between the Commons and the Lords.

To be able to discharge the wide responsibilities of the office, a Speaker requires firmness, fairness, a deep knowledge of the procedures of the House, a ready wit, a capacity to follow the course of a debate and, perhaps above all, the confidence of the House, whose servant he is. It was widely agreed that Mr Speaker Thomas, who retired in 1983, possessed all these qualities in abundance.

Other officials

The Chairman of Ways and Means, who is also an MP, is the Deputy Speaker. He frequently relieves the Speaker during sittings. When the whole House goes into committee, he presides in place of the Speaker. He is appointed only for the duration of a Parliament. The Clerk of the House of Commons is responsible for keeping records of proceedings and for advising MPs on matters of procedure. He is appointed by the Crown and is not an MP. The Serjeant-at-Arms is also appointed by the Crown. He has responsibility for helping to maintain order in the House by dealing with unruly MPs and visitors. He carries a sword and sits at the opposite end of the chamber from the Speaker. He attends the Speaker as he enters and leaves the chamber and carries the Mace.

Legislation

One of the functions of Parliament, as we have seen, is to pass legislation. Today the volume of legislation passed by Parliament is much greater than it used to be. In the 1975–6 session alone, 2800 pages were added to the statute book. Every law begins as a Bill and only becomes an Act of Parliament when it has been read and approved three times in both Houses and has received the Royal Assent.

Bills are of three kinds: Public Bills promoted by Government, Private Members' Bills promoted by MPs who are not members of the Government and Private Bills promoted by, for example, local authorities in their own interests. By far the greatest proportion of Bills are advanced by Government as part of its legislative programme.

How a Government Bill becomes law
The process by which a Government Bill becomes law is long and at times arduous, and it begins outside Parliament itself.

Preparation
The Government will have made clear many of its proposals in its election manifesto, and it is for the Cabinet, guided perhaps by the Cabinet legislation committee, to decide the priorities. Once a decision has been taken to include a Bill in the legislative programme for a session, reference to it is made in the Queen's Speech at the opening of Parliament. The Parliamentary Counsel — a group of experienced lawyers — then prepares the Bill line by line. This is a task requiring much skill, for it has to convey exactly the intentions of the Government. The Bill, once prepared, is returned to the Cabinet for approval, after which it is printed. Consultation then usually begins with the interests affected. The Bill may have to be rewritten in part in the light of these discussions. The initial drafting of the legislative proposals and the rewriting of them after wider consultation may take a period of about six months. Only then is the Bill ready to begin its progress through Parliament, and the minister responsible arranges with the Leader of the House a suitable time for its introduction.

First reading
This is a very brief formality. The Clerk of the Commons reads out the title of the Bill; the minister responsible, at the request of the Speaker, names a day — probably about two or three weeks later — for the second reading, and the Bill is then printed. Between the first and second readings MPs are able to familiarize themselves with its proposals while ministers continue their consultations with interested parties.

Second reading
This concerns the principles and objectives of the Bill. The minister opens the debate and is followed by either the Leader of the Opposition or the shadow minister. The debate lasts the whole day and sometimes

longer. At the end of the debate the House divides on the motion, 'That
the Bill be now read a second time'. If the motion is carried, the Bill
progresses to the next parliamentary stage.

Committee stage
The Bill is then usually sent to a standing committee (see page 76) where
it is discussed in detail under less formal procedure. Alternatively,
although infrequently, it may be considered by a committee of the whole
House. Amendments may be put, but only if they are consistent with the
main principles behind the Bill, which have already been approved on
second reading. It is nevertheless not unknown for the whole nature of a
Bill to be transformed by amendments in committee.

Report stage
If a Bill has been considered in committee by the whole House, report
stage is a formality unless the Bill has been amended, in which case a
further debate may take place. Report stage is more important when the
Bill is being returned from a standing committee, for it then affords an
opportunity for the whole House to consider the detailed provisions of the
Bill and to make any final amendments. The Government might also have
promised in committee to make certain amendments which the House
may now be able to confirm.

Third reading
This is a final opportunity to debate the principles of the Bill, after which,
if approved, it is sent to the House of Lords.

Amendments
In the House of Lords the Bill has to go through the same stages. If no
amendments are made, it becomes law immediately on receiving the
Royal Assent. If the Lords amend the Bill, the changes are considered by
the Commons. Some may be accepted, others rejected and sent back to
the Lords. Not until both Houses are in agreement can the Bill be passed
to the Sovereign, although under the terms of the Parliament Act 1949, if
a Bill is passed by the Commons and rejected by the Lords in successive
sessions, it may still be presented to the Sovereign for assent, provided
that at least twelve months have passed since the original reading.

Guillotine, closure and kangaroo
The pressures upon the parliamentary time-table and the knowledge that
Bills will lapse unless completed by the end of a session oblige
Governments at times to restrict by various means the time available for
debate. By the use of 'closure' any MP (but usually the Government
Whip) moves 'that the question now be put'. If the Speaker allows a

vote on the motion and if this is carried, the debate ends. At committee stage a Government can resort to other methods to quicken proceedings. By the use of the 'guillotine' a time limit is established for the consideration of certain groups of clauses, while the use of the 'kangaroo' empowers the chairman to select certain clauses for discussion and ignore others completely.

The Whips
Whips perform an essential role in the work of Parliament. Each party has its own Whips (chosen by the leader in the Conservative Party but elected in the Labour Party) drawn from the ranks of its own MPs. Those serving the party of Government are members of the Government although outside the Cabinet. Working together with the Leader and Shadow Leader of the House, they help to organize parliamentary business. They arrange for MPs who wish to absent themselves from the Commons on a particular occasion to be 'paired' with an absentee from the other major party, thus preserving overall voting strengths. They ensure that there is always a quorum in the House. Their most important functions, however, are carried out as servants of their party. Whips are one of the main channels through which party leaders and back-benchers are kept informed of each other's feelings. They can tell party leaders if back-bench opinion is unfavourable to a particular policy, and they can explain to back-benchers the views of the leadership. Thus Whips act as a potentially stabilizing force within parties. But although they occupy an interim position between the leaders and the rank-and-file, their main loyalty is to the former. Each week they circulate a memorandum to their party members outlining the week's business. If an item is underlined three times, that indicates to the MP that his support for his party in the division lobbies is absolutely essential. To ignore a 'three-line Whip' can be a very serious matter for an MP. A two-line Whip indicates that although the matter is important, support for it is not vital, while a one-line Whip carries still less force. The Whips play a central role in maintaining 'discipline' in both Houses of Parliament, and we shall have occasion to refer to them again.

Question
2 Having read the whole of this chapter so far, make a list of features of life in the House of Commons which are likely (a) to promote, (b) to detract from the quality of legislation.

Private Members' Bills
Ten Fridays in each session are allocated for Private Members'

legislation. MPs wishing to introduce a Bill may proceed in one of two ways. Either they may enter a ballot, held each session, to determine which Bills shall be introduced on the designated days, or, less frequently, they may proceed under the 'ten minute rule'. Here they hand in a motion requesting leave to introduce a Bill and, after question time on Tuesday or Wednesday, are called by the Speaker to make a short speech in its favour. One further brief speech may be made against the proposal, after which the House votes. If the motion is passed, the Bill is judged to have passed first reading.

Whichever method MPs choose, they face difficulties. Most obviously they cannot use the Parliamentary Counsel to draft the Bill, but must either do it themselves or employ lawyers with knowledge of parliamentary procedure to do it for them. They may also have difficulty in consulting the various interest groups affected by the Bill. Before they introduce it they must ensure that they have a quorum for the debate, and even if they manage to achieve that, they can do little to prevent the Bill from being 'talked out'. In short Private Members' Bills are unlikely to be successful unless they have the support of the Government and can persuade it to use some of its parliamentary time for them. In 1971 the Conservative Government made it clear that it did not intend to provide time for Private Members' Bills, but the Labour Government of 1964–70 showed a more tolerant attitude. The Sexual Offences Bill of 1967, the Medical Termination of Pregnancy Bill and a Bill to improve facilities for the chronically sick and disabled in 1969 were all the result of the encouragement given by the Government to Private Members. So too was Sidney Silverman's Bill in 1965 which led to the abolition of capital punishment.

Document: Private Members' legislation

Below is an extract from an article by Roy Jenkins, a leading Social Democrat and former Cabinet Minister, whose own Private Member's Bill became in 1959 the Obscene Publications Act.

What conclusions can be drawn? Private Members' legislation on a highly controversial subject is clearly still occasionally possible in the British Parliament. But it requires the following combination of circumstances. First, a certain amount of luck; second, a great deal of time and even more patience; third, some all-party support; fourth, a Minister who will be personally sympathetic at crucial times; fifth, some well-organized and determined allies both inside and outside the House of Commons; and sixth, an articulate and impressive body of extra-parliamentary support.

Roy Jenkins, *Essays and Speeches* (Collins 1967), pp. 108–9.

Question

3 From the examples given, what kinds of issues become the subject of Private Members' Bills? Why should this be so?

Delegated legislation

Not all the laws of this country undergo the procedure described above. Some laws of the European Economic Community, for example, are directly applicable in Britain without having gained the approval of Parliament (see page 199). Laws may also be made by ministers or local authorities exercising powers devolved to them by Parliament. This is known as delegated legislation and it has existed for centuries, but since 1945 its volume has increased. Today about 2000 rules and regulations are made each year by ministers.

There are many reasons why the practice is used as often as it is. One reason is simple necessity. Parliament has not got the time or even the competence to handle the complex detail which would have to be included in all legislation were the practice of delegation to cease. Moreover delegation allows a minister and his department to deal flexibly with problems arising from the implementation of an Act, some of which it will have been impossible to anticipate. And it has other virtues. It allows experts to be drawn in to give assistance with technical matters, or interest groups to be consulted on issues of concern to them, before detailed rules and regulations are established. It enables ministers to act swiftly to deal with emergencies such as floods or other natural disasters, the consequences of industrial action, a threat to the stability of the pound, or civil unrest in Northern Ireland. Last, it gives ministers or other authorities the ability to revise their powers to meet a changing situation without having to undertake the lengthy process of passing an amending Bill through Parliament.

Delegated legislation can take a number of forms. The most frequent practice is for a minister to exercise his right deriving from a particular statute to make law for certain purposes. The document expressing this law is known as a Statutory Instrument, and each one is given a number for the year. Full accounts of them are published annually by HMSO in chronological sequence. A further method is by Orders in Council. Here the Sovereign holds a Privy Council (see page 114) and by an Order in Council exercises a power allowed to her by Parliament. The best example is perhaps the power of the Crown under the Emergency Powers Act to declare a state of emergency. A final source of delegated legislation is by-laws. Local authorities or bodies such as British Rail are able to make by-laws which take effect once confirmed by the minister responsible.

The practice of delegated legislation is frequently criticized because of the considerable power it gives to ministers and because of the difficulty Parliament has in determining whether the powers it has delegated are being exercised properly or being abused. Some fear that in pursuit of efficiency delegation could give ministers too much power, free them from direct accountability to Parliament and open the way to arbitrary government.

These dangers have been recognized, and the Statutory Instruments Act of 1946 provides for various methods of parliamentary control. Parliament may, for example, revoke the authority it has given. Also each Act providing for delegation now stipulates how delegated powers shall be brought into force. Some regulations are simply laid before the House for information only and take effect immediately. Others require an affirmative resolution of the House for which the Government must find time. But the most common practice is for orders to be laid before the House and to take effect after forty days, providing that no 'prayer' of annulment has been successfully moved during the period.

In addition parliamentary supervision is assisted by the Select Committee on Statutory Instruments consisting of seven members of each House and chaired by a member of the Opposition. Its function is to keep Statutory Instruments under review, and it has the power to force a government department to justify a new order. Finally, any person may ask the courts to rule that a minister has exceeded his powers in the use of Statutory Instruments. The courts have the authority to declare a rule *ultra vires* (and therefore void) if they feel that provision for the power was not made in the parent Act.

The machinery for control therefore exists, but the bulk and complexity of delegated legislation, the lack of publicity and the shortage of parliamentary time make it difficult to scrutinize powers as closely as may be desirable.

Committees

There are two main kinds of committee in the House of Commons: first, those concerned with legislation passing through Parliament — generally standing committees — and, second, specialist or select committees set up to inquire into a specific aspect of the working of Government or administration.

Standing committees
A number of standing committees are appointed for each parliamentary session. They are known as standing committees A, B, C etc. One standing committees is reserved primarily for Private Members' Bills and

another for Scottish business. Committee usually consists of about thirty or forty MPs (chosen to reflect the distribution of party support in the House of Commons), a minister responsible for the Bill and a Chairman chosen by the Speaker. The proceedings of committees are rarely reported and committees meet in the mornings when some MPs are anxious to pursue their interests outside the House. Nevertheless, over 500 MPs usually make themselves available for standing committee work, although some will clearly be a great deal more active than others. The reason for this degree of involvement is twofold. First, although MPs are still subject to the party Whip (see page 73), proceedings in committee are less informal than in the Chamber of the House and give the back-bencher his best opportunity to influence the character of legislation. Secondly, it is by work on a standing committee that an ambitious MP might first draw himself to the attention of the Whips and, thus, prepare the ground for his advancement.

Select committees

These are of two types. The first, the ad hoc body, is set up to inquire into a specific and immediate issue and breaks up once its inquiry and report are complete. The second kind of select committee is more permanent and has responsibility for looking into the work of a department or a particular subject or even, in the case of the Committee of Privileges and the Committee on House of Commons Services, the working of the House itself. Through the work of such committees it has been possible for Parliament to acquire a deeper understanding of particular issues and therefore to criticize policy more effectively.

In the 1970s new select committees were established on, for example, European legislation and the work of the Parliamentary Commissioner for Administration (see page 148) and, most significantly of all, in 1979 twelve new select committees, each containing between nine and eleven members, were set up to examine the 'expenditure, administration and policy' of specific departments of Government. It is too soon to say how effective these committees will be but the signs are encouraging. Between 1979 and 1983 the total number of ministerial appearances before Departmental Select Committees totalled 224 of which 111 were by Cabinet Ministers. Officials appeared on 1681 occasions. In 1980–81 the Treasury committee subjected the then Chancellor of the Exchequer to a number of vigorous cross-examinations. The Energy committee has scaled down Britain's nuclear power commitment and the Home Affairs committee achieved the repeal of the 'sus' laws. Other committees have looked into issues such as the sale of council houses and economic policy. Although ministers cannot be compelled to attend committee meetings and have occasionally been reluctant to release official material, and although some MPs have argued against the expansion of the committee system on the grounds that it has tended to undermine the authority and importance of debates within the Chamber itself, the majority have welcomed the growth of committees because they have made the Commons more efficient. They have relieved the Chamber of detailed work for which it is not really suited. They have injected greater parliamentary influence into the policy-making process, as well as more effective scrutiny of it. What is also encouraging about such committees is the way they have operated. A select committee cannot be successful if it is subject to pressure from the Whips or if its members are primarily concerned with vindicating their political party. Some but not all select committees have been able to operate with neither of these constraints, and their usefulness is generally directly related to the degree of independence they have had.

A particularly important select committee, the Public Accounts Committee, is considered later (see page 80). The Scottish and Welsh Grant Committees do not fit easily into either of the two categories discussed here, and they will be considered in Chapter 9.

Figure 7   *Some aspects of the Parliament of 1980–81*

House of Commons		House of Lords	
Number of days sitting	163	Number of days sitting	140
Average daily hours of sitting	9hr 07	Average daily hours of sitting	6hr 34
Number of divisions	317	Number of divisions	184
Parliamentary questions: oral	8,175		
: written	22,688	*Parliament 1980–81*	
Select committees: number	41	Public Bills : introduced	151
: meetings	851	: received Royal Assent	71
: MPs involved	309	Private Bills: introduced	42
		: received Royal Assent	32
Standing committees: number	21	Private Members' Bills: introduced	78
: sittings	388	: received Royal Assent	14
: MPs involved	530		

Source: Adapted from *Social Trends* (HMSO 1983).

The control of finance

At the beginning of this chapter it was pointed out that one of the main responsibilities of Parliament is to control the raising and spending of money. In 1983–4 public expenditure in Britain amounted to £125,624 million and a broadly similar figure was raised in taxes. If this could take place without parliamentary approval we should have taken a great step towards arbitrary and authoritarian Government. Parliament must control the purse strings; it must be satisfied that the purposes for which money is raised, the amount that is raised and the way in which it is spent are all consistent with the public interest. This is thus done much less through the chamber of the House of Commons than through particular select committees. The following discussion will make this clear.

The raising of money

The financial year ends on 5 April. On the same day the Government's right to collect most — but not all — taxes expires. At about the same time the Chancellor of the Exchequer presents his annual budget to the House of Commons, and this is accompanied by a White Paper setting out the financial background to it. The budget is the product of months of preparation with the Treasury in the course of which consultation is widespread. The details, however, are a closely guarded secret, and although the Prime Minister will have been involved at all stages, the Chancellor only reveals his proposals to the full Cabinet the day before he presents his budget to Parliament. The budget speech consists of a broad review of the economic situation and, towards the end, the Chancellor's taxation proposals. The House of Commons is then invited to pass resolutions to give immediate effect to the proposals — but only for a period of ten days. During that period the budget is debated for about five days in the Commons, after which the Finance Bill is introduced incorporating its proposals. For these to remain in force, the Finance Bill must have received a second reading within twenty-five days and have passed through all its parliamentary stages within four months. Taxes once collected are paid into the 'Consolidated Fund' at the Bank of England. Thus the House of Commons gives to or withholds from the Government the right to raise money. But it is hardly in a position to make informed criticisms as it lacks detailed knowledge of the likely effects of tax policy.

The spending of money

The House of Commons is equally unable to exercise rigorous control of expenditure. During the summer months the total volume of public expenditure and the priorities for the coming financial year are determined by the Cabinet. In November 'estimates' for each department are submitted to and discussed with the Treasury. In February or March of the following year, after the estimates have been scrutinized by the Treasury, they are published and presented to Parliament.

Three days are now set aside specifically to debate the departmental estimates and the particular estimates to be debated are chosen by the liaison committee. While this arrangement may be preferable to the former practice of using 'supply days' to criticize Government policy in general (thus avoiding detailed scrutiny), it remains true that it is not on the floor of the Commons that close analysis and scrutiny of legisation takes place.

In July or August following the presentation of the estimates, the Appropriation Act is passed authorizing the withdrawal of money in the estimates from the Consolidated Fund. By passing 'votes on account' in March, the Commons enables withdrawals to be made from the Consolidated Fund before the passing of the Appropriation Act in July. Withdrawals themselves are closely supervised but not by the House of Commons. Departments make an application in the first instance to the Treasury. Once the Comptroller and Auditor General (see below) has approved the application, money is transferred to the department concerned. At the end of the financial year each department is audited to ensure that there are no irregularities in its expenditure. This procedure relates to supply services granted by Parliament for one year only and based on the estimates. A different procedure operates for 'Consolidated Fund Services' as these do not require annual parliamentary approval. The sums of money involved are relatively small and cover items such as the Civil List (see page 117) and salaries for the Leader of the Opposition, the Speaker and High Court judges.

The scrutiny of expenditure
The main responsibility for the scrutiny of finance is exercised not by the House of Commons as a whole (which, because of its size, is unsuited to the task) but by select committees of which the most important is the Public Accounts Committee (PAC). This has fifteen members and is chaired by a member of the Opposition. The committee works closely with the Comptroller and Auditor General, an officer of the House of Commons, who sits with the committee and whose reports to Parliament provide the foundation for its work. About 60 per cent of total public expenditure is scrutinized by the Comptroller and Auditor General. Outside his jurisdiction are Local Authorities, the nationalized industries and the health authorities. The Public Accounts Committee examines accounts of past public expenditure, ensuring that it has been used for authorized purposes and drawing attention to wasteful expenditure. Between 1965 and 1978, the PAC examined various departments on nearly 400 separate issues and made recommendations which, in 45 per cent of cases, produced a response from the department. Part of the reason for its success and for its position as the most prestigious select

committee at Westminster, is that its work is essentially non-political and its reports nearly always unanimous.

Until 1979 an Expenditure Committee reviewing future patterns of expenditure also existed. This was wound up on the establishment of the new departmental committees.

Questions
4 Using pages 75–81 of this chapter, consider the various ways in which committees are able to exercise control over the work of Government.
5 Examine the differences between the role of the House of Commons and the role of Commons' committees.

The back-bench MP

Becoming an MP
In Chapter 2 we saw that about 75 per cent of the seats may be regarded as safe in that they do not usually change hands from one general election to another. In these constituencies it is very frequently the case that to become the candidate of the strongest party is to become the MP. Moreover, once someone wishing to enter Parliament has been adopted in a 'safe' constituency, the biggest hurdle he or she is likely to find to a parliamentary career has been cleared.

The procedure for selecting candidates has already been described (see page 29), and we have seen that it gives considerable power to the local constituency parties. It is therefore important for a candidate once adopted to maintain a good relationship with his local party. That is certainly a more important consideration than the need to retain a close relationship with the electorate. The constituency party membership may not amount to more than about 200, and those actually involved directly in the selection of the candidate may be no more than twenty, but within their constituency their power is formidable. (The importance of this from the point of view of the freedom of the MP is considered below.)

Conditions of work
In 1986, an MP's salary was around £17,500. In addition, MPs may claim certain expenses. They are allowed free travel between their home, their constituencies and Westminster, and their spouses and children are entitled to fifteen free return journeys each year within a similar triangle. They have allowances for the use of a car within their constituencies, for accommodation in London and for secretarial and research assistance. In addition, they have free use of the postal and telephone services and an allowance for office equipment.

These allowances have improved substantially in recent years but the working facilities of MPs remain generally poor. Many do not have a private office and the parliamentary routine, according to one former MP, the late John Mackintosh, makes the life of an MP fragmented and lacking in coherence.

When Parliament is in session MPs work a long day. Most receive a daily mailbag of between fifty to a hundred letters from constituents, pressure groups or other organizations (see Figure 8). These are usually attend to in the mornings. Then too they may be serving on standing committees or preparing themselves for a debate in Parliament later in the day. In the afternoon and evening an MP may be fully occupied in the chamber, but he or she is more likely to spend a good proportion of that time in seeing constituents or other delegations visiting the Commons, in attending party or other meetings, in contacting ministers or civil servants about particular issues which he or she cannot deal with alone, or simply in discussing issues informally in the members' rooms in the House of Commons. At weekends the majority of MPs undertake duties in their constituencies. About once a month they hold 'surgeries' at which they see constituents and deal with their problems personally. They are often expected to participate in social or fund-raising activities. It is certainly true that a constituency — or to be more exact, a constituency party — expects to see its MP regularly and may be displeased with one who is seldom available for weekend engagements.

Figure 8 *Mr Benn's correspondence as MP for Bristol South-East from 1 April 1972 to 31 March 1973*

(a) *General breakdown*	From MP	To MP
Constituents and constituency organizations	1958	1266
On behalf of constituents	880	
About constituents in response to letters on their behalf		907
Total	2838	2173

(b) *Particular aspects of correspondence*	From MP	To MP
Central government	286	336
Nationalized industries and public agencies	72	85
Local government	424	420
Private sector	99	73

(c)   Mr Benn's total correspondence amounted to 5011 letters covering 1106 cases. The average number of cases being dealt with at any one time was 90.

Source: Frances Morrell, *The Electors of Bristol,* Spokesman Pamphlet No. 57 (1977).

Many MPs do have interests and occupations outside the Commons —
in, for example, the law, business or consultancy work — which give them
an additional source of income. In 1984, 179 MPs held 388 company
directorships, and Mr Parkinson, who left Mrs Thatcher's Cabinet in
1983, subsequently joined the boards of nine companies. But such
interests are becoming increasingly difficult to combine with parliamentary life. Today, the pressures upon MPs from Parliament, their
constituencies and pressure groups often restrict opportunities outside.
This has tended to make politics more of a profession and to make the
parliamentary salary the only source of income for many MPs. Although
an MP who loses his seat to find himself unemployed does receive his
parliamentary salary for a further six months, the effect of his dependence
upon his salary is to increase his dependence on the party he represents.

Questions
6 What impression of (a) the work and (b) the usefulness of the
  constituency MP emerges from Figure 8?
7 Why might the survey (which is the only one of its kind we have) not be
  entirely representative of the work of MPs within their constituencies?

The duties of an MP
Whose interests ought MPs to serve? Their own? Those of their party?
Those of their constituency association? Or those of the nation? This
has been a controversial issue in recent years, and some views on it are
set out below.

Documents: MPs and their constituents

1 Edmund Burke, 'Speech to the Electors of Bristol 1774', in Speeches and Letters on American Affairs *(Dent 1908), p.73*

Your representative owes you not his industry only, but his judgement; and he
betrays instead of serving you if he sacrifices it to your opinion. . . . Parliament is
not a congress of ambassadors from different and hostile interests . . . it is a
deliberative assembly of one nation, with one interest, that of the whole. . . . You
choose a member indeed; but when you have chosen him, he is not a member of
Bristol, but he is a member of Parliament.

2 Letter from Mr Frank Allaun MP (Labour) to The Times, 8 July 1975

Mr Allaun's letter concerned the attempt then being made by Newham

North-East Constituency Labour Party to force the MP for Newham, Mr Reg Prentice, to stand down at the next election.

What is in fact at stake are two principles which are basic to the democratic Labour movement, namely the right of a constituency Labour party to be represented by an MP of its own choice, and the ultimate accountability of such an MP to the party organization which was instrumental to his selection and election. . . .

3 *Letter from Lord Shawcross to* The Times, *10 July 1975*

In the days, now perhaps long past, when democracy meant more or less the same thing to most intelligent people, 'a constituency Labour party' certainly had no 'right to be represented by an MP of its own choice' as Mr Allaun puts it, nor was 'the ultimate accountability of such an MP to the party organization'. In those days the right of the constituency party was to promote a particular candidate. But if the candidate was elected as an MP his 'accountability' was not to his party organization but to the electors as a whole. And, occasionally, perhaps, to his conscience? . . .

It is partly because so many MPs . . . choose to reduce themselves to the status of mere delegates of a local chamber of commerce, trade union or constituency party representing a handful of partisans that there is nowadays so great a disillusion with our parliamentary institutions. . . .

All honour to those (and Mr Prentice may be one of them) who instead of constantly talking . . . about what the party wants occasionally talk of what the country needs and count that higher than what some constituency caucus may clamour for.

4 *From Tony Benn,* Arguments for Democracy *(Penguin 1982), p.190*

What is wrong is that there is a fundamental structural weakness in the way the party is organised in Parliament and in its relationship with the party in the country.

What is the answer of members of Parliament to this problem? Some just accept it, others do not. Others express a point of view that runs like this: 'Once I have been elected to Parliament, I represent everybody — not just the Labour Party.' But in what sense does a Labour MP represent everybody in his or her constituency? Geographically, of course, he or she does. Everyone in the MP's constituency will come to him or her for advice. Labour MPs must try to help all their constituents impartially. But we do not represent the views of people who did not vote for us. This is a very important distinction that must not be blurred.

In no sense can election to Parliament give a Labour MP the right to abandon his or her political commitment or the manifesto policy upon which he or she was elected. It is just because some Labour MPs have seemed to argue that they can do so that there has been a move to secure the accountability of a Labour MP to his or her constituency party by mandatory re-selection. The object of re-selection is not to get rid of members of Parliament. It is to introduce that same element of accountability of an MP to his local party that we want the Cabinet to have in respect of the parliamentary party. It is to secure greater power for the Labour MPs over the parliamentary leadership, and greater accountability for the constituency parties over the use MPs make of that power.

Questions

8 How do the views expressed by Allaun and Benn differ from those of Burke and Shawcross? Consider in particular their contrasting attitudes to democracy, party and Parliament.
9 Whose views do you consider to be the most 'democratic'? Why?

Today it is probably true to say that many MPs would like to see their responsibilities in Burke's terms. Many are drawn into politics by a certain idealism and have mature and considered views on the great political questions. Most have a clear vision of the kind of Britain they would like to help to create. It is understandable and proper that they should want to feel free as MPs to vote as their consciences tell them for what they perceive to be the national interest, rather than feel under an obligation to reflect the views of their constituents or of their constituency party, which on many issues will probably be less informed. Certainly, many of the most memorable parliamentary occasions have taken place precisely when MPs, conscious of the historic importance of their decisions, have spoken and voted in the House of Commons out of a sense of deep personal commitment rather than along local or party lines. In 1940, for example, forty-one of the Government's usual supporters voted against it in the Norway debate and a further sixty abstained. Neville Chamberlain, the Prime Minister, resigned. Similarly, in 1971, sixty-nine Labour MPs voted with the Conservative Government on the question of Britain's entry into the European Economic Community. On both occasions MPs recognised a higher loyalty than that due to their party and expressed it in the manner of their voting.

Nevertheless it would be foolish not to recognize that the majority of MPs today feel an instinctive loyalty to their party. This is easy to understand. Many have been life-long members of it. To fail to support it would seem a betrayal. They do not need to be 'whipped' into support; they are proud to identify with it. And there are other considerations as well. It is only by virtue of standing as the representative for a party that most MPs gained a parliamentary seat at all. The electorate has a reasonable expectation that the successful candidate will support the party in whose interests he or she fought the campaign. For an MP to adopt an independent stance, having stood as a party candidate, would constitute a breach of faith.

Opportunities open to a back-bench MP

Many people today are cynical about the value of the work of back-benchers in the House of Commons. Some writers, such as Richard Crossman, have stated that the only real job of a back-bencher 'is to support the front-bench', and Mr Woodrow Wyatt a former Labour MP has written that the back-bench MP performs trivial functions. It is certainly true that because our method of government is based upon the party system and because the party in power dominates the parliamentary timetable, the opportunities available to the back-bencher are limited. Nevertheless a back-bench MP does have certain opportunities to exercise influence. In the House of Commons he can table questions for ministers, speak in debates, try to introduce a Private Members' Bill, play a role on the committee stage of a Bill or on one of the twelve new Departmental Select Committees, communicate his feelings to the Whip, and most obviously he can, if he feels particularly strongly about an issue, vote against his party. This action is more likely to be meaningful if the Government is in a minority position in the House of Commons. In 1977 two Labour MPs, John Mackintosh and Brian Walden, were able to frustrate part of the Government's legislative programme by voting against the Dock Work Regulation Bill.

But in general, the main influence of the back-bench MP is exerted outside the chamber of the House of Commons. MPs are free to express their opinions in the press and on radio and television, where they are able to communicate with a wide audience. More importantly, they can raise issues and grievances at meetings of the Parliamentary Labour Party or, in the case of the Conservatives, the 1922 Committee. Here, free from the pressure of the Whips, back-benchers can seek to influence the leadership by argument but also by threats to withhold support. It was, for example, the feeling that the Parliamentary Labour Party might revolt which forced Mr Wilson to abandon his proposed trade union reform in 1969. It should also be remembered that both major parties in Britain now have formal procedures for electing their leaders. The importance of this was made particularly clear in 1975 when Mr Heath was deposed and Mrs Thatcher was elected leader of the Conservative Party. It was widely felt at the time that Conservative MPs had voted to give a new style and identity to the party after its two defeats in the general elections of 1974. So it proved to be.

Document: An MP's discontent

Mr Rose explained in his article why, after fifteen years as an MP, he was not intending to stand for re-election ('Why am I quitting', *Guardian*, 23 February 1979).

Of course, backbenchers have a role. When they combine to express a widely-felt dissatisfaction with Government policy they can become a formidable force. . . . But . . . the MP's life is so fragmented and disorganized, his back-up of half a secretary and occasional help on research so inadequate, that he can scarcely compete with the phalanx of specialists trained to deflect the probing eye from the Minister's obvious failures . . .

I believe that our present parliamentary system stifles individuality and innovation. It is illiberal and based on the flow of power from the top downwards. . . . For weaker mortals like myself, 15 years knocking one's head against a brick wall is long enough.

Question
10 In what sense is the work of a back-bench MP important?

The Opposition

The importance of opposition
One of the simplest hallmarks of a free society is to be found in the existence and status of an organized Opposition to the Government of the day. In Britain this status is recognized in the payment of an official salary to the Leader of the Opposition and the Opposition Chief Whip and also in the traditional courtesies which are extended by the Government to the Opposition and which are discussed below. The Opposition plays an essential role in the day-to-day affairs of Parliament, but more importantly it symbolizes the existence of free institutions.

The role of the Opposition
It is often said that the function of an Opposition is to oppose the Government. In a sense, this is true. The Opposition stood apart from the Government at the preceding general election and probably advocated policies and principles different from those espoused by the Government. It is natural and proper that it should oppose those with whom it disagrees.

But a good Opposition will not oppose the Government for the sake of it. Nor will it try to obstruct the Government's programme. Rather it will be alert and critical but also responsible. It will scrutinize the Government's actions and proposals and continually force the Government to account for the ways in which its powers are being used. It will also try to be constructive. It will seek to influence Government policy by advancing alternative proposals of its own, remembering that these proposals should present the Opposition as a credible alternative Government-in-waiting. The Opposition will lack credibility if its criticism is not thoughtful and considered. It should also remember that it represents political ideas and policies which, although rejected by the electorate as a whole, do nevertheless command substantial support in the country. It is the duty of the Opposition to keep these beliefs and policies alive, to develop them in the light of changing circumstance and to act as the spokesman within Parliament and in the country for that substantial proportion of the electorate which the Government does not represent. What these responsibilities mean in practice we must now see.

The work of the Opposition

The Leader of the Opposition sits opposite the Prime Minister in the House of Commons and acts as his or her 'shadow', just as members of the 'Shadow Cabinet' have the duty of replying to their ministerial counterparts. The Opposition has no right to introduce legislation into the House of Commons (although members of the Opposition may, of course, try to initiate a Private Member's Bill), but it still makes an important contribution to the work of Parliament. Government and Opposition together, through their respective Chief Whips and the Leader and Shadow Leader of the House, arrange the parliamentary timetable. Opposition spokesmen challenge ministers at question time and reply to them in debates. Moreover, the Opposition has the right to choose the subjects for debate in the nineteen days reserved for Opposition business and in reply to the Queen's Speech. Such occasions enable it to focus attention on an issue the Government may prefer to ignore or to choose subjects which will cause ministers the maximum possible embarrassment and win favourable publicity for the Opposition in the national press. They also serve to rally support and raise morale in both Parliament and in the country. More dramatically, the Opposition may table against the Government a motion of censure or no confidence. These are debated as soon as is possible — usually within days — and if the Government is defeated, it is expected to announce a general election. The Opposition also has a right of reply on radio or television to ministerial broadcasts.

But an Opposition must choose the ground on which to fight the Government very carefully. It is likely to have the maximum impact if it concentrates its efforts on a few areas of policy where the Government may be particularly vulnerable. It must also try to criticize the Government without over-committing itself in respect of future policies. It may choose, for example, to criticize the detail of a particular policy rather than the principle behind it. This Mr Wilson did in 1971 when, as Leader of the Opposition, he criticized the specific terms negotiated by Mr Heath's Government for Britain's entry into the European Economic Community but was careful not to attack the principle of membership. In this way his own future freedom of action on the European question was secured. Mrs Thatcher too, as Leader of the Opposition between 1975 and 1979, tended to avoid detailed policy statements.

The Opposition can also, as we have seen, use committees such as the Public Accounts Committee, of which a leading member of the Opposition is chairman, to scrutinize Government policies. In addition the Prime Minister will usually keep the Leader of the Opposition informed of developments concerning foreign affairs and defence where it is understood that there is a common interest.

Problems facing the Opposition

One of the most difficult problems facing the Opposition is that of its own morale. It is very easy for a party, having perhaps been rejected by the electorate on two or three successive occasions, to become bitter, divided and preoccupied with its own troubles to the point where its ability to present itself as a convincing alternative Government is diminished. This happened to a degree to the Labour Opposition between 1970 and 1974, although it did not prevent the Labour Party from returning to power in February 1974. Similar divisions within the party after 1979, however, probably did weaken considerably the party's prospects of success in the 1983 General Election in which Labour was heavily defeated. The major responsibility for maintaining morale inevitably falls upon the leader. The task is not an easy one. Government, for example, is a natural focus for publicity, the Opposition less so. The Government's confidence in the House of Commons is usually greater because it is making proposals rather than simply reacting to them and because when Government speaks, it is with the backing and expertise of the Civil Service. The Opposition does not have this facility and is invariably less well informed. Finally, if the Government has a comfortable majority in the Commons, it can pass its legislative programme whatever criticisms the Opposition may make. To be speaking and voting repeatedly in the Commons without any apparent effect on policy is bound to be dispiriting.

The Opposition is also, it appears, unable to do much to influence the result of the next election. A great deal of the evidence suggests that it is Governments which lose elections rather than Oppositions which win them. Thus Mr Gaitskell's leadership of the Labour Opposition between 1955 and 1959 won much praise, but it did not prevent Mr Macmillan's Government from being re-elected at a time when living standards for most of the people were, as Mr Macmillan pointed out, rising steadily. In contrast, although Mr Heath won the 1970 General Election, he had never been a particularly impressive Leader of the Opposition, and his success may rather be attributed to the electorate's dissatisfaction with the record of the Labour Government than to anything he did.

5 Government, Cabinet and Prime Minister

While it is convenient to consider Parliament separately from Government, there is, in Britain, no simple and genuine division between the functions of the two. The Government (and Cabinet) are drawn from Parliament and sit in Parliament. But questions about the distribution of power within Government, and about the ability of Parliament to control Government remain controversial. It will be part of the purpose of this chapter to explore them.

In the first place, however, we should make clear the terms we are using. 'Parliament' comprises Commons, Lords and Sovereign. Together they form the legislature. 'Government', on the other hand, refers to Cabinet ministers, ministers of state, under-secretaries and parliamentary secretaries who have been chosen by the Prime Minister from his or her party to hold office. Together they number about 100. A much smaller group of just over twenty form the Cabinet (the executive) at the head of which is the Prime Minister. The Cabinet stands today at the very centre of power in Britain. It is the most important and authoritative part of Government.

Government

During the twentieth century the responsibilities of Government have become increasingly complex. While the great offices of state are, as at the beginning of the century, the Exchequer, the Foreign Office and the Home Office, many new departments have since appeared as a result of the growing involvement of Government in a much wider area of our national life. The Departments of Employment, Energy, Environment, Health and Social Security, and Trade and Industry, to name the most obvious, are all relatively new.

This rapid expansion in the functions of Government has been accompanied, quite understandably, by an increase in the size of Governments. In the 1880s the Government consisted of thirty-five ministers, fourteen of whom were in the Cabinet. By 1939 the number of ministers had grown to fifty-nine, and today it is even larger. Mrs Thatcher's administration, formed in June 1983, consisted of twenty-one Cabinet ministers and a further eighty-four ministers outside the Cabinet. Most ministers have duties specifically related to the work of their departments, although some are free from departmental responsibilities and are given specific duties by the Prime Minister. Perhaps the best example of such a position is the office of Chancellor of the Duchy of Lancaster. In Mr Callaghan's Government this was held by Mr Harold Lever, whose main concern was economic policy, whereas when Mr Heath became Prime Minister in 1970, Mr Rippon was given the office and placed in charge of Common Market negotiations.

Although there is no statutory limit on the number of ministers a Government may have, no more than ninety-one ministers may have seats in the House of Commons. Mrs Thatcher's second administration contained twenty-one peers.

The Cabinet

Function

Although any minister wields greater influence on the formulation of policy than the ordinary MP, it is the Cabinet that is the centre of political authority in Britain. In Bagehot's famous phrase, the Cabinet is a 'combining committee — a hyphen which joins, a buckle which fastens, the legislative part of the state to the executive part of the state'. Its main purpose is to determine and co-ordinate the policy of Government. Without the sense of unity and coherence a good Cabinet can give to an administration, Governments can very easily become Governments of departments with each minister defending the interests of his department rather than considering Government policy as a whole. It is the responsibility of the Cabinet to reconcile the competing and at times conflicting claims of ministers, to establish priorities in Government action, to select those items from the party's manifesto which need to be dealt with urgently and to discard those which are of only secondary concern, to modify policy in the light of changing circumstance, to respond to unforeseen crises and to keep in mind a general vision of the future which it is part of the purpose of Government policy to bring about.

Choosing the Cabinet

The responsibility of choosing the Cabinet lies with the Prime Minister (although he or she might consult others, for example the Leader of the House and the Chief Whip). It is an important example of Prime Ministerial power. Through their choice, Prime Ministers can do a great deal to determine the character of an administration as well as the policy of major departments. Nevertheless, they are not entirely free in the choices they make. They will generally choose from the more experienced parliamentarians, although there have been a number of obvious recent exceptions. Mr Cousins became Minister of Technology on entering Parliament in 1964, and Mr Davies became Minister for Trade and Industry in Mr Heath's Government in 1970 without any previous parliamentary experience. Prime Ministers want individuals who are capable of dealing efficiently with affairs within their department, of taking decisions in the light of Government policy and of defending those policies with conviction in the House of Commons. They also want ministers able to work together as a team and to recognize that whatever their individual differences, they have a common responsibility to preserve the unity and strength of the administration. Two views on the responsibilities of a Cabinet minister are given in the documents below.

Documents: Two views of a minister's responsibility within Cabinet

1 *From R.H.S. Crossman,* Inside View *(Cape 1972), p.70*

The Cabinet Minister goes to the Cabinet as the champion of his Department and, therefore, goes supplied with a departmental brief. Where expenditure is concerned, a Department is usually well enough briefed to give him the arguments which the Chancellor is going to use, and the reply to them. (And, no doubt, the Chancellor has been briefed in the same way against him!) He is there to fight the battle of the Department in the absence of the Department.

The Department is at his mercy because no official is allowed to be present at the Cabinet meetings, apart from the Cabinet Secretary. One of the ways Ministers' reputations are established in Whitehall is through their success or failure in winning victories in the Cabinet. Any Minister knows his reputation depends on his doughtiness in the infighting in Cabinet.

2 *From P. Gordon Walker,* The Cabinet *(Cape 1971), pp.31–2*

My own attitude as a Minister always leaned to the view that the loyalty and interest of each member of a Cabinet is to its policy as a whole. ...

A conflict of departmental interests of a sharp kind arose in the long Cabinet discussions early in 1968 on large savings on proposed Government spending. As Secretary of State for Education I did not conceive it as my sole or prime duty to fight all out and at all costs in defence of my departmental Estimates as they stood. Each department in my view had to try and forward the Government's collective policy by agreeing to accept economies.

This attempt to take a governmental and not merely a departmental line was not popular amongst all departmental ministers and was attacked by some of them.

Question
1 Which of these two views do you prefer? Why?

Prime Ministers are concerned too with wider considerations. As party leaders they are anxious not to lose contact with their back-bench supporters. Because parties are coalitions, Cabinets must be coalitions, for if the debate within the Cabinet does not reflect the debate within the party, then the danger of the Government becoming remote from its supporters is considerable. It is indeed a positive advantage to a Prime Minister to have some critics in the Cabinet because of the control and influence he may then have over them and because of the assistance such colleagues may be able to give to the Prime Minister in winning the support of their wing of the party for unpopular policies.

But this does not mean that Prime Ministers have to balance wings of the party exactly. They will want to achieve a balance in favour of those like themselves. Mr Callaghan's Cabinet, for example, contained in Mr Foot, Mr Benn, Mr Shore and Mr Silkin, four prominent politicians identified with the left of the party, but they were easily outnumbered by those such as Mr Healey, Mr Jenkins, Mr Crosland, Mr Dell and Mrs Williams, who stood with Mr Callaghan on the centre-right of the party. Moreover, Mr Callaghan ensured that the office of Chancellor of the Exchequer, carrying influence over a whole range of policies related to the Government's economic strategy, went to a minister (Mr Healey) whose views corresponded to his own. At the same time, Mr Foot, a powerful and influential figure on the left of the Labour Party, was denied similar political influence through being appointed Leader of the House, in charge of the Government's devolution proposals and the parliamentary timetable. Equally, Mrs Thatcher's second administration formed in June 1983 had, like her first, a clear bias in favour of those whose political outlook accorded with her own. Of those who were doubtful of the wisdom of Mrs Thatcher's economic policy (often referred to as 'the wets'), only Mr Prior and Mr Walker remained, while other 'wets' such as Mr St John Stevas, Mr Carlyle, Mr Gilmour and Mr Pym, all members of her first administration, had been dismissed.

A Prime Minister will also want a balance of youth and experience to ensure that the Cabinet is again representative of the party, but also to prepare the next generation of party leaders. Mr Callaghan's appointment of Dr David Owen as Foreign Secretary at the age of thirty-eight in February 1977 may best be explained by his desire to bring to positions of power within the Labour Party young and promising men with views similar to his own.

The size of the Cabinet is another matter to which a Prime Minister has to give consideration. During the nineteenth century the average size was between twelve and fifteen, but the tendency in this century has been for it to be larger. Most Prime Ministers would probably like to keep the size of their Cabinets under twenty because it enables business to be transacted more speedily and because there are fewer views to reconcile. The very size of modern Government, however, makes this difficult. To reduce the size of the Cabinet much below twenty would require excluding ministers with important departmental responsibilities. But there is perhaps a further reason why the size of Cabinets has grown. To hold office is the ambition of many more MPs today than in the last century, and it is an aspiration which Prime Ministers are under pressure to satisfy. To restrict the size of the Cabinet (and also the Government) is to risk creating resentment on the backbenches. No Prime Minister would wish to do this unnecessarily.

During Mr Wilson's Government of 1964–70, the view was frequently expressed that an 'inner Cabinet' existed. It is certainly true that throughout much of the period of that Government, Mr Wilson was encouraged (by Mr Crosman in particular) to form an 'inner Cabinet' to give purpose and direction to governmental policy. It is doubtful, however, if such a group ever seriously existed, and Mr Gordon Walker, who was a member of that administration, has dismissed it as 'no more than an informal small group of friends or confidants of the Prime Minister drawn from members of the Cabinet'. Such groups probably exist within most Cabinets, and it is natural that they should. Prime Ministers should, however, be aware of the danger that too many informal consultations with a favoured minority could isolate them from the Government as a whole. During the Falklands War in 1982 Mrs Thatcher established a War Cabinet of five to handle the Government's response to the war from day to day. This inner-Cabinet was, however, disbanded when the war came to an end.

How the Cabinet works

The Cabinet generally meets once or twice a week, usually in the morning and in the Cabinet Room at No. 10 Downing Street, although Prime Ministers are free to summon Cabinets wherever and whenever they please. The usual custom is for the agenda and papers relating to a meeting to be circulated to ministers forty-eight hours in advance, but when Cabinets meet to discuss an emergency, business is raised orally.

The table around which the Cabinet meets is boat-shaped and seating is arranged by the Prime Minister and the Cabinet Secretary (see page 98). Certain placements are fixed by convention. Speakers in Cabinet are called by the Prime Minister, who will know whose views on a particular issue he or she would like to hear. Members refer to each other by the title of their office and speeches are brief — generally not longer than five minutes. A common practice is for notes to be passed from one minister to another commenting on proceedings or encouraging a minister to enter the discussion. The agenda, which is drawn up by the Prime Minister in consultation with the Cabinet Secretary, is of central importance, and it is one of the most obvious sources of Prime Ministerial authority. The Prime Minister may exercise his or her power to bring an issue before the Cabinet or may, as Mr Wilson did with the issue of devaluation between 1964 and 1967, exclude it from the agenda altogether. Furthermore, the Prime Minister can determine the sequence of items on the agenda, knowing that those at the bottom are unlikely to be considered as fully as the first few.

It would be dangerous, however, to exaggerate the power which the control of the agenda gives to the Prime Minister. In the first place, two items, parliamentary business and Foreign and Commonwealth affairs, are raised weekly. Second, there are some items which virtually choose themselves, such as crises upon which a Prime Minister would be reluctant to act without consulting his or her colleagues. Third, Ministers acting individually or as a group will freqently put pressure upon the Prime Minister to have a particular item included. The Prime Minister's influence on the agenda is considerable, but it cannot be exercised indiscriminately.

The Prime Minister will usually open a discussion by inviting the minister directly concerned to speak on the paper circulated to ministers. He or she will then invite the views of other colleagues and usually sum up the mood of the meeting at the end. It is incorrect to say that voting never takes place in the Cabinet, but it is highly unusual for it to do so. Mr Heath said shortly after leaving office in 1974 that in all the Cabinets in which he had sat throughout his political career, a vote had never taken place. Mr Attlee, the Labour Prime Minister between 1945 and 1951, never took a vote, but Mr Wilson between 1964 and 1970 sometimes made a note of the views of colleagues as they spoke and, according to Mr Gordon Walker, occasionally announced the result. There are two main reasons why voting is rare. First, by drawing attention to differences between members, it might threaten Cabinet unity. Second, and perhaps more important, it would give ministers parity of status, whereas in practice not all ministers in the Cabinet carry the same weight. In a discussion on economic strategy, for example, a Prime Minister will clearly attach greater importance to the views of the Chancellor than to the views of a minister less closely involved with the economy. The Cabinet is not and cannot be a democratic body.

Cabinet committees
The committee system has been one of the most important developments in the working of the Cabinet in the twentieth century. There are two main

kinds of committee: standing committees covering different areas of policy such as defence, home affairs, social services and the Government's legislative programme in general, and ad hoc committees, set up to deal with particular problems, possibly of a specialized or inter-departmental nature. Committees are appointed by the Prime Minister. Some writers, such as Richard Crossman, have suggested that the growth of the committee system has weakened the Cabinet in general and, through the right of appointment, strengthened the Prime Minister. It is certainly true — indeed it was intended — that committees reach decisions enabling some aspects of Government policy to be settled outside Cabinet. Whether this is undesirable is another matter. The pressure on a modern Cabinet is such that without committees it would be impossible for Cabinets to deal efficiently with all the business coming before them.

But the justification for the committee system does not rest purely on necessity. It enables the individual minister to work more quickly. It transfers much straightforward decision-making from Cabinet leaving it freer to concentrate on important decisions. It enables ministers outside the Cabinet to make a positive contribution to the work of the Government through participating in the decision-making process. Furthermore it ensures that when an issue does come to Cabinet, the discussion is much more informed, for papers and minutes relating to the work of every committee are circulated to ministers. In short, the committee system helps the Cabinet to be more efficient.

The chairman of each committee may or may not be the minister most closely involved in the work of the committee, but the usual practice is for the Prime Minister to appoint to the chair a senior Cabinet colleague without departmental responsibilities. Prime Ministers are usually anxious for committees to reach decisions, and this is the responsibility of the chairman, although where agreement is clearly not possible or where, for example, delicate party political issues may be involved, a chairman may decide to take the matter to Cabinet.

One of the main criticisms made of Cabinet committees concerns the secretive manner in which they operate. Very seldom is the composition of committees or even their existence known. In April 1984 *The Times* published a detailed analysis of Cabinet committees, extracts from which are set out in Figure 9. This identified 52 committees of which 27 are listed here. In all there are probably around 135 such committees and in view of the influence they exercise, such excessive secrecy is difficult to justify.

Figure 9 *Some major Cabinet committees (April 1984)*

Committee initials	Chairman	Functions
		Economic and industrial
EA	Margaret Thatcher (Prime Minister)	Economic strategy, energy policy, changes in labour law, the most important EEC matters
E(EX)	Margaret Thatcher	Exports policy
E(NI)	Margaret Thatcher	Public sector strategy and oversight of the nationalized industries
E(NF)	Nigel Lawson (Chancellor of the Exchequer)	Nationalized industry finance
E(PSP)	Nigel Lawson	Public sector and public service pay policy
E(DL)	Nigel Lawson	Disposal and privatization of state assets
E(PU)	Norman Tebbit (Trade & Industry Secretary)	'Buy British' policy for public purchasing
E(CS)	Peter Rees (Chief Secretary)	Civil Service pay and contingency plans for Civil Service strikes
		Oversea and defence
OD	Margaret Thatcher	Foreign affairs, defence and Northern Ireland
OD(E)	Sir Geoffrey Howe (Foreign Secretary)	EEC policy
OD(SA)	Margaret Thatcher	Committee on the South Atlantic, the so-called 'War Cabinet' of 1982
OD(FOF)	Margaret Thatcher	Committee on the future of the Falklands
		Home, legislation and information
L	John Biffen (Leader of the House)	Future legislation and Queen's speech
H	Lord Whitelaw	Home affairs and social policy, including education
CCU	Lord Whitelaw	The Civil Contingencies Unit of the Cabinet Office which plans for the maintenance of essential supplies and services during industrial disputes
H(HL)	Lord Whitelaw	Reform of the House of Lords
M10	Bernard Ingham (No. 10 Press Secretary)	Weekly meeting of chief information officers
		Intelligence and security
MIS	Margaret Thatcher	Ministerial steering committee on intelligence which supervises MI5, MI6 and GCHQ and fixes budget priorities
PSIS	Sir Robert Armstrong	Permanent secretaries' steering group on intelligence: prepares briefs for ministerial group
Official Committee on Security	Sir Robert Armstrong	Permanent secretaries' group on internal security
		Ad hoc
MISC 7	Margaret Thatcher	Replacement of the Polaris force with Trident
MISC 14	Nigel Lawson	Policy innovations
MISC 21	Lord Whitelaw	Ministerial committee which meets each autumn to fix the level of rate and transport support grants for local authorities
MISC 62	Lord Whitelaw	The 'Star Chamber' for forcing spending cuts on departmental ministers
MISC 79	Lord Whitelaw	Alternatives to domestic rates: rate-capping
MISC 87	Nigel Lawson	De-indexing of benefits
MISC 95	Margaret Thatcher	Abolition of the GLC and the metropolitan counties

Source: Adapted from *The Times*, 30 April 1984

Documents: Cabinet committees

1 Harold Wilson, The Governance of Britain *(Weidenfeld and Nicolson 1976), p.86–7*

We have seen that the development of Cabinet committees has been used by adherents of the Crossman school to suggest that the power of the Prime Minister is enhanced thereby. This is a facile view: what it does is to make the whole government more effective, and to shield Cabinet from over-absorption in detail. . . . The principal checks on over-delegation, or lack of co-ordination with other sectors of the government, are, first, the right of any minister to ask for the matter to go to Cabinet on appeal. . . ; second, the ability of the Prime Minister to direct that such and such an issue shall go straight to Cabinet . . . ; third, where the membership of an established committee seems inappropriate for a particular reference, a decision to make it more representative. . . .

2 *Edward Heath,* The Listener, *12 March 1976*

. . . the workload of the Government today is so great that every decision cannot possibly be handled by the Cabinet itself. You therefore have a number of major Cabinet committees. . . . Now every Prime Minister, I believe, wants to see these Committees work efficiently and reach agreed decisions; and that is the job of the chairman of the Cabinet committee. Where he finds that he cannot get agreement, he says to the minister: 'Very well, you will have to bring this to Cabinet', and with it will go a report from the committee of the differences of view. The Cabinet will then have to decide. In my experience, too many decisions came up from committees rather than too few, and there were too many cases where a chairman ought to have reached agreement but did not do so.

Questions

2 What advantage of the committee system is emphasized by both Wilson and Heath?

3 Consider the ways in which, according to Mr Wilson, over-delegation can be checked. How effective do you think these checks might be?

4 Consider carefully the role of the chairman of a Cabinet committee with reference to the text and to Mr Heath's comments.

5 Study Figure 9 carefully. What does it reveal of the priorities of Mrs Thatcher's second administration?

6 What does Figure 9 suggest about the power of the Prime Minister?

The Cabinet Secretariat

The smooth working of the Cabinet system is greatly facilitated by the Cabinet Secretariat set up in 1916. Its head is the Cabinet Secretary. Today it has a staff of just over one hundred recruited mainly from departments within the Civil Service. The functions of the Secretariat are to service the Cabinet, to provide information, to circulate the agenda and papers to ministers and to keep a record of Cabinet proceedings. Minutes are taken in the Cabinet room by the Secretary and two assistants and are subsequently recorded as 'conclusions' or Cabinet decisions. The minutes are brief and do not include conflict in Cabinet on party political questions. They are circulated to Cabinet members, and it is not unknown for ministers to try to change them.

While the Secretariat serves the whole Cabinet, the work of the Secretary involves more direct contact with the Prime Minister than with any other Cabinet member. Mr Gordon Walker has suggested that he is effectively a Permanent Secretary to the Prime Minister, preparing the agenda, briefing and advising him or her on, for example, feeling within the Cabinet on a particular issue or the adequacy of a particular memorandum.

From 1970 to 1983 Cabinet Ministers also received guidance from the Central Policy Review Staff (CPRS) or 'Think Tank'. It was a small body of about twenty and its purpose was to evaluate the effectiveness of a Government's policies in relation to its long term objectives. The CPRS was abolished by Mrs Thatcher after her election victory in June 1983.

Collective Cabinet responsibility

One of the most important conventions of the Constitution is that Cabinet ministers are responsible to the Prime Minister and to Parliament for everything which happens within their department. This doctrine of ministerial responsibility is considered fully in Chapter 7. A further and equally important convention is that ministers have responsibility as a group for all the policies of the Government. This is known as collective Cabinet or ministerial responsibility, and it became established in the nineteenth century. Its import is that although ministers will inevitably disagree in Cabinet, a decision once taken is the responsibility of all ministers and must be defended in public and Parliament by them. This applies to decisions of Cabinet committees as well. Any member of the Cabinet or Government who finds himself or herself unable to accept and defend a Cabinet decision must resign. The importance of the convention is that it allows the Government to present a united front to Parliament. Were this not so, then the Government could legitimately ask for the support of its back-benchers and party government through the House of Commons would become impossible.

The doctrine of collective responsibility does not, however, prevent the public from knowing something of the feeling and divisions within a Cabinet. Today through 'unattributable leaks' from ministers to the press, a good deal of information is readily available on Cabinet arguments. Ministers frequently make statements to the press on the understanding that their own names will not be mentioned in any newspaper report. During Mr Callaghan's administration leaks were so common that the Prime Minister apparently had occasion to inform his colleagues that he was becoming a little tired of reading accounts of Cabinet disagreements in the press. In Mrs Thatcher's administrations too, leaks have been frequent — mainly from those who question the wisdom of her economic policy and who have been anxious for Cabinet disagreements to be given an airing. Leaks should not be regarded, however, as erosions of collective responsibility for by their very nature they acknowledge that it is inappropriate for ministers to disagree publicly.

Yet the doctrine of collective responsibility is not absolute. In 1932 ministers of the National Government were allowed to differ publicly on the question of tariffs, and recently the doctrine has been further eroded. In 1975 ministers of the Labour Government were allowed to disagree publicly during the campaign leading to the referendum on the issue of Britain's membership of the EEC, and in 1977 ministers were again allowed to disagree on the question of direct elections to the European Parliament. Whether these events indicate that the doctrine of collective responsibility will no longer carry the force it once had is something upon which it would be premature to comment.

The Cabinet and patronage

One aspect of the power of Cabinet Ministers, and of the Prime Minister in particular, which has often been criticized recently is the amount of patronage they have at their disposal. Mr Benn has pointed out, for example, that between 1945 and 1976 Prime Ministers made 1494 ministerial appointments and created 568 hereditary and life peers. They also have a right to be consulted over the appointment of Chairmen of Royal Commissions and of Nationalized Industries. Mrs Thatcher, for example, was quite adamant in her desire that Mr Macgregor should be Chairman of British Steel (1980) and she later championed equally vigorously his appointment to the Chairmanship of the National Coal Board (1983). Prime Ministers are also consulted over senior judicial and Civil Service appointments. Again, Mrs Thatcher was influential in the appointments of Sir John Donaldson as Master of the Rolls in 1982, and over a number of very senior appointments in the Civil Service (see page 143). Between 1981 and 1983 eleven of the twenty-three Permanent Secretary posts in the Civil Service became available. Mrs Thatcher's interest in the new appointments went beyond that of her predecessors. She did not simply act on the advice of others. She backed her own instinct and judgement.

But patronage extends beyond the Prime Minister to ministers themselves. In February 1982, for example, the Secretary of State for

Employment replaced Sir Richard O'Brien with Mr David Young as Chairman of the Manpower Services Commission. According to Mr Edelman, then a Labour MP, in 1975 seven Cabinet Ministers had within their gift 4223 jobs on various administrative and advisory bodies (Quangos) worth £4,200,000 in salaries. Mr Edelman felt that the use of patronage on this scale impaired the quality and efficiency of administration and he suggested that a Public Service Commission should be appointed to control all public appointments through competitive entry. Since then, Mrs Thatcher's first administration did see a reduction in the number of Quangos and in paid appointments in them, but patronage remains an important aspect of the power of the Prime Minister and of her senior colleagues.

The Prime Minister

The office

Although the power of Prime Ministers in relation to their Cabinet colleagues has been a matter of debate recently, few would dispute that their personal prestige, authority and influence are considerable.

The Prime Minister is usually the leader of the party which commands a majority in the House of Commons and a very experienced politician. As Walter Bagehot said of the American Presidency over a century ago, 'The notion of employing a man of unknown smallness at a crisis of unknown greatness is to our minds simply ludicrous.' A British Prime Minister will probably be over the age of fifty. He or she will have been in Parliament for about fifteen to twenty years and will probably have held important ministerial office. Mrs Thatcher had been in Parliament for twenty years before becoming Prime Minister in 1979, and she had previously held the office of Secretary of State for Education and Science. Mr Callaghan's position, however, is unique. When he became Prime Minister in 1976, he had been in Parliament for thirty-one years and had previously held the offices of Chancellor of the Exchequer, Home Secretary and Foreign Secretary. No other Prime Minister has had this distinction.

Today, as both major parties have formal arrangements for electing their leaders, the Sovereign no longer chooses the Prime Minister; she simply ratifies a decision which others have taken. To become party leader is then to go a long way to becoming Prime Minister. The requirements of this office we must now consider.

Prime Ministers must be able to establish an ascendancy over the House of Commons, especially at question time on Tuesdays and Thursdays. They must have easy relations with MPs on both sides of the House. They must be good administrators with a capacity to delegate responsibilities to their ministers. At the same time, they must be available to guide ministers and to offer them quick and assured advice. They must be convincing both as national leaders and as party leaders — roles not always easy to reconcile. They need to build up the confidence and morale of their supporters in Parliament and the country while trying to unify the country and serve the national interest. Since the growth of radio and television, it has become accepted that Prime Ministers must have a good media image.

Perhaps the most important requirement of Prime Ministers, however, is the ability to co-ordinate the policy of their administration and create a genuine sense of unity and purpose. To this end, the choice of the Cabinet, the allocation of ministerial positions and the removal of unsatisfactory ministers are all important. One of the most serious criticisms Mr Crossman made in his Diaries of Mr Wilson's Cabinet (of which he was a member) was that the Government lacked a firm sense of purpose and direction. For this, Mr Crossman blamed the Prime Minister.

Question
7 Refer to pages 87–9 and compare the role of the Prime Minister with that of the Leader of the Opposition. What are the similarities and differences in the two positions?

The power of Prime Ministers
The power of Prime Ministers derives from their relationship with the Cabinet, the party, the Civil Service and the media. In this section we shall discuss — and perhaps exaggerate — the influence they may have. We shall then consider the limitations on their power, again perhaps over-stating the case. Finally, we shall try to evaluate how powerful Prime Ministers really are in relation to their colleagues.

Prime Ministers' authority within the Cabinet is seen most clearly in the fact that they are responsible for choosing the Cabinet, for dismissing ministers and for re-allocating ministerial positions. They also choose ministers of state and under-secretaries — though not yet parliamentary private secretaries. The influence this gives them over Government policy at every level is considerable. Moreover, the modern tendency to apply the doctrine of collective responsibility to all members of the Government and even to parliamentary private secretaries gives Prime Ministers a great amount of direct leverage on perhaps almost half of their parliamentary party.

Prime Ministers also have the exclusive right to summon a Cabinet at any moment or place of their choosing. In consultation with the Cabinet Secretary, they decide the agenda. Mr Wilson's use of this over the issue of devaluation between 1964 and 1967 has already been noted (see page 95) and Mrs Thatcher's first Cabinet did not consider economic policy until July 1980 — by which time she had been in power for fourteen months. Within Cabinet, it is the Prime Minister who invites ministers to speak, determines the point at which a decision shall be made and declares the collective view of the meeting. This need not always correspond exactly to the views of the majority within the Cabinet. Prime Ministers' influence over committees is also extensive. They decide which committees to chair themselves and determine the composition and chairmen of other committees. Their relationship with the Foreign Secretary is generally particularly close, but they have the right to intervene in the work of all departments. In October 1976, for example, Mr Callaghan, in a speech at Ruskin College, Oxford, spoke of his concern for education and in this way opened a 'Great Debate' which the Education Secretary, Mrs Williams, was obliged to conduct and on which she produced a Green Paper (a document for discussion) in July 1977. Mr Callaghan also appears to have taken an acute interest in the contents of the paper and to have insisted that certain parts of it be rewritten before publication. Moreover, no matter how strong a Prime Minister's determination not to intervene and to allow ministers great freedom within their departments, he or she may well become involved because of the pressure of those with whom Government has to deal. Mr Heath, for example, was initially reluctant to be drawn into the handling of industrial disputes, but by force of circumstance he played an important role in discussions with the trade unions in the great disputes of 1972–4.

A further aspect of Prime Ministers' power, it is often argued, is their relative safety from the threat of ministerial resignations. To resign is to risk terminating a ministerial career prematurely and it is never something undertaken lightly. In 1951 Mr Bevan and Mr Wilson resigned from the Labour Government; Anthony Nutting and Sir Edward Boyle resigned from the Conservative Government over the Suez question in 1956, and three Treasury Ministers, Mr Thorneycroft (now Lord Thorneycroft), Nigel Birch and Enoch Powell resigned in 1958. In 1968 Lord Longford, George Brown and Frank Cousins resigned from Mr Wilson's Labour Government. In the 1970s, Mr Prentice's resignation in 1977 was the only resignation of note, but Mrs Thatcher has twice faced significant resignations. Lord Carrington, Richard Luce and Humphrey Atkins resigned from the Foreign Office following the 'humiliation' of the invasion of the Falklands in April 1982, and Michael Heseltine and Leon Brittan resigned in 1986 over different aspects of the Westland Affair.

But not all of those in disagreement with major Cabinet decisions or strategies have resigned. Many have chosen to remain and to continue to fight from within the Government. Mr Varley, for example, the Industry Secretary in Mr Wilson's Government, was known to be unfriendly to the view that Government assistance should be given to the Chrysler

Company in 1975. He was overruled in Cabinet and the Government agreed to provide £162,500,000 for the company, but Mr Varley did not resign. Equally, a number of ministers in Mrs Thatcher's first administration (1979–83) were known to have serious doubts about the wisdom of the Government's economic policy but they chose to argue their positions from within the Government rather than to resign. The knowledge Prime Ministers have today that few ministers will sacrifice office and rank within the parliamentary party for the relative impotence of the backbenches helps to augment their power.

The authority of Prime Ministers derives also from the fact that they are leaders of a mass party and the figureheads for party members both inside and outside Parliament, a natural focus for loyalty and attention. In Parliament in particular the instinctive loyalty of MPs to the party enables them to win support even when MPs may have reservations about the wisdom of their policies. Mr Heath's handling of Britain's entry into Europe in 1973 and Mr Callaghan's handling of his Government's counter-inflation policy are just two recent examples of this. But as well as relying on the loyalty of their back-benchers, Prime Ministers can discipline them through the threat of a dissolution of Parliament. Whatever the reservations back-benchers may have about their own Government, they will invariably find it preferable to any alternative.

The third major prop of Prime Ministerial authority concerns relations with the Civil Service. In 1919 the Civil Service was unified under the Permanent Secretary at the Treasury. Today the Permanent Secretary, together with the head of the Civil Service and the Secretary to the Cabinet, exercises great influence over promotion within the higher ranks of the Civil Service. All three are responsible to the Prime Minister, who is minister for the Civil Service.

The final source of Prime Ministerial power is to be found in the facilities available to her (see Figure 10). We have already noted (see page 98) that the Cabinet Secretary, as head of the Secretariat, works more closely with the Prime Minister than with other ministers but, in addition, the Prime Minister has her own office at 10 Downing Street and her own Special Advisers. The Press Section of the Private Office is especially important for it enables the Press Secretary to offer a regular commentary upon Government policy in terms the Prime Minister will have helped to define. The press receives her views on Government policy rather than those of other ministers or even the Cabinet's collective view. But the media are also important in a second and more obvious sense. Prime Ministers have access to the media, and especially radio and television, at any time of their choosing. Their speeches are widely reported; they are, in short, projected by the media as the very pillar of Government and as the Government's most powerful and authoritative figure.

Figure 10 *Facilities available to the Prime Minister and Cabinet 1985*

Policy Unit
Started by Sir Harold Wilson. Purpose is long-term policy preparation. Has about 5 full-time staff together with Special Advisers, e.g. Professor Alan Walters has advised Mrs Thatcher on economic policy, and Sir Percy Craddock has advised her on Foreign Policy.

Political Office
Concerned with the PM's constituency and party relations and headed by her Chief of Staff. He is assisted by the PM's Parliamentary Private Secretary, a constituency secretary and other aides and advisers.

Private Office
Responsible for the PM's daily diary, correspondence and the planning of official engagements. The Private Office is headed by the Prime Minister's Principal Private Secretary (a senior civil servant).

Appointments Section
Handling honours and patronage and headed by a Secretary for Appointments.

Press Section
Responsible for the presentation of policy to the Press at press conferences and briefings. Headed by Press Secretary.

Prime Minister's Office (No. 10)
(68 Staff and 5 Special Advisers)

Prime Minister

Cabinet

Cabinet Office
Has about 600 staff headed by the Cabinet Secretary.

Cabinet Secretariat
This is the most important part of the Cabinet Office, consisting of about 100 senior civil servants. It services the Cabinet and Cabinet Committees.

Historical Section
Works on Official histories.

Central Statistical Office
Collects, prepares and presents information on many aspects of Government and Society in Britain.

Management and Personnel Office
Headed by PM and Secretary to the Cabinet. A major responsibility is the appointment of senior civil servants.

Constraints upon Prime Ministers

In the last section we tried to build up an impression of the kind of power
Prime Ministers have. We shall now consider the checks or constraints
which at times make some of the powers we have discussed less real.

One of the most obvious constraints is the need to retain party loyalty
and Cabinet support. Mr Gordon Walker has pointed out that if Mr Eden
in 1957 and Mr Macmillan in 1963 had not resigned office, considerable
pressure would have been brought to bear upon them because of feeling
within both the Cabinet and the parliamentary party. Similarly, Mr Wilson
in 1969 was unable to win complete support for his attempt to reform the
law relating to industrial relations. His proposals were quickly dropped.
Equally, Mrs Thatcher, while appearing to be completely dominant
within her Cabinet, has often given way to ministerial or Cabinet pressure.
In 1979, for example, she wanted to recognize Bishop Muzorewa's
Government in Rhodesia but was dissuaded from doing so. Thus while
Prime Ministers do, as we have seen, have means of controlling both
Cabinet and party, they cannot presume their support on all occasions. In
addition they are not entirely free in the choice of their Cabinet. They
must balance the various wings of their party, including those who
because of their authority and prestige either nationally or within the
party simply could not be excluded. Prime Ministers will also be careful
when they dismiss ministers for they could easily damage their own
authority rather than confirm it. When Mr Macmillan dismissed seven
Cabinet colleagues in 1962, it was generally agreed that he diminished his
own credibility. We have also seen how, despite the Prime Minister's
strong influence on the Cabinet agenda, they cannot be said to fashion it
entirely alone.

A further constraint is their need to retain the confidence of the House
of Commons. Constitutionally this ought to be the most serious constraint
of all but, as is argued below, because of the strength of the party system,
the need to retain the confidence of the Commons very frequently
amounts to nothing more than the need to keep the confidence of one's
own party. One rather obvious exception to this generalization would be
the position of Mr Callaghan's administration from March 1977. He then
negotiated an agreement with the Liberals to help sustain the Labour
Government in power, and accepted that because of the agreement he
and the Government would have to drop certain measures which won no
support outside the Labour ranks.

A third restriction, and one which is far more important for Labour
Prime Ministers than for Conservatives, is the power of the party and its
organization outside Parliament. As we saw in Chapter 3, the Labour
Party Annual Conference constitutionally has the power to determine
party policy. Of equal importance is the party's National Executive
Committee (NEC), which regards itself as the custodian of conference

decisions and is at times an irritant to Labour Prime Ministers.

A fourth constraint, but one which most Prime Ministers are happy to accept, is the Civil Service. The problem is not that the Civil Service will try to obstruct Prime Ministers. Rather, like all sensible ministers, they will not want to proceed until they have either won the argument with the Civil Service or satisfied themselves that despite the disagreement theirs remains the most sensible course. The Civil Service possesses an enormous amount of professional expertise, and it would be a foolish Prime Minister who did not try to use this, accepting that some of the ideas entertained when in Opposition might have to be modified.

A final and increasingly important constraint is the influence of pressure groups and other organizations using the accepted freedoms of a democratic society to protect and to promote their own interests. Government has to be responsive to opinion outside Parliament without surrendering its right to govern and to determine the national interest. The miners' strike of 1974, which led to the collapse of Mr Heath's Government, is an obvious reminder of the power which particular groups are able to wield.

Prime Ministerial Government?

The Prime Minister's powers are considerable, but they are not exercised in anything approaching an unfettered way. They must constantly be mindful of the reactions in Cabinet, party, Parliament and the country. Moreover, not all policy emanates from the Prime Minister. Policy is the product of a continuous debate involving parties, ministers, the Civil Service and outside groups and individuals. It is also in part fashioned by circumstances no Prime Minister could have anticipated when taking office. The power of Prime Ministers, then, perhaps inheres not so much in their command over the major institutions of Government as in their ability to influence the style and strategy of an administration in so many ways. It should also be remembered that while our discussion has concerned the office of Prime Minister in general, no two Prime Ministers wield power in the same way or in the same circumstances. The influence of personality and the context in which a Prime Minister is working should not be discounted in any appraisal of his or her power. Mrs Thatcher, for example, has, by common consent, been a powerful Prime Minister. She has established her ascendancy within the Conservative Party; she has removed many (but not all) of her critics from the Cabinet; she has tightened her grip, as we have seen, on the Whitehall machine and greatly reduced the involvement of the trade unions in the process of Government. As importantly, she has been faced, for virtually the whole of her Premiership, with a divided Opposition. These factors have augmented her power but they have not left her unchallenged. Many of the constraints mentioned in this chapter apply to her as well and she has been forced to bend to the feeling of her back-benchers over, for example, student grants in December 1984, to the feeling of the House of Lords over, for example, the abolition of the Metropolitan Counties in 1985 and to her Cabinet on many occasions between 1980 and 1983 when her zeal for cutting public expenditure was not matched by that of her colleagues. The issue of Prime Ministerial Government is explored further below.

Documents: Cabinet and Prime Minister

1 *From R.H.S. Crossman, 'Introduction' to W. Bagehot,* The English Constitution *(Fontana 1963), pp.51–2.*

The post-war epoch has seen the final transformation of Cabinet Government into Prime Ministerial Government. . . . His right to select his own Cabinet and dismiss them at will; his power to decide the Cabinet's agenda and announce the decisions reached without taking a vote; his control, through the Chief Whip, over patronage — all this had already before 1867 given him near-Presidential powers. Since then his powers have been steadily increased, first by the centralisation of the party machine under his personal rule, and secondly by the growth of a centralized bureaucracy, so vast that it could no longer be managed by a Cabinet behaving like the board of directors of an old-fashioned company.

Under Prime Ministerial government, secondary decisions are normally taken either by the department concerned or in Cabinet committee, and the Cabinet becomes the place where busy executives seek formal sanction for their actions from colleagues usually too busy — even if they do disagree — to do more than protest. Each of these executives, moreover, owes his allegiance not to the Cabinet collectively but to the Prime Minister who gave him his job, and who may well have dictated the policy he must adopt.

2 *From Richard Crossman,* The Diaries of a Cabinet Minister *(Hamish Hamilton and Cape 1975), pp.202–3 & 510–11*

Richard Crossman was Minister for Housing and Local Government in Mr Wilson's Government of 1964–6. Below are two extracts from his diaries on the period.

Sunday, 18 April 1965
. . .Cabinet hasn't really become a collective decision-taking body — we have been mainly dealing with secondary disagreements which have to be resolved. We were promised a discussion about general economic policy before the budget, but that discussion never took place. . . . Cabinet only heard about the budget on the day before it was presented to Parliament. This was equally true with regard to defence policy. . . . Harold Wilson has certainly allowed some of us a great deal of ministerial freedom in forging our own departmental policies. Nevertheless,

I would say that he has completely dominated foreign affairs and defence, as well as all the main economic decisions.

Mr Callaghan's Budget of May 1966 introduced a new tax — Selective Employment Tax. Below are Mr Crossman's reaction to the way in which it was introduced.

Sunday, May 2 1966
At eleven o'clock the Cabinet gathered to hear the Budget secrets and Selective Employment Tax was revealed to us.... There was bewilderment and consternation. Nobody could quite follow what he (Callaghan) was saying and he had the easiest time in the world.... There was virtually no discussion.... By far the most important aspect of the budget is the constitutional issue. It seems to me to make an absolute mockery of Cabinet Government and Cabinet responsibility to introduce S.E.T. in this way and tell none of us about it until it is too late to do anything.... I am preparing to write to Harold about it.

3 *From Harold Wilson,* **The Governance of Britain** *(Weidenfeld and Nicolson 1976), pp.20–1*

My own conclusion is that the predominantly academic verdict of overriding prime ministerial power is wrong. It ignores the system of democratic checks and balances, in Parliament, in the Cabinet, and not least in the party machine and the party in the country. The checks and balances operate not only as long-term safeguards, but also, in one way or another (often unpredictable), almost every day. ...
   Cabinet is a democracy, not an autocracy; each member of it, including the prime minister, seeks to convince his colleagues as to the course to follow. The Cabinet bears his stamp, it is true, on each and every policy issue, but it is the Cabinet not the prime minister who decides.

4 *From Edward Heath,* **BBC Radio 3,** *12 March 1976*

I always went to great pains to see that everything was thoroughly discussed in Cabinet, and that the members of the Cabinet were brought along. ... I was not prepared to rush into an initiative without the Cabinet being, all of them, absolutely satisfied that we were doing the right thing.

Questions

8 Read the documents above. Make a list of the reasons why Crossman believed the power of the Prime Minister to be so considerable.

9 Bearing in mind what you have read, especially pages 106–7, what do you feel are the main checks and balances to which Wilson refers?

10 On balance, do you feel that the evidence in this chapter supports those who suggest that we have a system of Prime Ministerial Government?

The ability of Parliament to control the executive

In Chapter 4 we considered the theoretical functions of Parliament in relation to the executive and saw that Parliament existed to question and expose the Government, to consider, amend or reject its legislative proposals and to control public expenditure. How effectively does Parliament discharge these duties today? Does Parliament still control the executive or has the executive been able to subject Parliament to its will? For some time there has been concern about the strength of the executive in relation to Parliament and in 1978 the Select Committee on Procedure noted. 'The balance of advantage between Parliament and Government in the day to day workings of the constitution is now weighted in favour of the Government in a way which arouses widespread anxiety'. This has a number of aspects.

The first, and possibly the most important, source of the executive strength is the power of the party. Whereas in the 1860s, for example, in only 31 per cent of divisions did over 90 per cent of the Conservative Party vote together, today it is rare for an MP not to support his party in the Commons. Between 1970 and 1974, for example, the average Conservative MP supported his party in 99.9 per cent of divisions. The main duty of MPs has become to support their leaders rather than to scrutinize their actions and the task of controlling the executive has, in many instances, been transferred from the whole House to the Opposition.

The second source of Parliament's weakness lies in its inability to exercise any noticeable influence on legislation. When a Bill reaches the floor of the House it tends to be looked on by ministers as the finished product and if amendments are made, it is very likely to be the minister responsible who initiates them. For example, between 1967 and 1971, 99.9 per cent of amendments to bills proposed by ministers were approved but only 4.4 per cent of those moved by the Opposition and 9.5 per cent of those moved by back-benchers in the governing party were successful.

Thirdly, the authority of Parliament has been diminished by changes in the procedure of the House of Commons. At the turn of the century, Question Time was developed to replace the previous practice whereby Private Members had the right to raise debates. After the Second World War, because of the volume of questions being tabled, each MP was restricted to one supplementary question. This considerably eased the burden upon ministers and protected them from detailed cross-examination. Evading the question became relatively straightforward. The Government's control of the parliamentary timetable and its ability to be able to curtail debate in order to hasten the passage of its legislation, has also enhanced its authority.

A final consideration is that ministers are so much more knowledgeable than back-bench MPs. The minister is supported by the Civil Service whose responsibility it is to enable him or her to defend the policies of the department in the Commons. The back-bencher, on the other hand, has few opportunities for research at his or her disposal and no right of access to the kind of information the minister gets from the Civil Service.

Parliament today, then, is no longer an impartial restraint upon the executive, but essentially a forum where Government explains its policies and where those policies are legitimized through being formally approved.

But while it would be wrong to ignore Parliament's weakness, it would be equally wrong to overstate it. Over the past decade, for example, there has been growing evidence of Parliament's readiness to assert itself. Thus, whereas between 1947 and 1963 Governments were defeated, on average, once every three years, in the Parliament of 1970–74 and 1974–9 the number of defeats attributable to back-bench rebellions in the governing party was six and twenty-three respectively. Between 1970 and 1974, 61 per cent of Conservative MPs voted at least once against their own Government and between 1974 and 1979, 81 per cent of Labour MPs behaved likewise. There were also a number of back-bench rebellions against Mrs Thatcher's Government between 1979 and 1983, causing one Government defeat in December 1982 on Immigration rules, and modifications to Government policy on about a dozen other occasions. MPs appear to be becoming more assertive and independent and their attempts to control the executive are also helped, as we have seen, by the new select committee structure (see page 77).

One Conservative MP, Timothy Raison, has argued recently that a change of attitude within the House of Commons would be every bit as useful as institutional change in putting power back into Parliament. That change of attitude appears to be taking place.

Questions

11 Given the weaknesses of Parliament to which attention was drawn in the last section, what use is it?

12 In the last section, four reasons are given for Parliament's weakness in relation to Government. Identify them and think of any reforms which may help to improve Parliament's position. Consider also the wider effects these reforms may have.

6 The monarchy and the House of Lords

The nature of the British monarchy

The British monarchy is not only the oldest of our national institutions, it has also proved itself to be one of the most flexible. It has two important characteristics. First, it is an hereditary monarchy. On the death of the Sovereign, the Crown passes to the eldest son or to the eldest daughter if there are no sons, although no Monarch may be a Roman Catholic or be married to a Roman Catholic. Second, the monarchy is constitutional; although it retains certain powers, these are largely exercised on the advice of ministers. The monarchy's political power has declined over the centuries, and as we shall see, it is now almost, but not completely, extinct. But this is not to say that monarchy is irrelevant or meaningless today. It may not exercise power directly but its influence not only in politics but in many other areas of our national life is considerable.

Moreover, the monarchy gives every indication of being the most popular of British institutions. It has its critics, most notably the Labour MP, Mr Willie Hamilton, but republicanism has never been a force in Britain. Occasions such as the wedding of Prince Charles and Lady Diana Spencer in 1981 and the celebrations of the Queen's Silver Jubilee in 1977 demonstrate clearly the affection and esteem in which the monarchy is held by ordinary people. For all those who regard it as outdated or divisive, there are millions who look to it with respect and admiration and to whom it gives a pleasure afforded by no politician.

The power of monarchy today

In theory the powers of the Sovereign to act without consulting Parliament (the 'Royal Prerogative') are very wide indeed. In practice they have become progressively more restricted and are now exercised on behalf of ministers rather than independently. In this section we shall examine the nature of the 'prerogative' and explain why, except in one very important respect, it is no longer of real significance.

Ministerial appointments

Ministers, including the Prime Minister, are formally appointed by the Sovereign, but in practice they are not chosen by her. Before 1965 her role was more significant. In 1957 and 1963, for example, two Conservative Prime Ministers, Mr Eden and Mr Macmillan, resigned because of ill-health. The Queen had to appoint successors. In both cases she felt obliged to seek and, it appears, to follow advice given to her. In 1957 she consulted Sir Winston Churchill and Lord Salisbury before inviting Mr Macmillan to form a Government, and in 1963 she visited Mr Macmillan in hospital in order that his advice could be given. This resulted in the appointment of Sir Alec Douglas Home as Prime Minister, but it is widely believed that had the Queen sought to ascertain feeling in the Conservative Party, Mr Butler would have been appointed.

Today, however, the Sovereign is denied even this small amount of influence. All major political parties now have provision for electing their leaders who, in the event of their party winning a general election or being in Government already, will become Prime Minister. This was illustrated very clearly in April 1976 when, following Mr Wilson's resignation as Prime Minister, the Parliamentary Labour Party elected Mr Callaghan to be his successor as party leader. The Queen promptly invited Mr Callaghan to form a Government. She had no choice.

The influence of the Sovereign over ministerial appointments, although small, is more important. Prime Ministers will have clear ideas about their Cabinet and Government even before an election victory. Out of courtesy, they will discuss these with the Sovereign, who may feel disposed to offer advice. In 1945, for example, when the Labour Party came to power, George VI advised the Prime Minister, Mr Attlee, to appoint Mr Bevin rather than Mr Dalton as Foreign Secretary. The advice, which was possibly contrary to Mr Attlee's intentions, was followed. Bevin became a respected Foreign Secretary. Today, such influence is still possible although a Prime Minister's greater knowledge of both his party and its policies make it likely that his judgement will prevail.

Parliament and legislation

The Sovereign has the power to summon, prorogue and dissolve Parliament but will, in each case, feel bound to accept the advice of the Prime Minister. At the opening of Parliament the Sovereign reads from the throne to the assembled Houses of Parliament a speech setting out the Government's legislative proposals for the session. The speech is written by the Prime Minister after consultation with his or her Cabinet. The Prime Minister's control of dissolution is equally clear. Not since 1834 has a Monarch dismissed a Government against its wishes. Moreover, it is widely recognized that a Monarch would be unwise to refuse a dissolution.

The question might arise if a newly appointed Prime Minister were to seek a dissolution immediately following a general election in order to give himself a clear parliamentary majority. Had Sir Harold Wilson, for example, in March 1974 sought a dissolution straight after the general election in February, the Queen might well have tried to restrain him. But of course it is improbable that a Prime Minister would make the request unless, first, he did not have a working majority and second, it was clear that no other party leader could form an administration.

The Monarch also possesses a theoretical right to veto legislation, but this was last exercised by Queen Anne in 1707. Its use is given further consideration below.

Patronage

The right to confer honours and to make certain official appointments is vested in the Sovereign, but it is exercised almost entirely on the advice of ministers. For example, the Monarch creates peers and awards other titles but is advised by the Prime Minister who will, in turn, have had wider consultations. (Two notable exceptions are the Order of the Garter and the Order of Merit, which are conferred by the Sovereign alone.) The most important constitutional aspect of patronage has been the creation of peers to resolve a conflict between the two Houses of Parliament. In 1832 and 1911 the King was ready to create sufficient peers to enable the Government to get its measures through the House of Lords. In both cases the threat was sufficient to persuade the House of Lords to give way and allow the legislation to pass. Today as the Lords is only able to delay legislation, it is unlikely that the Monarch's powers of patronage will be needed to resolve a conflict between two Houses.

The Sovereign also appoints judges, bishops and archbishops, commissioned officers in the armed forces and members of Royal Commissions, acting always on ministerial advice. Her patronage is wide but it is seldom of her choosing.

In other areas too powers are exercised for her rather than by her. The prerogative of pardon, for example, is exercised by the Home Secretary, while the power to declare war, make peace and conclude treaties is assumed by the Government as a whole.

The Privy Council

The Privy Council (or Queen's Council of State) has declined in political importance over the centuries. Today it is mainly an instrument for the convenience of ministers. The total membership of the Council is about 300, and members appointed by the Sovereign on the advice of the Prime Minister are known as the 'Right Honourable'. Cabinet ministers past and present, the Speaker of the House of Commons, the Lords of Appeal and retired High Court judges, important ambassadors, the Archbishops of Canterbury and York and members of the Royal Family are all 'Privy Councillors'.

The full Council meets only on the death or marriage of the Sovereign. The active members are current Cabinet ministers. About four attend typical Councils, which are presided over by the Sovereign. (A quorum is three.) About ten Councils are held each year. The Lord President of the Council (a Cabinet minister) is responsible for arranging the business, which is usually transacted swiftly. The main functions of the Council are to make certain Crown appointments and to give immediate effect to Cabinet decisions by issuing Proclamations or Orders-in-Council. These functions are purely formal, but particular committees of the Privy Council still do important work. The most important is the Judicial Committee of the Privy Council, which consists of the Lord Chancellor, the Lord President of the Council, the Law Lords and other Privy Councillors who have held high judicial office, together with leading members of the judiciary from Commonwealth countries. It deals with appeals from courts of the Channel Islands and the Isle of Man, Commonwealth courts, Ecclesiastical courts and the Disciplinary Committee of the General Medical Council. (In 1975, for example, it heard ninety-four appeals from overseas courts alone.) The Privy Council also establishes special committees to enquire into particular problems.

The influence of monarchy today

If the Royal Prerogative is today exercised only indirectly, the influence of monarchy remains considerable.

Political influence

During the course of a normal reign a Monarch acquires a depth of political knowledge and experience which may well exceed that of the Prime Minister. The present Queen, for example, has been served by eight Prime Ministers. She spends up to three hours each day reading state papers. She sees Foreign Office despatches and the Cabinet agenda in advance of meetings. All Cabinet minutes and papers are forwarded to her. She also receives a short daily report of proceedings in Parliament. At her weekly meeting with the Prime Minister (usually Tuesdays at 6.30 p.m. in Buckingham Palace), she is not only informed of proceedings in Cabinet and Parliament, but will often tender advice of her own. Sir Harold Wilson has said, 'She is astonishingly well informed on every detail.' It is impossible to define precisely the degree of influence a

Sovereign might have at these meetings, but a wise Prime Minister will listen to advice which is probably as impartial as any can be, which is not prompted by narrow party political considerations and which in the case of the present Queen, for example, derives from an extensive familiarity with the problems and processes of government.

But the Sovereign exercises political influence in other areas as well. She is hostess and guest on behalf of the nation. She entertains foreign and Commonwealth heads of state and, together with other members of the Royal Family, makes both official and private visits abroad which help to promote good relations between Britain and other countries. In 1903, for example, King Edward VII made an official visit to France which prepared the ground for the famous Entente Cordiale of 1904. More recently the Queen's state visit to France in 1972 anticipated Britain's entrance into the European Economic Community in 1973, while President Giscard D'Estaing's state visit to Britain in 1976 enabled both him and the Queen to call publicly for a new Entente Cordiale. Later the President and Mr Callaghan, then Prime Minister, agreed that there should be annual consultations between the two countries.

Social influence

The social influence of the Sovereign is harder to define. For many people the attraction of monarchy lies in its difference — its pomp, colour and splendour — but also in its image — warm, honest, dignified, yet remote. As Bagehot recognized in 1867, 'Its mystery is its life.' Monarchy appears to satisfy a popular need. It has a remarkable capacity to evoke respect, enthusiasm and loyalty.

And it is a symbol of stability and continuity. Monarchs change but the monarchy survives. The Sovereign is also the embodiment of the idea of national unity. This is expressed most clearly in the Christmas broadcast to the peoples of the Commonwealth, begun in 1932 and now very much a part of the festive season. (It is usual for the Queen to consult her Private Secretary over important speeches and broadcasts as well as on broader constitutional questions.) In her 1977 broadcast, for example, the Queen claimed that the Silver Jubilee celebrations had shown '. . . that we can be a united people'. She went on, 'It showed that all the artificial barriers which divide man from man and family from family can be broken down,' and said she felt that 'the real value and pleasure of the celebration was that we all shared in it together'.

But the Sovereign's social role is not purely symbolic. She does much of practical importance as well. Visits to parts of the country to open schools, factories and civic centres are common. In the war King George VI visited bombed areas to demonstrate his concern and help raise the morale of his people. The Duke of Edinburgh, whose main task is to accompany, support and escort the Queen, has himself played a very prominent role throughout her reign. He has been strongly identified with youth, conservation, technology and industry. To encourage industrial exports, the Queen's Award to Industry was introduced in 1966. In 1976 the Queen and Prince Philip began the practice of inviting representatives of successful firms to receptions at Buckingham Palace.

In recent years the whole style of the monarchy has become less formal and more relaxed. In 1969 a television film was made on the life of the Royal Family, and in 1973 on a visit to Australia the Queen went on a 'walkabout' to meet the people of Sydney. This was repeated in London in the celebrations of 1977. Since 1958 the Queen has given three garden parties each year, inviting about 8000 guests to each. Informal lunches were started even earlier, in 1956. About six are held each year, and it is usual for eight guests to be invited and to be entertained by the Queen, Prince Philip and perhaps two other members of the Royal Family.

The financing of monarchy

In 1761 George III agreed to surrender his income from the Crown Estate (the lands owned by the Crown) in exchange for a regular annual grant from Parliament. Until recently the annual grant was agreed at the start of a reign and paid throughout it. When a new Monarch came to the throne, the grant (known as the 'Civil List') was revised.

During the present Queen's reign, the Civil List has been revised on a number of occasions because of inflation, and in 1984 it stood at £3,850,000. About 75 per cent of this money is paid to staff of the royal household. In addition, Government departments incur expenses from the maintenance of the royal yacht, the Queen's flight and the royal palaces.

But money from the Civil List is not the only source of royal wealth. The Queen owns the royal treasures (although these yield no income to her and cannot be sold). More importantly, she enjoys an income each year from the Duchy of Lancaster, and the Prince of Wales has an income from the Duchy of Cornwall. In 1969, Prince Charles voluntarily surrendered half of this to the Consolidated Fund (see page 79). Separate allowances are paid to the Queen Mother, the Duke of Edinburgh, the Queen's children and other members of the royal family. All royal income is exempt from tax and death duties.

Conclusion

Walter Bagehot, in a famous passage, claimed that the rights of the Monarch were 'to be consulted ... to encourage ... to warn'. In his memoirs the Duke of Windsor (who, as King Edward VIII, abdicated in 1936) put the same point more simply and directly. 'The Royal power in British politics,' he wrote, 'is limited to the power of suggestion.'

This appraisal needs one important qualification. It is frequently argued that the Monarch has reserve powers which, in a time of crisis, would be very useful as a constitutional safeguard. Events in Australia in 1975 provide a clear illustration of this. Mr Gough Whitlam, the Labour Prime Minister, was unable to get his budget through the Senate. This created a constitutional impasse which Whitlam refused to resolve by offering his own resignation. Accordingly the Queen's representative, the Governor-General Sir John Kerr, dismissed Whitlam and his Government in November 1975 and invited the Opposition leader, Mr Fraser, to form an administration.

It is unlikely, but not unthinkable, that a similar position could arise in Britain. If, for example, a Government tried to extend the life of Parliament without good reason, the Sovereign might well be justified in dissolving Parliament in order that the electorate could be consulted. The power of veto may not have been exercised since 1707, but that is not to say that it could never be exercised. It has not been used precisely because Governments have accepted and worked within the spirit of the Constitution. They have sought neither to exceed their legitimate powers nor to perpetuate them. They have understood the importance of means in politics as well as ends. Should this trust ever be violated, then the Monarchy, against which Parliament struggled in the seventeenth century to achieve liberty, could become the guardian of liberty itself.

Thus the Monarchy represents not only an agreeable spectacle and a major source of pleasure and curiosity, but an important constitutional safeguard. In 1974 the American head of state, President Nixon, was forced from office as a result of the 'Watergate' scandal after two years of political uncertainty. In Britain we may be fortunate in having a head of state who is not, as is the American President, at the heart of politics, but above politics. President Nixon's disgrace cast a shadow over the whole American system of government, and the crisis which led to his resignation had crucially weakened his administration for two years previously. The British political system is doubtless capable of producing corruption, but at its worst, it would be corruption in the Prime Minister and not the head of state. The former could be removed and a successor appointed with far greater ease than proved possible in America. Thus the neutrality of the monarchy is constitutionally its most distinctive and important characteristic.

Questions

1 What case could be made against monarchy today?

2 If monarchy were abolished, what aspects of its work, both social and political, would be most missed?

Nature and composition of the House of Lords

The House of Lords is the upper house or second chamber in Parliament and comprises the Lords Spiritual and Temporal (see page 121). Unlike the House of Commons which, as we have seen, was gradually transformed by the Reform Acts of the nineteenth and early twentieth centuries, the House of Lords remains essentially what it has been for centuries, a House based on the peerage of the realm, themselves appointed by the Crown on the advice of the Prime Minister.

Until the beginning of this century the power of the House of Lords equalled that of the Commons. Its veto was absolute, although its powers had been seldom abused. As the House of Commons became increasingly representative of the people in the nineteenth century, any interference came to be regarded as obstructing the will of the people and was deeply resented. Towards the end of the century it became clear that the Conservative-dominated House of Lords were ready to obstruct the work of Liberal Governments in the Commons. In 1893 the Lords rejected the Second Home Rule Bill for Ireland, and betwen 1906 and 1910, 18 out of 210 Bills put forward by the Liberal Government failed to become law. Some of them, such as the Education Bill of 1906, the Licensing Bill of 1908 and the budget of 1909, were absolutely central to the Government's strategy. It was the rejection of the budget which confirmed the Government's intention to restrict the power of the Lords. This was done through the Parliament Act of 1911, which abolished the Lords' power of veto and its right to interfere at all with money Bills (defined by the Speaker). The passage of other Public Bills it could delay for a maximum period of two years.

In 1949 by a further Parliament Act the power of delay was reduced to twelve months. But there are two important qualifications to both Acts. First, the provisions apply only to Public Bills. Second, for any Bill to extend the life of Parliament, the House of Lords retains an absolute right of veto. How important a constitutional safeguard this is, given that the Lords could only delay for one year a Bill to abolish itself, may be doubted.

The composition as well as the power of the House of Lords has also been affected by recent legislation. Today most people feel that a House founded essentially on the hereditary principle is difficult to justify and in need of reform. Although, despite frequent inter-party discussions, major reform has not been achieved, two recent measures have had an impact on the composition of the House. The first is especially important.

The Life Peerage Act 1958

Well before the 1950s it was widely recognized that to choose members of the second chamber purely on the basis of birth was not only unjustified but inefficient. It represented the distribution of power of an age which had long since passed, and it meant that many groups in the community were either under-represented or without representation altogether. The abilities of those outside the peerage were not being used, and the House did not represent a cross-section of the community. What Bagehot had said in 1867 remained true nearly a hundred years later, 'for a revising legislature, it is far too uniformly made up.' He had seen that life peers, chosen on the basis of ability and aptitude and not passing their titles on to an heir, were needed to inject new life into the chamber.

The Life Peerage Act of 1958 made possible what Bagehot had hoped for. It drew men and women of distinction and wide experience into public life. It could have provided a sound basis for a reformed second chamber. It was a step in the right direction, but it has not changed the upper house as much as some felt it would do. There are a number of explanations for this. First, although the Act allowed peers to claim an attendance allowance and travelling expenses for each day spent at the House of Lords, allowances are a poor substitute for an actual salary. Many life peers have had a poor attendance record precisely because they have been unable or unwilling to allow parliamentary work to interfere with their business or other commitments. In the 1978–9 session eighty-five life peers attended fewer than ten times and 119 life peers did not speak at all. Second, by granting peerages to people distinguished in various fields, many of whom were likely to be elderly, the Act tended to strengthen the natural conservatism of the Lords. John Grigg, a former peer, has pointed out that of twenty-five peers who took part in a debate on the economy in June 1976, twelve were in their late sixties and nine were over seventy. He maintains that the Life Peerage Act has 'done more than anything to give the House of Lords the character of a geriatric institution'. Third, although, as Figure 11 makes clear, there are now over 300 life peers, they are still a small proportion of the whole House. Moreover, the bias of the House of Lords towards the Conservative Party persists, if not among life peers, then certainly among the hereditary peerage who still predominate. The Act was passed as a temporary solution to an awkward problem. Its impact has been less than expected and has not been followed by bolder reform.

The Peerage Renunciation Act 1963

The second important reform of the House of Lords in recent years was the Peerage Renunciation Act of 1963. Prior to that year, anyone inheriting a peerage was prevented from having a seat in the House of

Figure 11   *Composition of the House of Lords 1985*

	Dukes	25	Hereditary peers by succession	763
Lords Temporal	Marquesses	28	Hereditary peers of first creation*	31
	Earls and Countesses	156	Life peers	364
	Viscounts	104		
	Barons and Baronesses	842	Conservatives	418
			Labour	136
Lords Spiritual	Archbishops and Bishops	26	Liberal	41
			SDP	41
	Total	*1181*	Cross-benchers	219

*No hereditary peers were created between 1964 and 1983 but in June 1983 two new hereditary peers, Viscount Whitelaw and Viscount Tonypandy, were created. As both men are without male heirs, their titles will not be passed on.

Source: Dod's Parliamentary Companion 1985.

Commons. In 1950, for example, Quintin Hogg was compelled against his wishes to succeed to his father's title and forfeit his seat in the House of Commons. In 1960 the Labour MP for Bristol South-East, Anthony Wedgwood Benn, inherited his father's peerage as Viscount Stansgate. This disqualified him from the Commons, but Benn fought and won the subsequent by-election in Bristol. He was prevented from taking his seat, and his Conservative opponent, having come second in the poll, was declared elected.

Mr Benn's campaign to renounce his peerage achieved success when the Peerage Renunciation Act was passed in 1963. This allowed an hereditary peer to disclaim his title within twelve months of receiving it, although existing peers were given only six months to decide and those with seats in the House of Commons one month. The Act extended to peeresses a similar right to disclaim. Finally, any act of renunciation was not to affect the right of an heir to the peerage his father had surrendered.

The results of the Act have hardly been dramatic. Since 1963 only about fourteen peers have disclaimed, although the loss has been mainly of those who would probably have been figures of influence in the Lords had they chosen to say, including, for example, Mr Grigg.

The working of the House of Lords

The House of Lords meets from Monday to Thursday in the Palace of Westminster on about 120 days each year. The chamber is far less austere and proceedings are conducted in a more leisurely way than in the Commons. The House meets at 2.30 p.m. and adjourns at about 7 p.m.

(although occasionally, as in 1971 when the House was debating the Conservative Government's Industrial Relations Bill, sittings proceed beyond 10 p.m.). The House has no question time and is not strictly divided on party lines. Each party has an organization and a leader, but many peers are cross-benchers (those without any declared party ties). Discipline is less severe and the Whips less evident than in the Commons. There is no arrangement for 'closure' (see page 72). Members have no constituencies to worry about, no prospect of losing their seats and fewer division bells to answer. (In the session of 1982–3, for example, there were only eighty-nine divisions.) A quorum is three, compared with forty in the Commons. The average daily attendance is about 290. (See also Figure 7, page 78, for statistics on the House of Lords.)

Meetings are presided over by the Lord Chancellor who sits on the 'Woolsack' — a square couch before the empty throne. His position is closest to that of the Speaker in the House of Commons, but there are important differences between them. The Lord Chancellor is not outside party controversy. As head of the judiciary he is a member of the Cabinet, and he takes part in debates on behalf of the Government, leaving the Woolsack to do so. He also presents the Queen with her speech at the opening of a new parliamentary session to hear the Government's intentions.

It is at the State Opening of Parliament that Black Rod is prominent. His main responsibility is to enforce order in the House of Lords, for which purpose he carries an ebony stick. But Black Rod also performs more ceremonial duties. When the Queen is seated on the throne in the House of Lords, he is sent to summon the Commons from their own chamber to hear her speech. As he approaches, the doors to the Commons are slammed. Black Rod knocks three times, whereupon the doors are opened and MPs make their way in pairs to the upper house. Occasionally Black Rod summons the Commons to hear the Royal Assent being given to a Bill. The exclusion of the Sovereign from the Commons arises from the constitutional struggles between the King and Parliament in the seventeenth century. In 1642 Charles I entered the Commons to arrest five Members of Parliament. No Monarch has been allowed in since.

Question

3 Before reading the next section, ask yourself what kind of work the House of Lords is best suited to.

Functions of the House of Lords

Those who argue for the abolition of the House of Lords and for government through a single chamber ignore the great amount of valuable work done by the Lords which, if not done there, would have to be done by an already burdened House of Commons. It is true that some of the official functions of the House of Lords could be separated from it. The ten Law Lords, for example, headed by the Lord Chancellor, form the final court of appeal in the country. There is no practical or constitutional reason why this work requires the existence of a second chamber. Moreover, some functions of the House of Lords, although useful, are not necessary. It is a convenient place of retirement for elder statesmen for whom a Prime Minister or party leader can no longer find a prominent position in the lower house. In 1975, for example, when Mrs Thatcher became leader of the Conservative party, she did not offer Mr Carr (a prominent minister in Mr Heath's Government) a place in her Shadow Cabinet. Mr Carr's acceptance of a peerage enabled him to begin a new career in the Lords without the humiliation of having been 'sacked'. Nobody, however, would suggest that this consideration alone justified a second chamber.

And yet there is very strong justification for the second chamber which was made clearly in 1918 in the Bryce Report. Bryce suggested that the House of Lords performed four functions: the examination and revision of Bills brought from the Commons, the initiation of Bills of a non-controversial nature, the delaying of certain Bills to allow the opinion of the country to be expressed on them, and finally the full and free discussion of important issues, such as foreign policy or individual liberty, for which House of Commons can very rarely find time. Is the analysis in the Bryce Report still valid?

Examination and revision

The work of the Lords in examining and revising legislation matters so much because debate in the Commons can so often be curtailed (see page 72). Today it is not uncommon, even at committee stage, for whole sections of Bills to be ignored or forced through without full consideration. In the session of 1978–9, for example, the Bill to devolve new powers to Scotland reached the House of Lords with 61 of its 83 clauses unconsidered. Amendments too may be moved in the Lords for which, quite simply, no time could be found in the Commons. They may also arise from the Government's anxiety to meet points agreed to in the Commons or even to correct anomalies which have arisen through other amendments. In 1975 the Lords made 186 amendments to the Labour Government's Community Land Bill, of which all but 29 were accepted. But it is not only legislation from Labour Governments which has been modified. In the 1979–80 session the House of Lords made 1319 amendments to Government Bills of which all but a few were accepted by the Commons. One Bill, the Local Government Planning and Land Bill, underwent 265 amendments. Similarly, the Conservative Government's

Industrial Relations Bill of 1971 underwent 351 amendments after more than one-third of the Bill had never been debated at committee stage in the Commons. Moreover, some amendments have been very important. The Housing Finance Bill of 1972 was amended to provide better rebates for disabled tenants, and local authorities were required to send to each tenant individually a notice of fair rent. Similarly, in 1980 the House of Lords, by an amendment, exempted from the Government's 'right to buy' legislation, council accommodation designed or adopted for the elderly. This amendment affected 220,000 dwellings. In the same year the House of Lords rejected by 216 votes to 112 a clause in the Education Bill allowing local authorities to charge for school transport, and in 1984, the Government's wish to cancel elections for the Greater London Council and the Metropolitan Counties and to have nominated bodies administer the Councils until their abolition in March 1986, was defeated by 191 to 143.

In the parliamentary session of 1983–4 the Government was defeated in the Lords on no fewer than twenty occasions. It is difficult to avoid the conclusion that if the House of Lords did not exist, the quality of legislation would deteriorate.

Initiation of non-controversial Bills

A considerable proportion of time in the House of Commons is devoted to the passing of legislation. In the session from October 1976 to October 1977, for example, 178 Public Bills were introduced into the Commons of which 53 became law. The burden on the Commons is partly relieved by the introduction of non-controversial measures into the Lords. In the session from 1973 to 1974, 44 Public Bills were introduced in this way. In the previous session, something as important as the National Health Service Reorganization Bill was also first introduced into the Lords. Finally, about half the Private Bills before Parliament (such as those from local authorities) are treated in the same way.

Delaying legislation

The power of the House of Lords to delay legislation cannot exceed twelve months. Thus eventually the will of the House of Commons prevails whatever the judgement of the Lords might be. But this is not to say that the power remaining with the Lords is useless or that it can never be exercised in the public interest. The history of the Trade Union and Labour Relations (Amendment) Bill of 1975 demonstrates clearly, as Lord Goodman (who was closely involved with the issue throughout) has said, that the House of Lords does have a role to perform. The details are instructive.

The Bill was introduced into the Commons in November 1974. Its main purpose was to give to trade unions the right to organize closed shops (see

p. 250). Concern was voiced both in the country and in the House of Lords not only about the morality of closed shops but also about the effect they might have in the newspaper industry (see also page 250). The Labour Government therefore agreed that a charter on press freedom should be negotiated within the industry. The Lords insisted that the charter be made enforceable at law, the (Labour) Government preferred not to allow the Bill through in that form but deferred it to the next session instead. The Bill finally became law in March 1976. The House of Lords had been defeated, as it always will be, but it had asserted an essential principle of democracy — the freedom of the press. It had debated and brought to public attention a question of personal liberty and had proposed a possible solution in the field of journalism. Without the work of Lord Goodman and other peers, the Bill would have been passed more quickly but its implications would have been less fully understood.

Discussion of important issues

The House of Commons has little leisure. It is precisely the pressure of time which often prevents it from debating issues of principle which bear directly on the quality of public and private life. Now it is in this area that the House of Lords, relatively free from the constraint of time, excels. In 1973, for example, the Lords debated the Younger Report on Privacy, drawing attention to the fact that twelve months after the publication of the Report, the Government had taken no steps to implement it. But what matters quite as much as what the House of Lords debates is the knowledge and expertise it brings to this task. Lord Hailsham, himself a highly influential peer and one deeply committed to the value of the Lords, has written, 'The real value of the House of Lords . . . is as a forum and focus for specialist and informed opinion.' A very good example of this was the debate in 1975 on Direct Grant Schools, in which Lord Butler (the author of the 1944 Education Act), Lord James (a former High Master of Manchester Grammar School), Lord Eccles (a former Minister of Education), Lord Wolfenden (a former headmaster) and four other speakers directly involved in education all took part.

Document: The virtues of the House of Lords

Below is a short extract from Lord Hailsham's autobiography, *The Door Wherein I Went* (Collins 1975, pages 191–2). Lord Hailsham draws attention to the wealth of experience in the Lords.

. . . a debate in the House of Lords on an important subject, let us say economics, will contain, apart from the speeches from the front benches, contributions from three and possibly four ex-Chancellors of the Exchequer, two or more trade union leaders of experience, one or two chairmen or ex-chairmen of nationalized industries and several industrial chiefs in the private sector. A similarly impressive array of experience and talent can be brought to bear on Foreign Affairs, Defence, Industrial Relations, the Environment, Education, Law, Local Government, Aviation, or any other major topic of controversy or public interest. There are, of course, eccentrics and bores, as there are in every other deliberative assembly in the world. But there is no uproar, no disorder and, by and large, there is civilized and well-informed discussion.

Questions
4 Do you feel that the present House of Lords is suited to exercising the kind of responsibilities described on pages 123–6? Consider each function in turn.
5 Is the House of Lords helped or hindered in its work through being non-elected?

Reform of the House of Lords

The House of Lords has already undergone modest changes during the present century, as we have seen, but radical reform, although long recognized as overdue, has not been made. It is important to remember for just how long the idea of reform has been discussed. In the 1850s Lord Palmerston's Government proposed the creation of life peers — a measure introduced a hundred years later. In 1908 the Rosebery Committee reported in favour of the 'reform and reconstitution of the House of Lords', and suggested that the simple possession of a peerage should no longer afford the right to sit and vote in the House. In 1948 the leaders of the main parties agreed to nine principles for reform, of which the most important stated that the second chamber should complement but not rival the House of Commons, that no one party should have a permanent majority, that an hereditary peerage should not guarantee a seat in the Lords, that life peers should be included and that members should be paid for their services. The proposals were not acted upon.

In 1967 the Labour Government seriously took up the idea of reform. After abortive consultations between the major parties, the Prime Minister, Mr Wilson, announced that the Labour Party would introduce legislation of its own. A White Paper was published in November 1968 recommending a working chamber of about 230 peers of first creation with, in normal circumstances, a majority for the Government of the day. Hereditary peers were to have the right to attend and to speak but would not vote unless they had been specially designated life peers. The White Paper also proposed salaries for life peers and a reduction in both the Lords' power of delay and the number of Lords Spiritual.

Strong opposition came from both sides of the Commons. Concern was expressed over the potential increase in the Prime Minister's powers of patronage, for if the Government were expected to have a working majority, then a substantial number of life peers might have to be created to achieve this. Moreover, if the strength of parties in the House of Lords were to be 'arranged', then the House could hardly be regarded as being capable of independent action or judgement. Concern was also expressed, especially by Conservatives, about the proposal to pay life peers. (The idea was later dropped.) The Labour left too, led by Mr Foot, was strongly critical. Mr Foot argued, 'The powers of the Lords are to be retained pretty well as they are, but the possibility of using them will be greatly enhanced because the place will have been made much more respectable.' Mr Foot made clear then, and has repeated since, that his solution to the problem of the House of Lords is to abolish it. In April 1969 Mr Wilson gave up the attempt to force the measure through a hostile Commons and the Bill was abandoned.

Since then further proposals for reform have been floated. Professor Crick has suggested that the Lords' power of delay should be removed and that the House be devoted to debate, scrutiny and investigation. One former MP, Bryan Magee, has suggested that it should become 'a senate of the ablest people in the country'. Another proposal has been that it should become a pressure group second chamber, including representatives not only of all the main interest groups such as trade unions and employers, but others as well, such as farmers, doctors, teachers, solicitors, the church and even British members of the European Parliament. In the summer of 1977 a group of Labour peers under Lord Champion produced further proposals. They suggested that membership of the Lords should be confined to life peers, peers of first creation, the Law Lords, ten bishops and such peers by succession as were nominated for life peerages. From these, a body of about 250 salaried voting peers would be chosen by the parliamentary parties to reflect the party balance in the Commons. Non-voting peers would be able to take part in debates and serve, but not vote, in committee. The power of the Lords to delay legislation was to be reduced to six months. Lord Wedderburn, another Labour peer, has suggested the abolition of the Lords and the development of a more effective committee system in the Commons to provide the necessary scrutiny for legislation. Whether such committees would be capable of offering an independent view may be doubted. They may well simply reflect the view of the majority party in the Commons.

In 1978 a committee of Conservative peers and MPs headed by Lord Home produced proposals of their own. They were prompted by the passing of a resolution at Labour's Annual Conference in October 1977 in favour of the abolition of the Lords and by the knowledge that unless something was done to reform the Lords, its critics might pursue the more radical policy of abolition. Lord Home's committee suggested that the new chamber should have a membership of 430, of whom 268 would be elected through a system of proportional representation and 134 appointed by the Crown on the advice of the Prime Minister and an all-party committee of Privy Councillors. Numbers would be made up by Bishops and Law Lords. One peer, Lord Boyd Carpenter, is notably unenthusiastic about such proposals.

Document: A defender of the House of Lords

Below is an extract from a letter to *The Times* (1 July 1977) from Lord Boyd Carpenter, arguing against any fundamental change in the character of the upper house.

Both the strength and reputation of the present House of Lords are very much connected with the fact that it includes in its membership Peers equipped with unchallenged experience of almost every human activity who can and do turn up to speak and vote when matters on which they are expert are before the House, but who do not feel under any obligation to turn up and act as lobby fodder for any political party. It is this characteristic which enables the House to bring unparalleled expertise to bear on public issues without tying it at all rigidly to the disciplines or loyalties of the party system. Whether those Peers who make this sort of contribution would really be very interested to turn up and contribute when they knew that their views would be voted down by a salaried party phalanx is at least doubtful. What is beyond doubt is that such a situation would greatly diminish the prestige and standing of the House.

A Labour MP, Mr Eric Heffer, takes a very different view of the Conservative proposals.

Document: The views of an abolitionist

Below is an extract from an article by Mr Heffer in *The Times*, 30 January 1978.

It is Labour's contention that a second chamber is unnecessary. On the other hand, the Tories, it seems, would like a reformed Lords with a membership of between 400 and 500, two-thirds of whom would be elected, and one third life or hereditary peers.

The Tory proposals raise several important issues. Firstly, even though the second chamber would be partially democratically elected, it would continue to contain an undemocratic element. Secondly, how would the second chamber be elected? Would it be on the basis of proportional representation, or would it be first past the post, and if so, how would the constituencies be drawn up?

Then there is the vital question of the second chamber's powers. It is obvious that an elected second chamber, even if only partially elected, would not be content with the limited powers of the present House of Lords and would inevitably demand greater powers.

The two houses could, and most probably would, become involved in conflict arguing over which was the senior. Such proposals are therefore a recipe for almost continual constitutional strife, unless we are very careful in getting rid of the Lords, we could end up with a second chamber not fully democratic and with additional powers, which in many ways would be worse than the present situation.

Ideas on reform abound and yet nothing has been done. Moreover, it is probably wise for nothing to be done until agreement has been reached on the purpose a reconstituted House of Lords is to serve. The essential problem is one of function rather than composition. But it is precisely on this issue that it has been impossible to reach agreement. Some see the purpose of reform as being to weaken the Lords. Others want to strengthen it. The latter have a lot of sympathy with the idea of an elected second chamber believing, in the words of a *Times* leader of October 1977, that the House of Lords 'lacks the legitimacy that only elections can confer in a modern democratic state'. They argue that if it were elected, it would be able to use its powers with far greater conviction than it is able to at the moment. The Labour Party has been strongly opposed to the idea of an elected second chamber, fearing, as Mr Heffer suggested, that once the Lords had a power base in the country, the authority of the Commons would be undermined. Some Conservatives too have been doubtful about election because it would eliminate altogether the hereditary element and, far from reforming the present chamber, would bring into existence a completely new one.

The greatest danger remains that which Bagehot so accurately perceived over a hundred years ago — that the House of Lords may never be reformed. Certainly for as long as it remains in its present form, the prospect exists that some future Government will simply abolish it. We should probably be less well governed as a result.

Questions

6 Do we need a second chamber and, if so, what for?

7 Which, if any, of the very different arguments advanced by Lord Boyd Carpenter and Mr Heffer against an elected upper chamber do you regard as persuasive?

8 Divide your page into three columns, making the middle column the narrowest of the three. Head the columns (a) The proposal, (b) Elected,

non-elected or mixed, (c) Possible weaknesses. Analyse the proposals
for reform discussed in this section under these three headings, and try
to decide which of the many proposals considered provides the most
hopeful foundation for change.

7 The Civil Service and Government departments

What is the Civil Service?

Civil servants are employees of the Crown (not holding political or judicial office) whose salaries are paid directly from money voted by Parliament, and who work in a civil capacity in a Government department or some other independent body set up by the Government. (An example of the first is the Department of Education and Science and of the second is the Advisory Conciliation and Arbitration Service.)

The modern Civil Service only came into being in 1870. Before then appointment was by patronage rather than ability, but following the recommendations of the Northcote-Trevelyan Report in 1854, recruitment by competitive examination and promotion on merit were introduced in 1870. A further change which has come about over the past hundred years is in the size of the Civil Service. In 1853 there were only 16,000 civil servants in Britain. In 1977 there were 746,000. The main reason for this increase was the growing involvement of the Government in so many aspects of our national life. Before about 1870 Governments took the view that their responsibilities went no further than maintaining an army and a police force, regulating conditions in mines and factories, and providing workhouses for the poor, reasonable sanitary conditions in towns and reliable population statistics. Today these responsibilities have been greatly extended. Government is now directly involved in fields such as education, employment, health, social security, industry, the environment and transport. Mrs Thatcher's administrations have brought about a marked reduction in the size of the Civil Service. She has been determined to streamline Whitehall and to make it more efficient. By 1985, the size of the Civil Service had been reduced to 599,000. By far the most important and politically influential group of civil servants are those who work in central Government, advising ministers on the details of policy and implementing their decisions. The work of this elite is considered later (see pages 135–9). But what should also be remembered is that nearly 75 per cent of civil servants work outside London, and many of these have active daily contact with the public. They

Figure 12 *Ministers and their departments 1985*

Department	Cabinet ministers	Minister of State	Under-Secretary of State	Parliamentary Secretary	Civil servants
Agriculture, Fisheries and Food	1m	2		1	12,100
Defence	1s	3	1		174,000
Duchy of Lancaster (Chancellor of)	1				
Education and Science	1s	1	2		2,400
Employment	2†		3		54,700
Energy	1s	1	2		1,100
Environment	1s	3	3		35,800
Foreign and Commonwealth	1s	4	1		9,800
Health and Social Security	1s	2	3		94,900
Home Office	1s	2	2		36,600
Law Officers	1c	4 other members of the Government			9,000
Management and Personnel Office	1*				1,400
Northern Ireland Office	1s	1	3		
Privy Council Office	2**	1			
Scottish Office	1s	1	3		13,000
Trade and Industry	1s	3	3		14,000
Transport	1s	1	3		14,400
Treasury	2@	3		1	8,900
Welsh Office	1s		2		2,300
Other Civil Departments e.g. Inland Revenue					124,200

s   Cabinet minister with the title of Secretary of State
m   Cabinet minister with the title of minister
c   The Lord Chancellor
†   The Secretary of State for Employment, Lord Young, and the Spokesman on employment in the House of Commons, Mr Kenneth Clarke
*   The Prime Minister who also holds the titles of First Lord of the Treasury and of Minister for the Civil Service
**   The Lord President of the Council and Leader of the House of Lords
     The Lord Privy Seal and Leader of the House of Commons
@   The Chancellor of the Exchequer and the Chief Secretary to the Treasury

The Government in November 1985 consisted of 22 Cabinet ministers, 61 Departmental ministers outside the Cabinet and a further 25 ministers without Departmental responsibilities.

Sources: Adapted from *The Times*, 5 November 1985 and *Annual Abstract of Statistics* (HMSO 1985).

may be involved, for example, in paying benefits at a regional office of the Department of Health and Social Security or the Department of Employment. If they are working for the Department of Trade and Industry, they will probably have close contact with local companies and will act effectively as Government spokesmen. If they are working as membersof the schools' inspectorate, they will spend much of their time in contact with teachers and local authority administrators. They are anything but faceless and anonymous.

Departments of state

The structure of departments

Most civil servants are attached to departments of state (see Figure 12). Some of these, such as the Exchequer, the Home Office and the Foreign Office, have a very long history. Others, such as the Department of the Environment, the Department of Energy and the Northern Ireland Office are of comparatively recent creation. Others, such as the Colonial Office, have been closed because of a change in national circumstances, and still more, such as the War Office, the Admiralty and the Air Ministry, have been merged. Because departments or ministries exist to serve the needs of Government, it is one of the Prime Minister's responsibilities to change the 'machinery of Government' to reflect the priorities of his or her administration.

Departments differ greatly in size. Some, such as the Department of Energy, are relatively small. Others, such as the Department of Health and Social Security, are large and have regional and area offices. Some ministries, such as Defence, have virtually no dealings with local authorities, while others, such as the Department of Education and Science, are in frequent contact with them. Very frequently departments have come into conflict with each other. For example, the Departments of Health and Social Security or Education and Science, both of which are 'spending' departments, may well compete with each other for resources. Either could meet resistance from the Treasury. As we have seen in Chapter 5, one of the functions of the Cabinet, many of whose members are themselves responsible for major departments, is to reconcile such conflicts.

The departmental minister works closely with his most senior civil servant, the permanent secretary, who is responsible to the minister for the work of the department and who supervises and directs its activities, mindful always of ministerial policy. The permanent secretary is also responsible for the finances of his department and may be called before bodies such as the Public Accounts Committee (see page 80) on this subject.

During the last two decades, there have been many changes in the structure of departments. Before and during the years of Mr Heath's Government of 1970–4, the general tendency was towards merging departments with similar areas of responsibility. Thus, whereas in 1956 there were twenty-six main departments, in 1972 there were only seventeen. Of these, five — the Departments of Health and Social Security, Trade and Industry, Environment, Defence, and the Foreign and Commonwealth Office — were 'giants'.

The justification for the mergers, about which Mr Heath in particular was enthusiastic, was that policy- and decision-making would be more efficient because issues which were clearly interrelated, such as housing and transport, could be considered together rather than separately. In this way, potential conflicts could be avoided, and departments could co-ordinate their work more effectively, identifying clearly their own strategies and priorities.

But the 'giants' have not been universally popular, and they have created a number of problems affecting both the Civil Service and the minister. Most obviously, the problem of internal departmental organiza-tion and communication has often been acute, and there has been a tendency in some departments for decisions which should have been taken lower down the hierarchy to be pushed up to the top. Permanent secretaries too have been obliged to give their attention to the general strategy of the department and to ignore some of the traditional day-to-day responsibilities. Finally, the burden on ministers has been intense because of the sheer breadth of the field with which they have had to concern themselves. Much has depended on the quality of the individual minister, and it has now been recognized that no department should be so large that it is difficult for one person to be accountable for all its work to the Cabinet and to Parliament.

Because of these problems and the particular circumstances in which Labour came to power in 1974, two of the five giants were broken down. In 1976 the process was taken a stage further when Mr Callaghan re-established the Department of Transport. The age of the 'giant' ministry appears to have been short-lived, although the process of change will doubtless continue in response to new problems and priorities.

Questions
1 Look at the list of departments in 1985 in Figure 12. Since then have any departments disappeared and have any new ones been created?
2 Which departments are likely to remain irrespective of changes in Government?
3 Why do departments differ so greatly in size?
4 Make a note of the arguments for and against 'giant' departments.

The Treasury

The Treasury today is the most important department of state. Together with its ministerial head, the Chancellor of the Exchequer, it is responsible for the management of the national economy, the raising of revenue, and the oversight and control of public expenditure, Government borrowing and the national debt.

The Treasury has considerable influence over the financial proposals of each department. Every year the major spending departments submit their estimates to the Treasury for approval (see page 79). Since 1962 the Treasury has reviewed public expenditure and allocated resources to departments on a five-yearly basis, through the Public Expenditure Survey Committee (PESC), which is composed of the principal finance officers of all the main spending departments and is chaired by a senior Treasury official. Two former Ministers of Education, Edward Boyle and Anthony Crosland, have both acknowledged the importance of obtaining Treasury consent for any programme of expansion, and both have pointed out that the minister's desire to promote expansion is often in conflict with the Treasury's desire to contain public expenditure. In July 1979 for example, spending ministers were forced to make substantial cuts in their expenditure programmes because of the Chancellor's determination (strongly backed by the Prime Minister) to reduce the overall level of public expenditure.

The Chancellor of the Exchequer is assisted by the Chief Secretary to the Treasury (currently a Cabinet minister) who has particular responsibility for the preparation of the estimates which are presented to Parliament annually, having first been subjected to thorough discussion in Cabinet. It is the duty of Cabinet to establish, following the guidance of the Chancellor, the total sum available for public expenditure and then the distribution of resources among departments. Unless a Cabinet minister can get the support of a substantial proportion of the Cabinet, he is unlikely to be the victor in a conflict with the Chancellor. In 1975, for example, Mr Mason, the Secretary of State for Defence, resisted defence cuts but, lacking solid backing in the Cabinet, was defeated by the Chancellor, Mr Healey.

The relationship between ministers and the Civil Service

The role of the Civil Service

It is often said that the main difference between ministers and their senior civil servants is that the former have responsibility for deciding policy and the latter for implementing it. This is true in the sense that the minister is always responsible to Parliament for policy, but it is also a dangerous over-simplification of the actual position. For reasons which we shall examine, civil servants today play an important role in formulating as well as in implementing policy. Very frequently they become aware, in the normal course of their duties, of areas where a new policy initiative or development might be appropriate. They are so familiar with the work of their department that improvements almost suggest themselves. Anthony Crosland, a former Labour minister, has said, 'A large part of any department's work, which does not at that moment raise acute controversial issues, will go on without the minister being involved at all.' Similarly a former Conservative minister, Edward Boyle, has acknowledged that the decision taken in 1963 to expand teacher training could be attributed almost entirely to the forceful advocacy of civil servants.

So what exactly is the role of the higher civil servant? In very general terms, it is to help the minister to conduct the business of Government. Lord Rothschild, a former head of the 'Think Tank' (see page 99), has said that the Civil Service must 'ensure that ministers' decisions are based on a full study of options, information and arguments'. Lord Boyle's views were similar. The top level civil servant, he has said, 'identifies key issues for ministers, orders the relevant facts and figures and sets out possible courses of action'.

But senior civil servants do much more than try to put the minister into a position in which he can handle the issues before his department. They must try to anticipate problems before they arise, which is what they were doing for Edward Boyle in 1963 on the question of teacher training to which we have already referred. They must draw attention to any difficulties they foresee in the event of a particular course of action being adopted. They must warn the minister if a policy to which he and his party are committed conflicts with other objectives. As Richard Crossman observed in his diaries, 'There is a constant debate as to how the minister should be advised.'

Their day-to-day responsibilities are also complex. They deal with much of the minister's correspondence and conduct negotiations on his behalf with businessmen, industrialists, local authority spokesmen, representatives of pressure groups and foreign visitors. They consult interested parties about proposed legislation, prepare Bills and help the minister to see legislation through Parliament. They prepare and sometimes write speeches for him, research answers to parliamentary questions and brief him thoroughly for any important official engagements. Sometimes they may give guidance to the minister on purely political questions. Generally speaking, however, the minister would see this as an area in which he was uniquely qualified to judge.

One final point should be made about the role of civil servants — their relative anonymity. The names of the senior civil servants are known to the politically aware public, but the advice they give to ministers is offered in the strictest confidence. The reason for this secrecy we must now discuss.

The role of the minister

A minister has both administrative and political responsibilities. He is responsible for the management of a department of state and accountable to Parliament for the work of his department. In addition he has wider political responsibilities to the Government as a whole.

A minister's relations with his department are governed largely by the doctrine of ministerial responsibility, which means quite simply that once a department has made a decision, the responsibility for it belongs exclusively to the minister. If the decision was a good one, whether the minister made it or not, he will gain credit; if it was an unfortunate one, the minister cannot blame the Civil Service for incompetence. He must accept responsibility himself.

The doctrine has attractions for both ministers and civil servants. It strengthens the minister by linking the Civil Service to him in a kind of conspiracy of silence against the outside world. If the deliberations of civil servants and ministers were widely known, then the minister's position would be weakened because so much more information would be available to his critics. The secrecy of the Civil Service and the doctrine of ministerial responsibility are inseparably connected.

For civil servants the attraction of the doctrine is that it not only leaves them free from any direct responsibility for policy, but that it enables them to advise the minister openly, frankly and in confidence. In his diaries Richard Crossman put this point in a rather exaggerated form when he said that, at times, it was the minister who had to guide the civil servant away from irresponsibility! But what role does the minister play within his department? That depends to a great extent upon the minister. Civil servants generally like ministers to have clear ideas and to be firm and decisive. If they have these qualities, most ministers will get loyal support and co-operation from their civil servants. A minister's first duty then on coming into office is, as Anthony Crosland said, 'to lay down clearly what his party's policy is'. He must establish the values and principles to which he is committed. Having done that, he must, again in Crosland's words, 'create a sense of impetus'. He must try to address the energies and abilities within the department to issues he has identified and make the department believe that the issues are worthwhile. A minister must also be sufficiently flexible to alter his position in the light of thoughtful criticism. He should be ready to exercise his political judgement and to defend his department in Cabinet, Parliament and the country. He is the spokesman for his department and, more than anyone else, can advance its image.

The strength of the Civil Service

One of the aspects of the Civil Service most frequently commented on is its power in relation to the minister. Richard Crossman, whose attitude to civil servants was always, at the very least, critical, claimed that their first loyalty was to the ministry rather than to the minister. Others have pointed to the possibility of the Civil Service controlling the minister by restricting the supply of information to him or by presenting it in such a way as to limit his options. Although it would probably be quite wrong to regard these habits as general, it remains true that, for mainly practical reasons, the Civil Service has considerable power.

First, whereas senior civil servants tend to be permanently attached to a Government department, a minister has no such security. Not only will he be removed if his party loses a general election, but he can be dismissed by the Prime Minister or transferred to another department. Since 1945 there have been sixteen Chancellors of the Exchequer and twenty-one Ministers of Education. The latter have each held office for an average of only twenty-two months. Given that, as Anthony Crosland said, '. . . it takes you six months to get your head properly above water, a year to get the general drift of most of the field, and two years to really master the whole of a department', it is easy to understand why a new minister should be at a disadvantage in relations with his permanent officials who, unlike their American counterparts, retain their positions after a change of Government. In circumstances where, as in 1964, a party coming to power has been out of office for some considerable time, very few ministers will have had any previous experience. This too can strengthen the position of the Civil Service. Moreover, whenever there is a change of Government, the incoming minister is prevented from seeing the papers of his predecessor. Because of these considerations, as Richard Crossman pointed out, each change in Government provides a sharp, if temporary, increase in Civil Service power.

A second reason for the strength of the Civil Service concerns the complexity of issues facing modern Governments and the sheer volume of work with which they are confronted. The wise minister will select what appear to be the crucial issues and concentrate on them. Lord Crowther-Hunt, a minister of state in Mr Wilson's Government of 1974–6, has pointed out that, faced as he was with between 200 and 300 decisions each month, a very considerable proportion of the work had to be handled by the Civil Service. These pressures are particularly acute in the first year of office when a minister, unfamiliar with his department, may be disposed to accept the advice he is offered. They may also arise within 'giant' departments, where the burden on the minister can be unusually heavy.

Third, it should be remembered that handling the day-to-day affairs of his department is only a part of the minister's job. As a member of the Cabinet, he is expected to contribute to the formulation and development of Government policy in general, and, as a leading member of the party in power, to speak in the country as well. The process of decision-making within departments must continue in his absence.

General conclusions

It is clear that some of the main constraints on a minister come not from the Civil Service but from pressure of time and force of circumstance. These we have considered, but other factors may be mentioned briefly. One is that ministers do not always come to office in circumstances of their choosing. Very frequently, a new minister will find his options restricted by problems left by the old administration and of which he was previously unaware. Moreover, neither ministers nor civil servants conceive policies in a vacuum. Both are responsive to public and informed opinion, and their policies are often modified accordingly. Lord Boyle has emphasized that this is particularly important in education where many policies derive from the influence of teachers, academics and administrators. Policy decisions then come not from any one source but from many. Moreover, there is no uniformity of procedure, and it is often difficult to identify the exact moment when decisions take place.

Two final points should be made. The first concerns the great tradition of integrity and impartiality which exists in the Civil Service. Generally speaking, civil servants have a remarkable capacity for transferring their allegiance from one minister or Government to another and serving each as best they can. As Anthony Crosland said, 'It's very rare that you meet real resistance or obstruction'. The second point is that for a department to function efficiently, mutual confidence between civil servants and ministers is essential. The relationship is one of partnership rather than struggle, and there are considerable reserves of goodwill, knowledge, experience and expertise in the Civil Service for the minister to tap.

Documents: ministers and the Civil Service

Richard Crossman and Anthony Crosland were ministers in Mr Wilson's Labour Government of 1964–70. Their attitudes to the Civil Service were different as is revealed in the following passages.

1 *From Richard Crossman,* **The Diaries of a Cabinet Minister** *(Hamish Hamilton and Cape 1975), pp.21–22*

Thursday 22 October 1964
. . . already I realise the tremendous effort it requires not to be taken over by the Civil Service. My Minister's room is like a padded cell, and in certain ways I am

like a person who is suddenly certified a lunatic and put safely into this great, vast room, cut off from real life and surrounded by male and female trained nurses and attendants. When I am in a good mood they occasionally allow an ordinary human being to come and visit me but they make sure that I behave right and that the other person behaves right; and they know how to handle me.

Of course, they don't behave quite like nurses because the Civil Service is profoundly deferential — 'Yes Minister! No, Minister! If you wish it, Minister!' — and combined with this there is a constant preoccupation to ensure that the minister does what is correct.

It's also profoundly true that one has only to do absolutely nothing whatsoever in order to be floated forward on the stream . . . I turned to one of my private office (secretaries) and said, 'Now you must teach me how to handle all this correspondence.'

And he sat opposite me with his owlish eyes and said to me, 'Well, Minister, you see there are three ways of handling it. A letter can either be answered by you personally, in your own handwriting; or we can draft a personal reply for you to sign, or, if the letter is not worth your answering personally, we can draft an official answer.'

'What's an official answer?' I asked. 'Well, it says the Minister has received your letter and then the Department replies. Anyway, we'll draft all three variants,' he said, 'and if you just tell us which you want . . .' 'How do I do that?' I asked. 'Well you put all your in-tray into your out-tray', he said, 'and if you put it in without a mark on it then we deal with it and you need never see it again.'

I think I've recorded that literally, I've only to transfer everything that's in my in-tray to my out-tray without a single mark on it to ensure that it will be dealt with — all my Private Office is concerned with is to see that the routine runs on, that the Minister's life is conducted in the right way.

2 *From Anthony Crosland,* **The Politics of Education** *(Penguin 1971), pp. 177–82*

The Minister can't possibly control everything and shouldn't try. A Minister has to decide what to be interested in and what to delegate. The worst sort of Minister is the one who tries to control it all, and stays up till 3 a.m. each night going through endless red boxes and getting himself bogged down in detail. You must rigorously pick and choose the crucial subjects that you're going to concern yourself with . . . For example, even after two years at the Board of Trade I had no contact at all with the Patent Office and practically none with Weights and Measures. But I never lay awake at night thinking 'Gosh, I wonder what those chaps at the Patents Office are up to' . . .

Generally I found it perfectly simple to establish good relations with civil servants — why shouldn't it be? . . . An experienced civil servant can always tell when the argument is over and he's lost the battle. But of course there are many other cases where a decision emerges naturally from discussions between the Minister and his officials. The officials know what the government's broad policies are, and they tender advice in the light of them. It's a great mistake to think there's a continuous battle going on . . . a Minister who knows how to utilize his civil servants — and some Ministers conspicuously don't, they are too touchy and defensive — will acquire a strong feeling of camaraderie with the good ones amongst them. As to a dialogue, I never found the slightest difficulty in getting one, especially at Education. We had a sustained dialogue, for example, about the terms of reference of the Public Schools Commission. Nobody had an absolutely clear view and the senior officials were divided among themselves. There was another occasion, during the 1966 election, when I said that I wanted all Under-Secretaries and upwards to give me their views in writing on the age of transfer, and the result was a totally frank and extremely valuable exchange of views.

Questions
5 How, according to Crossman, does the Civil Service influence the minister?
6 Identify two ways in which Crosland's civil servants were able to help him.
7 How does the image of the Civil Service depicted by Crossman differ from that of Crosland?
8 Using pages 135–9 and the two documents above, try to decide whether the Civil Service represents a threat to the minister or is a valuable partner in carrying out the work of Government.

The Civil Service today

The structure of the Civil Service
The structure of the Civil Service today and the pattern of promotion within it are set out in Figure 13. Responsibility for all permanent appointments rests with the Civil Service Commission which advertises vacancies, conducts examinations and interviews candidates. Recruitment, as Figure 13 indicates, takes place at three main levels and one of the most interesting recent developments has been the recruitment of graduates as executive officers. At the moment, this accounts for one third of all entrants to this category. The most important and prestigious recruits are the 250 to 300 young people who enter the Service each year as administration trainees. 60 per cent are new graduate entrants, but the remaining 40 per cent are recruited from within the Service. Candidates in both groups are selected by the same rigorous procedures.

Recent changes in the Civil Service
In 1968, as a result of the recommendations of the Fulton Report, a Civil Service Department was created to improve the internal organization and management of the Service. This survived until 1981, when the Treasury

Figure 13 *Pattern of promotion within the administration group and numbers employed at each level (January 1982)*

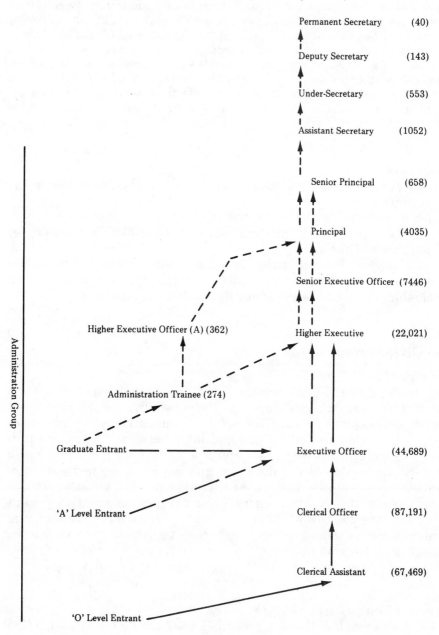

Source: Adapted from E. Russell-Smith, *The Home Civil Service: Modern Bureaucracy* (Longman 1974), p. 20.

regained control of Civil Service manpower, while the Prime Minister herself remained Minister for the Civil Service with responsibility for organization, management, efficiency, recruitment and training. She now heads a new Management and Personnel Office with the Secretary to the Cabinet as the most senior official. Together they exercise considerable influence over senior appointments. Mrs Thatcher, for example, developed the practice of choosing her own Permanent Secretaries when vacancies arose rather than acting on the advice of others. Her preference was often for those who identified with her own political viewpoint, such as Peter Middleton, who became Permanent Secretary at the Treasury and Michael Quinlan, Clive Whitmore and Kenneth Couzens, who became Permanent Secretaries at the Departments of Employment, Defence and Energy respectively.

Mrs Thatcher has also approached more seriously than any of her predecessors the issue of waste in Government Departments. During her first administration she set up, within the Cabinet Office, a small unit headed by Sir Derek Rayner to conduct an in-depth scrutiny of the work of Government Departments with a view, where possible, to eliminating waste. In December 1982, Sir Derek returned to his former employment at Marks and Spencer, having identified potential economies totalling £274 million.

Managerial efficiency has been another of Mrs Thatcher's concerns. Her view (which many others have shared) is that too few civil servants are skilled managers. She has also felt that senior officers spend perhaps too much time in policy analysis and too little in actually managing their own Departments. With her encouragement, there has been a greater emphasis upon management skills (the Civil Service College in Berkshire, established in 1970, offers training to civil servants at various stages of their careers) and some move away from the former practice of relying almost exclusively on 'amateurs' and 'all-rounders' (criticized by the Fulton Committee). The modern trend is towards the greater use of individuals with specialist skills in particular areas. In 1983, Sir Alex Atkinson, working within the Management and Personnel Office on the issue of recruitment, produced a Report calling for a 'new profile' civil servant and the greater use of 'outsiders' on selection boards.

Mrs Thatcher's own feeling that many of the internal practices of the Civil Service could be improved will now be clear. But she has also been distrustful of the traditional detachment of the Civil Service, of its ability to see and to present both sides of a case. Her preference, more often than not, has been for commitment to the policies she and her Government were trying to pursue, and some of the changes she has made are felt to have 'politicized' the Civil Service in a manner which many consider unhealthy. Mrs Thatcher has also (like previous Prime Ministers) sought to counter the weight of the Civil Service through the use of 'advisers' of her own. These are political appointees whose function is to add a political dimension to the advice ministers receive from civil servants. Between 1974 and 1979 about thirty such appointments (some part-time) were made. The practice has continued in Mrs Thatcher's administrations, if perhaps on a reduced scale. She herself, for example, appointed Professor Alan Walters as her economic adviser, Sir Anthony Parsons as her adviser on foreign affairs, and Dr Oliver Letwin as her adviser on education. In addition, she has frequently taken counsel from independent bodies such as the Centre for Policy Studies, the Institute of Economic Affairs and the Adam Smith Institute — all organizations sharing Mrs Thatcher's own political standpoint. It can obviously be of value to all ministers to have a source of advice which is independent of the Civil Service, but the use of advisers has been criticized by some on the grounds that it extends patronage (see page 100) and raises questions about the role of back-bench MPs who have traditionally seen themselves as the essential source of political guidance to ministers.

But despite her own often serious reservations about it, Mrs Thatcher is not the most radical or extreme of critics of the Civil Service today. Sir John Hoskyns, who headed her Policy Unit from 1979 to 1982, has been much more searching in his analysis and far-reaching in his prescription. He has attacked ministers for failing to define policy objectives more clearly, and civil servants for taking the rather pessimistic view that the problems confronting Britain are insoluble. He has also challenged (see Document on page 145) the tradition of political neutrality in the Civil Service and suggested that many senior civil servants should be replaced by politically appointed officials leaving the career civil servants to focus their attention on the day-to-day management of the Department. He argues that opposition parties should be financed to allow them to maintain shadow teams of officials who could then be brought into Government when the Opposition returned to power. These proposals have, not unnaturally, been criticized by, for example, Sir Douglas Wass, a former joint Head of the Home Civil Service, who has argued that the Civil Service has shown itself capable of adapting to changing circumstances and of looking at problems afresh. He also claimed that if the higher Civil Service was more political then the, 'time-horizon over which policy is formulated would become biased towards the short-term', that the 'collective and historical knowledge' of a Department would be lost, that young people of ability would not be attracted to the full-time career Civil Service and that smooth changes of Government, without major dislocation, would be made impossible.

What is quite clear is that the Civil Service is going through a period of major change and that many of its traditional 'virtues' are being called into question. Its future is likely to remain an issue of public debate.

Document: *Sir John Hoskyns,* A Criticism of Civil Service Neutrality *(adapted from 'Whitehall and Westminster' in* Parliamentary Affairs *Spring 1983)*

I believe that the present system of career politicians serviced by career officials is a failed system. How can senior officials work wholeheartedly for a Thatcher government for four or five years and then turn about and do the same thing for, say, a Benn government? They can only do so, I suggest, by cultivating a passionless detachment, as if the process they were engaged in were happening in a faraway country which they service only on a retainer basis. Difficult problems are only solved — if they can be solved at all — by people who desperately want to solve them: not by people who had been fully prepared, until polling day, to make those self-same problems worse, rather than better. The commitment, the urgency and energy must be provided by just ninety-odd ministers and a handful of special advisers — about a dozen in this Government and between thirty and forty in the last. The latter figure is less,I am told, than the number of people employed in storing and changing the pictures in ministers' offices.

Questions
 9 The practice Mrs Thatcher has adopted of effectively choosing her own Permanent Secretaries is felt to have 'politicized' the Senior Civil Service. What does this mean?
10 Having read pages 135–45, make a list of arguments for and against the traditional political detachment of the Civil Service.

The political freedom of civil servants
Another major issue concerning the Civil Service relates to the degree of political freedom given to civil servants. Special advisers are free to engage openly in political activities, but civil servants are subject to various constraints. There are three main categories for civil servants:
1 The 'politically free' group (29 per cent of all civil servants) includes all members of the industrial non-office grades. They may engage in any political activities, although they would have to resign from the Service if elected to Parliament.
2 The 'politically restricted' group (26.3 per cent) includes all staff above the level of executive officer. They are debarred from national politics but may apply for permission to take part in local political activities.
3 The 'intermediate' group (44.7 per cent) includes all the other staff in the Service. They may apply for permission to take part in national or local political activity.

The Armitage Committee recognized, in its Report of 1978, that if, for example, Permanent Secretaries or other senior officials directly involved with ministers were given greater freedom and, as a result, became recognizably politically partisan, this might tend to undermine public confidence in the Civil Service. On the other hand, the committee also recognized that civil servants were intelligent, articulate and informed, and that if they were given greater political freedom, they would not only be able to offer a substantial contribution to the political life of the nation, but would probably be helped in their official duties by gaining a wider experience. The committee recommended some modification to the existing arrangements. It proposed that the 'politically free' group should remain unchanged but suggested that the restricted group should be confined to the 3 per cent of civil servants at the level of principal and above. Certainly the restrictions on those who are not involved in giving top-level advice to the Government appear irksome and unnecessary.

Open government

The view that the whole machinery of Whitehall may be unnecessarily secretive and that some relaxation of the present tight controls on the supply of information would be in the interest of good Government is one very often expressed today.

Some aspects of the habit of secrecy we have already seen. The advice tendered by civil servants to ministers and the exchanges which take place between them are confidential. The work of PESC (see page 135), which is so important in deciding the allocation of resources, is conducted secretly, and incoming Governments are prevented from seeing the papers of their predecessors. But there are other examples too. State papers are only made available to the public after thirty years and, most important of all, Governments are protected by the very broad and general terms of the Official Secrets Act of 1911.

It is important to remember that this Act, which has few friends today, was passed through all its parliamentary stages in 1911 in less than twenty-four hours. Far from being the product of the mature judgement of the House of Commons, it was conceived in panic and passed in haste. Section 1 of the Act is unexceptionable on the whole. It makes it an offence, punishable by fourteen years' imprisonment, to engage in any activity which might threaten the safety of the state. (It also makes it an offence to approach, enter or inspect a 'prohibited place'.) Most criticisms of the Act, however, have been directed at Section Two, which makes it an offence, punishable by two years' imprisonment, to retain without permission information obtained in employment under the Crown, to communicate such information to 'unauthorized persons' or even to receive such information. According to the late Professor de Smith, this section creates 2324 'offences', many of which could not possibly be prejudicial to the State — for example, the passing on of information relating to internal departmental proceures. It is also a highly ambiguous section, giving no clear guidance on what is, or is not, illegal.

It was under Section Two of the Act that recently two cases were brought to court. In 1984, Sarah Tisdall, a clerk at the Foreign Office, was convicted and sentenced to four months' imprisonment for passing information to *The Guardian* on the arrangements which were being made for the arrival of American 'cruise' missiles in Britain. Shortly afterwards, a much more senior civil servant in the Ministry of Defence, Clive Ponting, was charged, again under Section Two of the Act, with passing documents on the sinking of the Argentinian cruiser *General Belgrano* during the Falklands War, to a Labour MP, Tam Dalyell. Mr Pointing did so because he felt the Government had been less than honest in what it had revealed to Parliament over the issue. Mr Ponting was acquitted.

Many people (always outside Government) feel that the obsession with secrecy is difficult to justify. Recently, many voices have been raised with proposals for reform, including those of two former heads of the Home Civil Service, Lord Armstrong and Lord Croham. Lord Croham, in a widely publicized radio talk in August 1978, argued that secrecy was harmful to good Government and that policies should be 'more fully exposed and deliberated' before decisions were taken. He also claimed that greater openness would act as a restraint on Governments perhaps too anxious to reverse the work of their predecessors. Lord Croham's main proposal was that it should be made easier for MPs to scrutinize the work of Government, Lord Crowther-Hunt, a former minister, has gone further and suggested that it ought to be possible for MPs, political parties and other interested bodies to make a much more active contribution to policy making. His suggestion (endorsed by the Select Committee on Commons Procedure in 1978) was that select committees should be appointed to scrutinize the work of each Government department and that these committees should have access to the policy recommendations of the Civil Service. These committees were actually set up in 1979 (see page 77) but not quite with the powers suggested by Lord Crowther-Hunt. They do not have access to all the policy recommendations of the Civil Service and a minister may decline to make papers available to them. Staffing levels and research facilities could also be more generous.

Despite these reservations the new select committees undoubtedly mark a step towards better control of Government. There have been other developments too. One small movement towards a more open system of Government has been the use of Green Papers, which are discussion documents, published by the Government, inviting public comments before any policy commitments are made. So far, however, their use has been limited.

It was widely expected that the publication of the Labour Government's

White Paper in July 1978 would mark a further step to open Government, but these expectations were not fulfilled. The White Paper proposed the revision of Section Two of the 1911 Act, making disclosures about Government economic information and the receipt of official information free from criminal sanctions. It also proposed a new category of protected information entitled 'security and intelligence', but it left the classification of such information to ministers. The White Paper did not go as far as the Franks Committee had gone in 1972 when it recommended that Section Two of the 1911 Act should be replaced by an Official Information Act which would restrict criminal sanctions to areas of major importance, such as information on defence, security, foreign relations and currency, Cabinet documents and information violating the confidentiality of information supplied to Government or facilitating criminal activity.

Franks disappointed many by failing to recommend that further publicity should be given to official information, but the White Paper of 1978 disappointed even more people, most notably Labour back-benchers.

The truth is that although political parties have pledged themselves in advance to more open Government, in practice little has changed. This can be attributed to the anxiety of Governments to preserve arrangements which make their lives easier and which shield them from informed and detailed criticism, but it should also be remembered that any attempt to make the system of Government more open would mean that the Civil Service, which as we have seen is responsible for many policy decisions, would have to be subjected to much closer scrutiny by Parliament. This in turn would probably destroy the doctrine of ministerial responsibility, which lies at the heart of the present system. The idea of 'open Government' has many friends, but its implications are more serious than is sometimes recognized.

Questions
11 Make a list of the advantages and disadvantages of more open Government.
12 What steps could be taken to make the Government more open without threatening the security of the state?

The Ombudsman and the redress of grievances

Means of obtaining redress
The growing involvement of the Government in so many aspects of the life of the nation has not only brought the citizen into more active daily contact with civil servants and departments of state, it has also increased the possibility of administrative injustice. The Department of Health and

Social Security and the Inland Revenue, for example, handle millions of claims each year. The possibility of occasional mistakes is evident. In the welter of bureaucratic organization, the rights of individuals can very easily, if unintentionally, be lost. It is clearly right and proper that individuals should have some channel available to them through which they can seek redress. In Britain today there is not one such channel, but many. If the grievances concerned, for example, an incorrectly assessed benefit or a tax problem, the citizen could write to or visit the department concerned. He could write to his MP and ask him to make an approach to the department or its minister. 50,000 letters pass between MPs and ministers each year. If the matter raised some genuine issue of principle or pointed to some anomaly in, for example, the payment of benefits, the MP might choose to table a parliamentary question to the minister or to raise the matter in an adjournment debate. He might also be able to draw attention to the need for new legislation to correct an abuse.

But these, of course, are not the only remedies available. There are now a whole series of tribunals (see pages 214–17) dealing with issues such as rents, rates, pensions, supplementary benefits and employment. In addition if a citizen is in conflict with a department over a planning question, he may well be able to get the minister's support for a local enquiry before any decision is reached (see pages 217–18). Moreover, although the procedure can be costly and time-consuming, it is possible in some circumstances for an individual to use the courts to settle a grievance. For example, an application to squash a compulsory order on the grounds that it was *ultra vires* (beyond the legal authority of a minister or other authority) would be heard before a High Court judge.

Since 1967 a number of significant additions have been made to these personal, political, administrative and judicial means of obtaining redress. Following the practice already established in countries such as Sweden, Finland, Denmark, Norway and New Zealand, Parliament set up in 1967 the office of Parliamentary Commissioner for Administration (the Ombudsman) to investigate cases involving maladministration by a government department. In 1973 the Ombudsman was given further responsibilities as Health Service Commissioner for England, Wales and Scotland, in which capacity he investigates complaints that individuals have suffered injustice or hardship at the hands of the National Health Service. He has, however, no right to question the clinical judgement of staff within the Health Service. In 1974 the idea of the Ombudsman was given further encouragement with the appointment of three Local Commissioners for England and one for Wales.

The powers of the Ombudsman

The powers of the Parliamentary Commissioner for Administration have been described by Sir Idwal Pugh, a former Ombudsman, as 'to investigate, disclose, report and recommend'. These powers may be exercised only in relation to maladministration by authorities engaged in activities for which ministers are responsible to Parliament — Government departments.

Precisely what constitutes maladministration is not always easy to say, although it was defined by Mr Crossman, the minister responsible for setting up the office of Ombudsman, as 'bias, neglect, inattention, delay, incompetence, ineptitude, perversity, turpitude, arbitrariness'. Clearly the Ombudsman himself retains a considerable amount of discretion concerning what lies within and outside his field of competence.

The Ombudsman has the power to require ministers or officials to produce documents relating to a particular case. His inquiries are generally rigorous. He makes an annual report on his work to the Select Committee on the Parliamentary Commissioner. As Figure 14 makes clear, neither he nor the other Ombudsmen is overburdened with cases.

Question
13 What conclusions can be drawn from Figure 14 concerning the work of the Parliamentary Commissioner for Administration?

Weaknesses of the Ombudsman
One of the most important weaknesses of the Ombudsman concerns the area of his own jurisdiction. His powers are confined entirely to maladministration by Government departments. He has no power to investigate complaints against legislation or against Government policy. Complaints involving local Government, health, nationalized industries and the police are also outside his jurisdiction. In the case of the first two, as we have seen, separate provision has now been made, while in respect of the nationalized industries, the Act of Parliament providing for nationalization has established a separate procedure for complaints (through, for example, the Gas Consumers' Council). As Figure 14 shows, 67 per cent of cases referred to him between 1971 and 1983 were outside his jurisdiction.

A second weakness relates to the way the whole system operates (shown in Figure 15). In the first place, although as Health Service Commissioner the Ombudsman can be approached directly by the public, as the Parliamentary Commissioner for Administration, he can only be approached through a Member of Parliament. This provision was drafted into the 1967 Act because it was felt that the role of the MP as the defender and servant of his or her constituents ought to be preserved. Few would deny that this has tended to reduce the number of cases taken to the Ombudsman. Ministers, for example, are unlikely to want to refer a

Figure 14 *Complaints to Ombudsmen 1971–83*

	1971	1975	1977	1979	1981	1983
Complaints to the Parliamentary Commissioner for Administration – United Kingdom						
Received during the year	548	928	901	758	917	751
Dealt with during the year						
Rejected	295	576	504	541	694	605
Discontinued after partial investigation	39	19	24	22	7	6
Reported upon Maladministration leading to justice found	67	167	177	84	104	90
Other	115	154	141	154	124	108
Total dealt with during the year	516	916	846	801	929	809
Complaints to the Health Service Commissioner – Great Britain						
Received during the year		504	584	562	686	895
Complaints to the Commissioners for Local Administration – Great Britain						
Received during the year		2,629	1,927	2,584	3,210	3,717
Total complaints	548	4,061	3,442	3,904	4,813	5,363

Source: Social Trends (HMSO 1985).

grievance of one of their constituents, if this might cause embarrassment either to themselves or to a colleague. It is probably also true that the instinct of most MPs is to try to settle personally the problems of their constituents. Moreover, just as a citizen cannot approach the Ombudsman, so the Ombudsman cannot inform the complainant directly of the outcome of his case. He too must use the MP. After his inquiry the Ombudsman sends two copies of his report and recommendations to the MP (one to be forwarded to the complainant) and another to the department concerned.

A third difficulty is that the Ombudsman has no power to enforce his recommendations. In principle, a minister or his department could simply ignore his report. Sir Idwal Pugh has, however, pointed out that it is very unusual for a recommendation to be ignored, and that if this does happen, it can be taken up by the MP and given publicity on the floor of the House. Alternatively the Ombudsman could report to Parliament through the Select Committee on the Parliamentary Commissioner.

Figure 15 *The Ombudsman and the redress of grievances*

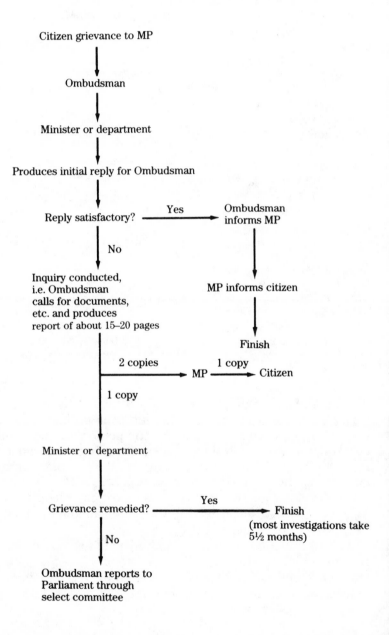

This brings us to the final difficulty facing the Ombudsman, that he has failed to capture the imagination of the public. The relative obscurity and anonymity of the office is only made worse by the lack of publicity given to the Ombudsman's reports. He does not publish these himself (as his one function is to redress legitimate grievances), and therefore the public hears very little of his work unless either an MP or the complainant chooses to make it an issue.

Conclusion

It is still perhaps too early to make a firm judgement on the work of the Ombudsman. In particular cases he has done a great deal. For example, a soldier invalided out of the Army in 1943 was awarded nineteen years of pension arrears totalling over £3400 because of the Ombudsman's inquiries. In another instance he revealed negligence in the handling by the Department of the Environment of a citizen's appeal for the conservation of a row of cottages and he secured — albeit too late — an unreserved apology for the complainant from the Department. But the machinery for redressing grievances remains complex and often confusing and there is a strong case for a uniform system supported by a much greater amount of public understanding.

Question

14 Is the Ombudsman a genuine citizen's man or a relatively ineffectual check on the work of Government departments?

8   Local government

Decentralization and the case for local government

It is neither practicable nor desirable for Government and administration to be conducted entirely from Westminster and Whitehall. It is not practicable because, given the rapid expansion in the responsibilities of Governments in the present century, the centre is already overburdened. To add to this load would probably create inefficiency and delay. It is not desirable for a number of reasons. Most obviously, different towns, cities and regions in Britain have different needs. Only by a form of local government is it possible for priorities to be established among the needs and wishes of the local community. Moreover, certain services which affect the daily lives of citizens, such as refuse collection or the condition of local roads and pathways, are obviously better dealt with by those with a feel for and interest in the locality than by civil servants in London. Finally, what is at stake in the question of local government is an essential principle of democracy, that people ought to be able to exercise influence over matters of close concern to them. For many the local community is a source of pride and satisfaction. It might offer facilities such as parks or sports centres which are distinctive and which are a product of the diversity made possible by local control. If everything were conducted from the centre, Government would be more impersonal and far more remote.

Local authorities are responsible for providing and administering services within their area (see page 161) and for doing what they can to improve the quality of life within a framework determined by Parliament and subject to the law of Parliament. Moreover, they are accountable to the people in the locality. Just as a Government can be removed at a general election, so the composition of a council (and the political control of the council) can be changed at local elections.

Of course local authorities provide only one example today of the devolution of political or administrative responsibilities from Westminster and Whitehall. Large Government departments (such as those of Trade and Industry, Environment, and Health and Social Security) have regional offices which enable them to carry out their work more efficiently. Also in Scotland and Wales the respective Secretaries of State exercise administrative powers already devolved by Westminster (see page 178). And there are other public bodies, such as the Regional Health and Water Authorities (see page 181) which, while set up by Parliament and while providing important services, are free from direct central control, independent of the local authorities and not directly accountable to the electorate.

In short the decentralization of power in Britain is haphazard rather than co-ordinated. It is also far less extensive than some critics would like. Many people feel that Britain is too centralized and that there is a very strong case not only for devolving greater power to the local authorities but also for developing greater regional self-government subject to more rigorous democratic control. These are some of the issues which will concern us in this chapter and the next.

Local government structure

The defects of the system before 1972

The structure of local government in England and Wales today owes much to the 1972 Local Government Act. This changed much that had become familiar and has since been heavily criticized and revised (see pages 156–9). But it is important to remember why the 1972 Act was considered necessary at all. Its roots lay in the weaknesses of the old system.

First, the structure (see Figure 16) was unsatisfactory in that it tended to enforce a division between country and town at a time when the two were becoming increasingly interdependent. Moreover, although the county boroughs themselves provided a comprehensive range of services, in the county councils there was considerable duplication of functions, confusion and conflict between tiers. The structure had been created in the nineteenth century when the duties of local authorities were more restricted. The great increase in scope of their activities in the twentieth century necessitated a tighter organization.

Figure 16 *Local government organization before 1972*

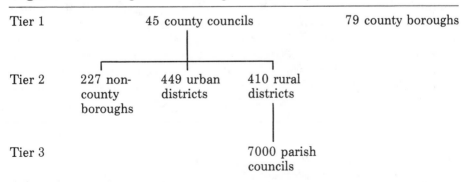

Figure 17 *The Redcliffe-Maud proposals 1969*

---

8 provincial councils

(To coincide with the existing economic planning regions and to be
responsible for the strategic framework within an area)

58 unitary authorities

(Population 250,000–1,000,00
embracing town and country and
responsible for almost all major
decisions and services)

3 metropolitan authorities

(Based on Manchester, Liverpool
and Birmingham and all having
populations in excess of one
million)

Local councils

(To put forward the views of the
local community and to provide
amenities)

20 metropolitan districts

Optional local councils

Second, there were considerable differences in the size and resources
of top tier authorities. Lancashire had a population eighty times as great
as the county of Rutland. The county borough of Birmingham had a
population of over a million while thirty-three other county boroughs had
populations of under 100,000. Many of the small authorities were too
poor to provide the services they were supposed to. The Department of
Education and Science estimated that it was difficult to organize an
effective education service in an authority with a population below
300,000. Yet seventy of the seventy-nine county boroughs had populations below that level. Smaller authorities also had difficulty in recruiting
highly qualified staff and in providing an attractive career structure.

Third, the relationship between local government and the wider
community was unsatisfactory. Local government did not appear to
interest the electorate. The turnout at local elections was low — about
30 per cent — and many elections were not contested. Also many felt that
the degree of central control over local government was too great, largely
because authorities were becoming increasingly dependent on Government grants. What was the nature of the reform enacted in 1972 and how
satisfactory was it?

Redcliffe-Maud and the 1972 Local Government Act
In 1966 the Labour Government set up a Royal Commission under Lord

Redcliffe-Maud to look into the structure of local government. The Commission reported in 1969 and its main recommendations are set out in Figure 17. The Commission had come to general agreement with interested parties that major services could only be provided satisfactorily by authorities with populations of at least 250,000. The report also suggested that if authorities had a population in excess of 1,000,000 then close contact with the locality would be difficult to preserve. It was quite explicit on two other important matters as well. First, the division in the old system between town and country was artificial, and the new structure ought to recognize their growing interdependence. Second, it was far better to have services provided by one authority within an area than for responsibilities to be split. On this last point, however, the Commission recognized the need for flexibility. The level of population in the conurbations around Manchester, Liverpool and Birmingham necessitated a two-tier structure and a division of responsibility.

Figure 18 *The structure of local government: the 1972 Act and today*

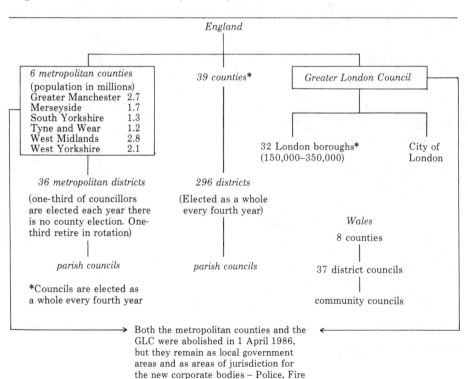

Figure 19 *Counties created by the 1972 Act*

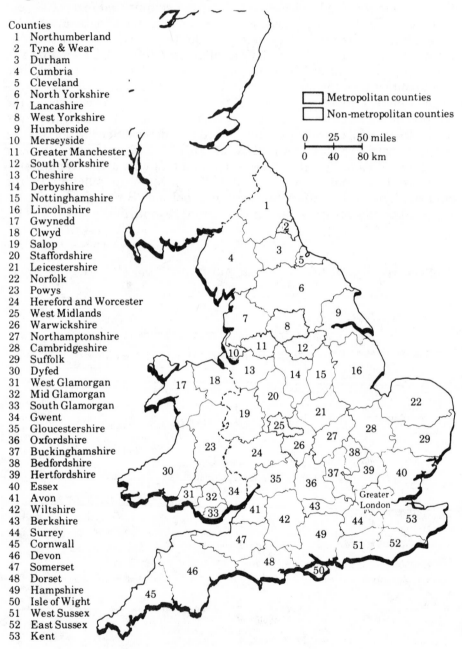

Counties
1 Northumberland
2 Tyne & Wear
3 Durham
4 Cumbria
5 Cleveland
6 North Yorkshire
7 Lancashire
8 West Yorkshire
9 Humberside
10 Merseyside
11 Greater Manchester
12 South Yorkshire
13 Cheshire
14 Derbyshire
15 Nottinghamshire
16 Lincolnshire
17 Gwynedd
18 Clwyd
19 Salop
20 Staffordshire
21 Leicestershire
22 Norfolk
23 Powys
24 Hereford and Worcester
25 West Midlands
26 Warwickshire
27 Northamptonshire
28 Cambridgeshire
29 Suffolk
30 Dyfed
31 West Glamorgan
32 Mid Glamorgan
33 South Glamorgan
34 Gwent
35 Gloucestershire
36 Oxfordshire
37 Buckinghamshire
38 Bedfordshire
39 Hertfordshire
40 Essex
41 Avon
42 Wiltshire
43 Berkshire
44 Surrey
45 Cornwall
46 Devon
47 Somerset
48 Dorset
49 Hampshire
50 Isle of Wight
51 West Sussex
52 East Sussex
53 Kent

☐ Metropolitan counties
☐ Non-metropolitan counties

0   25   50 miles
0   40   80 km

Source: Adapted from R. Maud and B. Wood, *English Local Government Reformed* (Oxford 1974).

One final and distinctive proposal of the Commission was that the whole system should be superintended by eight provincial councils consisting of representatives from the various councils in the region, together with other members co-opted from industry, the trade unions and the professions. These provincial councils should exercise responsibility for strategic planning, further education, tourism and cultural and recreational services.

As Figure 18 shows, the structure of local government in England and Wales which emerged from the 1972 Act differed substantially not only from the previous system but also from the Redcliffe-Maud proposals. First, it reduced by two-thirds the number of local authorities in England, while the number of councillors fell from 35,000 to 22,000. (The Redcliffe-Maud proposals, it should be noted, would have gone even further and reduced the number of authorities by over 90 per cent.) Second, despite the Commission's firm recommendation, the Act did not establish unitary authorities. Some functions, such as planning, continued to be shared and this created confusion, duplication and waste. Third, although the Act established fewer (and therefore larger) authorities, the Redcliffe-Maud recommendation (that an authority needed to have a population of at least 250,000 to be able to provide major services satisfactorily) was not observed. Only eight of the twenty outer London Boroughs (reorganized in 1964 and left unchanged by the 1972 Act) and only twenty of the thirty-six metropolitan districts are of this size (see Figure 19).

For these reasons the 1972 Act had many critics and in 1983 the Conservative Government made clear, in a White Paper, its intention to return to the question of reform. The Government's target was the Greater London Council and the Metropolitan Councils (both of which were eventually abolished in March 1986). The argument against the Councils may be summarized briefly. First, the Government was concerned about the problem of overlapping functions which created unnecessary bureaucracy. Second, it argued that the responsibilities of the councils were relatively minor and certainly were insufficient to justify a separate tier. Third, it maintained that there were likely to be considerable savings by returning, in the GLC and the metropolitan counties, to the Redcliffe-Maud principle of unitary authorities. Fourth, the Government argued that the Councils had been over-spenders — often on projects which bore little relationship to their statutory responsibilities. Cynics also suggested that a further motive for abolition was that all the authorities were Labour-controlled!

The revised structure of local government in England and Wales came into force on 1st April 1986 but the arguments will continue. Many people felt that the Government's handling of the reform was insensitive and it remains clear that little genuine consensus has emerged yet about the structure, responsibilities and power of local authorities.

Figure 20 *Metropolitan districts in Greater Manchester*

Source: Adapted from R. Maud and B. Wood, *English Local Government Reformed* (Oxford 1974).

Question

1 Consider the main differences between the Redcliffe-Maud proposals and the structure of local government in Britain today.

Local government work

Services and expenditure

Local authorities provide a wide range of important services. Some of these, such as the education service and various environmental health services, they are obliged to provide by law whereas others (such as recreational facilities) are provided at the discretion of the local authority. The broad allocation of the services is set out in Figure 21. As a result of the reorganization of local government in 1985–6 many of the former responsibilities of the GLC and the metropolitan counties (such as planning and road safety) have been transferred to the District Councils and the London Boroughs, while others have been transferred to new joint authorities. Each of the metropolitan counties (broadened in the case of Tyne and Wear to include Northumberland) has three separate authorities for Police, Passenger Transport and Fire and Civil Defence. These authorities (or boards) consist of councillors nominated to serve on them by each of the metropolitan districts in the county. One third of each

Figure 21 *Broad allocation of the main local government functions in England and Wales*

	District Council	County Council	District Council	London Borough Councils
Planning				
structure plans	*	*		*
local plans	*		*	*
development control	*		*	*
country parks	*	*	*	*
national parks	*	*		*
derelict land	*	*	*	*
Transport				
transport planning	*	*		*
highways	*	*		*
traffic regulation	*	*		*
road safety	*	*		*
parking	*	*		*
public transport	JB	*		LRT
Education	*	*		*[2]
Social services	*	*		*
Housing	*		*	*
Fire service	JB	*		LFCDA
Police service	JB	*		HS
Consumer protection	*	*		*
Environmental health				
building regulations	*		*	*
clean air	*		*	*
control of disease	*		*	*
food hygiene	*		*	*
refuse collection	*		*	*
refuse disposal	*[1]	*		*[1]
street cleansing	*		*	*
Libraries	*	*		*
Museums and the arts	*	*	*	*
Recreational facilities	*	*	*	*
Encouragement of tourism	*	*	*	*
Cemeteries and crematoria	*		*	*
Footpaths	*	*	*	*
Allotments	*		*	*
Land drainage and flood prevention	*	*		TWA
Administration of Justice	*	*		*
Appointment and payment of Coroners	*	*		*

TWA	Responsibility lies with Thames Water Authority
LRT	London Regional Transport Authority
JB	Joint Boards manage the services within metropolitan counties
HS	Home Secretary exercises responsibility for Police in London
LFCDA	London Fire and Civil Defence Authority
[1]	Joint arrangements are made by boroughs and districts
[2]	For Inner London Education Authority (ILEA) 58 directly elected members

of the police authorities consists of Justices of the Peace who together constitute a Joint Magistrates Committee. In the case of London, responsibility for the police continues to be exercised by the Home Secretary and for transport by the London Regional Transport Authority (LRT) but London does have a separate Fire and Civil Defence Authority. The Inner London Education Authority continues to exist but, for the first time in May 1986, became a directly elected body with 58 members.

Question

2 Look at Figure 21 and make a note of the authorities or boards responsible for the provision of your local services.

Because of their wide responsibilities local authorities are big spenders of public funds. They have two main forms of expenditure; revenue spending on, for example, salaries and heating costs, and capital expenditure on buildings and major items of equipment (see Figure 22). Their combined expenditure (revenue and capital) amounts to about 20 per cent of all public expenditure in Britain. Revenue spending is financed through grants from central government, rates and income from charges made by local authorities for some of the services and facilities they offer, such as public transport, swimming baths and civic restaurants. In recent years education has absorbed more than one third of revenue spending. Capital spending is financed mainly by loans from various sources and, to a much smaller extent, from grants. The most substantial capital item is housing. We must now consider the sources of local authority income, rates, grants and loans, in more detail.

Local authority income
Rates
Rates are a form of local taxation levied on houses and buildings and industrial premises. The rateable value of each unit (based on the annual rental value) is determined by the inland revenue and periodically reviewed. The last two reviews were in 1963 and 1973. Any ratepayer may appeal against the valuation to a local valuation court. Towards the end of the financial year each local authority assesses the gap between its proposed expenditure for the coming year and its non-rate income and imposes an appropriate rate to be paid on each pound of rateable value. Thus if a property has a rateable value of £240 and a rate of 75p imposed, then the tenant will be required to pay £180 in rates for the year.

Rates provide local authorities with their only independent source of revenue and they have a number of distinct advantages. They are well understood, easy to calculate, impossible to evade and extremely

Figure 22 *Distribution of revenue and capital spending by local authorities in England and Wales 1982–3*

Item of expenditure	Revenue £m	%	Capital £m	%
Education	12,694.3	35.1	474.2	7.8
Libraries, museums and art galleries	418.8	1.2	29.2	0.5
Health and social services	2,647.8	7.3	106.7	1.7
Police	2,600.2	7.2	80.6	1.3
Fire	573.5	1.5	32.2	0.5
Administration of justice	295.8	0.8	9.9	0.2
Refuse collection and disposal	704.9	2.0	64.2	1.0
Agriculture and fisheries	132.7	0.3	112.1	1.8
Highways, lighting and parking	2,574.8	7.1	700.8	11.5
Parks and open spaces	935.2	2.6	202.9	3.3
Environmental health	383.2	1.0	18.5	0.3
Town and country planning	573.6	1.6	298.0	4.9
Housing	5,995.6	16.6	3,308.3	54.1
Trading services	966.0	2.6	298.7	4.9
Other services	900.7	2.5	126.3	2.0
General administration	3,727.1	10.3	249.2	4.1
Total	36,124.3		6,111.8	
As a percentage of total expenditure	85.5%		14.5%	

Source: Annual Abstract of Statistics (HMSO 1985).

economical to collect. It is also argued that they are fair in the sense that those who occupy the largest houses, with high rateable values, are those who can most easily afford to pay. Last, the rating system has the considerable virtue of flexibility. No rates, for example, are levied on agricultural land. Untenanted properties are also usually exempted, and registered charities pay only half the standard amount for their properties. Moreover, rate rebates are available to those in financial hardship.

But rates today probably have more critics than friends. As they are based on property values, they tend to yield more money in the wealthier authorities where the need for services may be less great. For example, in 1976 rateable values per head of population were £86 in Durham, £96 in Lancashire and £159 in Surrey. Also, rates are a regressive form of taxation, being based only very roughly on a person's ability to pay. Thus although the owner of a large house will pay more in rates than the owner of a small house, his contribution may be much less in proportion to his total income. And rates lack buoyancy. Whereas the yield through income tax to the inland revenue increases with every increase in personal income, the rating system does not provide for automatic increases in local authority revenue. Simply to maintain the same level of services as in the previous year, a local authority will probably be obliged, because of inflation, to increase the rate.

Grants from Government
Government grants help to equalize the resources of local authorities. Between 1966 and 1980, the foundation of financial assistance from central government to local government was the Rate Support Grant (RSG), an elaborate and flexible provision which was calculated in relation to three elements:
1   domestic — a subsidy to reduce the cost to domestic ratepayers
2   resources — a grant to authorities where rateable values, per head of population, were below average
3   needs — a grant in recognition of the special needs of certain areas and calculated mainly in accordance with *past expenditure*.
RSG was replaced, through the Local Government Planning and Land Act 1980, by a Block Grant based upon an assessment *by central Government* of the spending requirements of each local authority rather than upon an authority's past expenditure. Thus, the former inducement to local authorities to raise expenditure in one year in order to obtain a higher grant in the next, has been removed. Central government now determines the Block Grant by considering the expenditure which an authority with similar circumstances and characteristics would incur in providing a normal service. Central government also specifies for each authority an appropriate level of rate (x pence in the £) and these two elements, the one national, the other local, together produce what central government believes to be a level of expenditure appropriate to the local authority. If a local authority seeks to exceed that figure without good cause by increasing the rate, then central government is able to reduce the Block Grant accordingly. The Act placed firmer financial disciplines on local authorities and has been regarded by some as being a serious erosion of their independence (see also pages 174–5).

Borrowing
Local authorities are entitled to borrow money to finance capital expenditure, subject to the approval of the Department of the Environment. The main source is the Public Works Loan Board, financed by the Treasury. Other sources include banks, insurance companies, superannuation funds and bonds.

Local income tax
What is at issue in the question of local authority finance is much more

Figure 23 *Revenue and capital income of local authorities in England and Wales 1972–83*

Source	1972–3 (£m)	(%)	1978–9 (£m)	(%)	1982–3 (£m)	(%)
Revenue income						
Rates	2,179.6	27	5,323.3	25	10,693.7	30
Government grants	3,135.0	38	10,103.8	47	14,246.5	40
Miscellaneous income	2,900.2	35	6,122.6	28	10,370.6	30
Total Revenue income	8,214.8		21,549.7		35,311.0	
Capital income						
Loans	2,150.9	75	2,751.0	63	3,572.6	49
Government grants	130.2	5	380.1	9	456.8	6
Sales and other sources	562.9	20	1,210.7	28	3,277.2	45
Total capital income	2,844.0		4,341.8		7,306.6	
Total income	11,058.9		25,891.6		42,617.6	

Source: Annual Abstract of Statistics (HMSO 1985).

than the ability of authorities to find money for the services they provide. Of equal importance are questions such as whether the system is fair and whether it gives the central government too much overall control.

In 1974 a committee chaired by Mr Frank Layfield was appointed to look into the issue of local authority finance. Its report, which appeared in 1976, affirmed very forcefully the general principle that those responsible for spending money should also be responsible for raising it. Layfield wanted the growing dependence on the central government to be halted, and argued that if local authorities were to be made more responsible for raising money, then a form of local income tax would be needed to supplement the income from rates. To alter the balance between central and local funds in this way, Layfield suggested, would help to strengthen local democracy by making councillors more directly accountable to the electorate.

Of course, Governments are reluctant to surrender the controls they have over local authority expenditure because to do so would not necessarily be in the best interests of the poorer authorities and because, since local authorities are such significant spenders, to lose control over them would weaken the ability of Government to manage the national economy. Although many ideas for restructuring local government finance have been floated in recent years (such as abolishing the rates and finding new sources of local taxation), little has been achieved and major changes in the near future are unlikely. Over the past decade the instinct of central government (see pages 174–5) has been to try to find ways of curbing local expenditure rather than to try to find new and more lucrative sources of revenue for local authorities. It is not an emphasis which is likely to change.

Questions
3 Consider pages 160–3 and Figure 22 in particular. Suggest various ways in which a local authority wishing to reduce its overall expenditure could do so.
4 How ought local authorities to be financed? Should they receive more or less of their income from central government?

Local government work: councillors and committees

Councillors and the community
To be eligible for service as a councillor one must be a British subject, over the age of twenty-one, not an employee of the local authority in question, not a civil servant in the 'politically restricted' category and not a person with a recent and serious criminal record. It is unnecessary for a person seeking election to be on the electoral roll for the area, as anyone who has occupied land or premises in the area over the previous twelve months is entitled to stand. So too is any person who travels into the area regularly to work.

Generally speaking, to be a councillor is not a full-time occupation. The majority of councillors combine their responsibilities as elected representatives with those of their normal work. Councillors receive allowances for attendance and loss of earnings. It is nevertheless probably the absence of adequate remuneration which explains why the Maud Committee found in 1964 that over half the councillors in England and Wales were over the age of fifty-five. Finance may also help to explain why there is a dearth of people wishing to become councillors. All parties experience difficulty in finding suitable candidates.

Although independent candidates are still common in country areas, the majority of candidates (86 per cent in the county elections of 1977) now represent political parties. The franchise corresponds to that in general elections (see page 26) but peers are entitled to vote as well. The results are more difficult to analyse. They often reflect the standing of the parties in the country as a whole, but it is difficult to separate national from purely local issues or from personalities. A candidate with high personal standing may be worth more votes to his party than a good candidate at a general election.

All councillors serve and represent the community, but it is the mayor who is figurehead. Councils hold an Annual General Meeting, usually in

May, at which the chairman (known in districts which have borough status as the mayor) is chosen. He presides over meetings of the full council, but his office has dignity rather than power. He generally plays no part in party political conflict during his one year of office and acts instead as leader of the community, attending local functions, opening new public buildings and generally identifying himself with things worthwhile.

Committees

The main work of local government is not carried out by the council acting as a whole. The council appoints the mayor and decides the composition of committees, but it is the committees themselves which exercise the main responsibility for policy-making. Most county councils have between six and ten committees, while district councils have between five and six (see page 168). If a party has a majority on the full council, then it will expect to command a majority on each committee and to appoint each committee chairman. Committees may in turn delegate their powers to subcommittees.

Two interrelated criticisms are often made of committees in local government. The first, that committees transfer power from the full council to small groups with specialist enthusiasms, thereby preventing the council from exercising its proper responsibility for policy-making, is fairly straightforward to answer. As with the central government, some form of committee system is necessary because of the volume of complexity of the work with which councils are concerned. Moreover, although the council delegates authority to committees, it does not surrender its control completely. It is the council which decides the degree of freedom each committee will have. If it finds a particular committee unsatisfactory, then it can dismiss it. The council can also reserve to itself the right to determine policy after having received a committee's recommendation. Party groups often meet before full council meetings to consider their position on committee recommendations. Although many recommendations are accepted without debate, any recommendation which fails to satisfy the council as a whole may be fully debated. Finally, the council controls the purse-strings. The power to raise money is one it cannot delegate.

The second criticism of committees is that, preoccupied with their own particular field, they may make the task of the council in co-ordinating the work of different committees extremely difficult. The force of this argument was recognized by the Maud Committee in 1967, which maintained that the existing committee structure was too complex (with the average county councillor serving on nine or ten committees) and that there were too many specialist policy committees (vertical committees) and not enough general or horizontal committees with interests in all areas of local authority policy. Maud claimed that the strength of vertical committees prevented local authorities from developing a clear perspective on their responsibilities. Maud recommended the establishment of a Management Board consisting of between five and nine elected members to co-ordinate the work of committees. It was largely because of this that many authorities subsequently established a Policy and Resources Committee (see Figure 24) to co-ordinate the work of departmental committees. The recommendations of the Bains Report also helped to push local authorities further in this direction (see page 170). The problem of over-specialization is being faced.

Figure 24 *Committee structure of a non-metropolitan county*

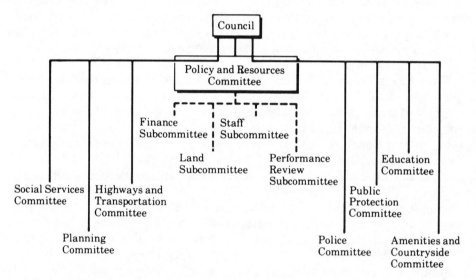

Source: Martin Cross and David Mallen, *Local Government and Politics* (Longman 1978), p. 108

Committees, however, possess considerable virtues of their own. First, they help to make the process of decision-making more efficient. They allow matters of detail, which may not be of great concern to many councillors, to be argued out before an issue is referred to the full council. In this way they save time for the council, allowing it to concentrate on general strategy. For councillors, often trying to fit their responsibilities into a busy life, committees afford the opportunity to specialize in a field of particular interest to themselves and thus to use their time profitably. Second, committees help to bring councillors and local government officials together in active co-operation. The chief officer within a department (or another senior officer) is usually present at committee meetings to give reports and offer advice, though not to vote. This helps to make the work of committees more informed, and it also subjects paid officials to 'democratic' control. Finally, through the committee system, local authorities are able to draw on the expertise of people outside the council. Such persons are co-opted on to committees and are entitled to vote. Thus teachers may serve on the education committee or doctors on the social services committee. While it is probably true that co-opted members have, almost by definition, a preoccupation with the one issue to the exclusion of others, that is probably a small price to pay for the specialized knowledge they are able to bring.

Questions
5 Consider the various ways in which councillors can influence work in local government. Draw on examples from your own area.
6 Can you find any examples within your own area of conflict between political parties on local issues? What issues and principles were at stake?

Local government: the role of officers

Local government needs full-time officers to give advice to elected members on professional or technical questions which councillors have not the competence or knowledge to handle themselves and to carry on the day-to-day administration of the large range of services which local authorities offer. To find the right balance between officers and elected representatives is a difficult but important task of local government. Just as it is too simple to say that ministers determine policy and civil servants carry it out, so it is equally facile to say that of councillors and officers respectively. The reality is that there is no clear distinction between policy and administration, and that although a wise officer will probably make the committee feel that it has made the decision, like the civil servant, the officer is often able to influence the outcome by presenting information to the committee in a particular way.

And yet it would be a mistake to exaggerate the similarities between local government officers and civil servants. For example, the chief officers in the main departments of local government serve a committee representing different shades of political viewpoint and not a single minister. They are brought into closer contact with elected representatives than are civil servants and they are much less anonymous. Very often, they are prominent public figures strongly identified with particular policies. This is largely because they are usually experts in a particular field. A chief education officer, for example, will probably have had not only lengthy experience of educational administration, but experience as a teacher as well. The 'generalist' or 'amateur', so common in the Civil Service, is relatively unknown to local authority administration. Moreover, whereas civil servants often move between departments, the pattern in local government is for promotion to take place within departments either inside or outside the authority.

It is easy to see why, just as there is a need for machinery to co-ordinate the work of committees, there is also a need for the work of departments to be co-ordinated as well. This was recognized by the Bains Report of 1972. While some authorities already had such machinery, many more have developed it since. Bains emphasized the importance of the corporate approach to management — of policy being formulated to serve the purpose of the authority as a whole rather than any single department. This required a management team consisting of about five or six chief officers headed by an chief executive who would maintain a close working relationship with the chairman of the Policy and Resources Committee (see page 168). The chief executive and his team were to prepare plans and advise the council on matters of general policy, helping it to realize its long-term as well as immediate objectives. Today most local authorities in England and Wales have such teams (see Figure 25).

Question

7 What effects are the developments of Policy and Resources Committees and management teams likely to have on policy-making in local government?

The relationship between central and local government

Some of the responsibilities exercised by local authorities may seem trivial in themselves, but together they amount to a wide influence. For example, planning decisions, such as whether to close parts of a town centre to traffic, are made by local authorities. So too are decisions on subsidies to public transport or on many aspects of education. Figure 26 shows the distribution of power in the education service at three levels: the Department of Education and Science (DES), the local education authorities (LEAs) and the schools.

Question

8 Study Figure 26 carefully and try to decide in each of the six areas

Figure 25 *Departmental structure of a non-metropolitan county*

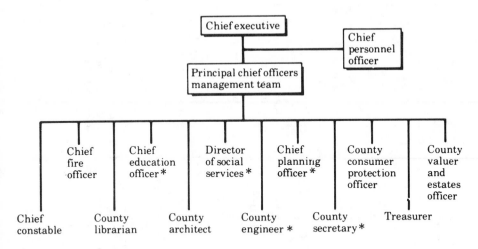

*Members of management team

Source: Martin Cross and David Mallen, *Local Government and Politics* (Longman 1978), p. 111.

where the real centre of responsibility rests. What *kind* of control does the DES exercise?

Local authorities also exercise influence unobtrusively. They are often drawn into discussion by departments of central government. In this way they are able to promote their own Private Bills at Westminster and thus have special powers on a particular issue. If a resolution has been approved by two successive council meetings, it can be laid before Parliament in the form of a Bill and passed in the normal way. The bulk of the work on it will be done at committee stage at Westminster.

But despite the importance of the influence local authorities are able to exercise, they are subject to a number of very tight constraints from central government. These may be usefully considered in three broad categories: judicial, financial and administrative.

Judicial

By far the biggest restriction on the freedom of local authorities is the doctrine of *ultra vires* — that local authorities have no powers other than those conferred by Parliament. They are able to spend, without statutory authority, as much money as they are able to raise through levying a rate of 2p in the pound, but they cannot use such money for purposes

Figure 26 *Decision-making in education at three levels*

Tasks	*DES decisions*	*LEA decisions*	*Institution decisions*
Decisions on structure of education – age of entry, age of compulsory retention	DES makes law on school-leaving age and it may seek to impose a particular form of education. The Education Act of 1976 sought to make the secondary system comprehensive	Able to vary the age of transfer between primary and secondary schools and to decide the structure of education subject to DES regulations	Decides structure within schools, for example, whether to 'stream' pupils or to adopt mixed ability groupings
Decisions on finance of education	DES negotiates elements of rate support grant through Department of Environment	Local Authority decides proportion of income to devote to education. LEA allocates money to individual projects	Decides how to spend money allocated for books and equipment
Building	DES decides, within Treasury constraints, total amount for building projects. DES decides list of major projects on basis of LEA proposals	LEA decides which major projects to propose and which minor projects to build	School draws attention to areas of need and tries to win support of LEA

Teaching and learning processes	Controls: (a) length and number of school days (b) acts of worship and religious education (c) pattern of secondary school examinations. Influence on the character of education through Her Majesty's Inspectors (HMIs)	Influences style and content of education through appointment of heads and through subject and general advisers. Helps to organize in-service training for teachers	Free to determine internal organization, the curriculum, and the style of education, for example teaching in a formal or informal manner
Provisions of teachers	(a) Control of total numbers reaching and leaving colleges and university education departments (b) party to salary and conditions of service negotiations	Controls staffing levels for each institution and appointments of heads and deputies. Influences promotion of teachers and helps in in-service training	(a) Helps decide on recruitment and nature of staff (b) allocates teachers' duties (c) recommends special responsibility allowances to LEA
Development of system	Influences the system through law, through circulars, through HMIs, and through courses organized	Decides the general response of the education service to the needs of the area, establishing priorities, and allocating resources, etc.	Responsible for deciding many of the objectives within schools and the general tone, for example, relationships with pupils, the local community, and parents

Source: Adapted from M. Kogan, *County Hall* (Penguin 1973), pp. 34–5.

forbidden by Parliament. They can also make their own by-laws, but these must receive ministerial approval before they can come into force.

A good recent illustration of the constraint which law can place on the activities of a local authority arose over the Greater London Council's 'Fares Fair' policy in 1981. The GLC wished to reduce fares on London transport by 25 per cent and subsidize transport from the rates. The Conservative-controlled London Borough of Bromley contested the legality of this policy in the courts and the Appeal Court ruled in favour of Bromley on the grounds that the Transport Act 1969 required services to 'break even'.

In respect of capital expenditure, local authorities now have greater flexibility as a result of the Local Government Act of 1980. Although central Government determines the amount an authority may borrow for its capital projects, the allocation of those resources is a matter for the local authority.

Financial

The financial dependence of local authorities on funds from central government has already been noted. The Block Grant provides authorities with a substantial proportion of their revenue income, and grants can very easily be withheld in order to control an authority. For example, in 1976 the Labour Government threatened to withhold RSG from any authority granting pay increases above the £6 per week limit recommended by the Government. Similarly, in September 1981, Mr Heseltine, Secretary of State for the Environment, announced that fourteen local authorities could be penalized for failing to reduce their expenditure. In 1982, the Local Government Finance Act banned the imposition of supplementary rates.

But despite these measures the Government's own spending targets for the years 1979–83 continued to be exceeded. Within those four years rates rose, on average, by 91 per cent while the retail price index rose by only 55 per cent. This, as we have seen, was one of the factors which caused the Conservative Government to abolish the GLC and the metropolitan counties (on the grounds that they were extravagant) but it also prompted the Government to introduce its most severe form of rate control — the Rates Bill of 1983. This sought to control both spending and rates in 'extravagant' authorities while giving additional powers to the Secretary of State to control spending in all councils should this be felt necessary. The Bill was strongly criticized in Parliament but became law. Eighteen councils were chosen to be 'rate-capped', of which only two, Brent and Portsmouth, were Conservative-controlled. The financial constraints within which local government now operates are more severe than they have ever been and have helped to bring about, within the past few years, a substantial shift in the balance of power between central and local government.

Central government also controls local authority borrowing. Authorities must obtain loan sanction from the Secretary of State for the Environment for most projects involving capital expenditure. Moreover, Governments will not approve projects, however worthwhile, if to do so would threaten their overall economic targets. They might even order a cutback in local authority spending as did Conservative Governments in December 1973 and 1979. And control is also exercised by means of audit. Each year local authority accounts must be audited either by a district auditor appointed by the Department of Environment or by a private auditor approved by the Secretary of State. If any illegal expenditure has been incurred, the auditor is entitled to impose a 'surcharge' on the councillors' or officers' own pockets!

Administrative

Administrative controls take many forms. The police, education, fire and social services, are subject to inspection by officials appointed by central Government. Appointments of chief constables and chief fire officers are subject to the approval of the Home Secretary. Before any authority appoints a Director of Social Services, the short list of candidates must be approved by the Secretary of State for the Social Services. Moreover, ministers, although not always possessing powers to require authorities by law to carry out certain policies, can nevertheless seek to influence the policy of local authorities through circulars. For example, the Labour Government's education circular 10/65 in 1965 'requesting' local authorities to submit schemes for comprehensive reorganization in their area contributed to a rapid expansion in comprehensive education over the next five years. It is interesting to note, however, that a number of Conservative-controlled authorities were still making strenuous efforts to resist such reorganization in 1979.

Ministers also have the last word on planning decisions (see page 218), and some Acts of Parliament give them special powers in circumstances where a local authority refuses to carry out its statutory responsibilities. For example, the Housing Finance Act of 1972 gave the minister the power to appoint commissioners to collect rents in areas where the local council (as at Clay Cross in Derbyshire) was refusing to implement the Act.

The relationship between central and local government is usually one of partnership and co-operation rather than conflict. It is nevertheless clear that a variety of pressures keep the real centre of power in Westminster and Whitehall.

Questions

9 Why are the controls exercised by central government over local authorities so rigorous? Why does local government resist these controls?

10 Can you find any recent examples (in your own area or elsewhere) of a conflict arising between local and central government? Why did it occur and what was the outcome?

9 Devolution, regionalism and privatization

Devolution and regionalism

Many people consider Britain to be an overcentralized state. Too many decisions are taken in Westminster and Whitehall and too few at local level. Government, or so the argument runs, needs to be taken closer to the people. In this chapter we shall be concerned with a number of aspects of this problem. We shall consider firstly the rise of nationalism in Scotland and Wales and the proposals in the late 1970s to devolve more power to those two countries. We shall then consider critically some other aspects of the devolution of power in Britain concerning, for example, the Health and Water Authorities, and examine the arguments for and against the introduction of a regional element into British Government.

The rise of nationalism

The rise of nationalism in Wales and especially Scotland was one of the main political issues in Britain in the 1970s. As a movement it had a number of causes. It was in part a response to cultural differences, and in Wales it was stimulated by the Welsh language. It was prompted too by economic considerations. Although the claim of the Scottish National Party (SNP) that Scotland had been unfairly treated in relation to other areas of Britain is questionable, it certainly is true that living standards in Scotland — as in other parts of Britain — had not improved as rapidly as had been expected. Both the Scots and the Welsh felt that London was remote and that they were the best judges of their own interests — interests which could only be promoted by giving them substantially more control over their own affairs. And, finally, in the case of Scotland there was oil, discovered in the early 1970s in the North Sea and offering Scotland (if she could rightfully claim it) the prosperity she had been denied.

The nationalist movements began to gather strength in the late 1960s. In 1966 the Welsh Nationalists won a by-election at Carmarthen, and the following year the Scottish Nationalists won a similar victory at Hamilton.

In the General Election of 1970 the SNP vote doubled, and in November 1973 the party wiped out a 16,000 Labour majority in the Govan by-election. In the General Elections of February and October 1974, SNP support rose first to 22 per cent and then to 30 per cent of the Scottish electorate. By 1976 the party appeared to have displaced Labour as the most powerful in Scotland. The progress of the Welsh Nationalists was less marked, although they did win three seats in the General Election of October 1974.

These successes were of obvious concern to the major parties. The Labour Party was particularly concerned as Scotland and Wales were traditional Labour strongholds. In October 1974, for example, twenty-three out of thirty-six seats in Wales and forty-one out of seventy-one in Scotland had gone to the Labour Party. If the force of nationalism continued to rise, that supremacy would be threatened. Something clearly had to be done, not only out of deference to nationalist opinion but out of self-interest as well. By 1974 all the main parties accepted the need for 'devolution', for giving more power to Scotland and Wales to control their own affairs while preserving the unity of the United Kingdom.

The current position

As a number of anti-devolutionists have pointed out in recent years, Wales and, to a greater extent, Scotland already exercise considerable influence over their own affairs. By reorganization in 1973 Scotland was divided into twelve regions with powers corresponding broadly to those of the English counties. The regions are further divided into districts similar to those in England. In 1975 a Convention of Scottish Local Authorities was set up to consider legislation proposed at Westminster affecting local government in Scotland.

But the devolution of power to Scotland already goes much further than simply granting her local powers similar to those in England. Unlike any of the English regions, Scotland and Wales have their own Secretaries of State, both of whom have seats in the Cabinet. They exercise responsibility for the work of the Scottish and Welsh Offices, staffed by 6500 and 1000 civil servants respectively.

To these offices a considerable amount of administrative devolution has already taken place. The Secretary of State for Scotland, for example, is responsible for agriculture and fishing, for stimulating industrial investment, for education (except the universities), for the administration of the National Health Service in Scotland, for housing and for a wide range of other important functions. Moreover, the Scottish Grand Committee (consisting of the seventy-two Scottish MPs and a sufficient number of English MPs to make the party balance comparable to that in

Britain as a whole) debates matters of concern to Scotland and takes the second reading of Bills dealing exclusively with Scottish affairs. A similar committee exists for Wales. In addition it should be remembered that Scotland has education and legal systems which are quite independent of those in England and Wales.

The degree of administrative devolution is then already considerable, but what it does not provide is control by locally elected representatives through a national assembly. Neither have Scotland and Wales been granted legislative devolution — the right to make laws in certain areas. These changes were proposed by the Labour Government in 1977.

The devolution proposals

During the Parliament of 1974–9 two efforts were made to devolve further powers to Scotland and Wales. The first came to an end in February 1977 when the Labour Government failed to win a majority in the House of Commons for a guillotine motion which would have allowed the legislation to pass through Parliament more quickly. That Bill grouped Scotland and Wales together, but when the proposals were later reintroduced, Scotland and Wales were treated separately. The Bills were duly passed by Parliament but not before a group of Labour back-bench MPs had managed to insert clauses into both Bills preventing them from coming into force until they had been approved in a referendum by at least 40 per cent of the electorates in Scotland and Wales. The referenda were held in March 1979. In Scotland devolution was approved but by a narrow majority (32.5 per cent were in favour and 30.4 per cent against.) In Wales only 11.8 per cent were in favour. The devolution Bills were withdrawn.

The proposals collapsed eventually because of feeling in the two countries. But from the start many MPs had had considerable doubts about the wisdom of the Government's proposals. The Scotland Bill, which will concern us here, was the most heavily criticized.

The Bill proposed an Assembly of 142 members in Edinburgh to be elected every four years using the first-past-the-post system (see pages 27–34). The Assembly was to choose its own executive headed by a Prime Minister, and broadly speaking it was to have jurisdiction over those matters which had been the responsibility of the Scottish Office. The Bill affirmed the unity of the United Kingdom and the sovereignty of Parliament. This it protected in a number of ways. The Assembly was to have no powers of taxation. Instead an annual block grant was to be made to the Assembly by Westminster. Westminster could also prevent or restrict increases in housing rents. Moreover, it could set aside Assembly Bills if they affected adversely matters outside the Assembly's responsibility or if they were contrary to any of Britain's international obligations or to her obligations arising from membership of the European Economic Community. If Westminster felt that a Bill from the Assembly exceeded its legal power, the Bill could be referred to the Judicial Committee of the Privy Council (see page 115), the decision of which had to be accepted by both sides.

The Bill attempted to provide for a measure of legislative devolution while preserving the ultimate authority in Westminster. It attracted a number of powerful criticisms. First, the rejection of proportional representation in elections to the Assembly created the possibility of the SNP obtaining a majority of seats (and using this as a platform from which to demand full Scottish independence) having obtained only about one-third of the votes cast. Second, the Bill invited the prospect of an annual confrontation between Westminster and the Assembly in the negotiations over the size of the block grant. Any development project not undertaken could be blamed on Westminster and used as a further lever in the bid for independence. Third, although the Bills established a new tier of government for Scotland and Wales (but not for any other part of the United Kingdom), they did not propose any reduction in Scottish and Welsh representation at Westminster despite the fact that the two countries were already over-represented per head of population. Finally, although all Scottish MPs would have been able to vote at Westminster on all issues, English MPs would not have had similar privileges on matters transferred to the control of the Assembly. In many ways the proposals were extremely unsatisfactory. They were concerned with the short-term problem of containing the growth of the SNP rather than the long-term problem of providing better government for Britain. The problem of the SNP receded in significance with the reduction of SNP representation at Westminster from eleven to two in the General Election of 1979. To the long-term problem we now turn.

Question
1 Why did the Labour Government decide to introduce a measure of devolution for Scotland and Wales in 1977 and why did its attempts to create separate Assemblies fail?

Devolution and accountability

We have already seen, in Chapter 8, that Parliament has chosen to devolve some powers and responsibilities to local authorities. But there are many other public authorities which are required by Parliament to exercise administrative responsibilities or to provide services in the regions and districts of Britain. The Scottish and Welsh Offices, the regional outposts of many of the main departments of central Government (such as the Department of Health and Social Security or the Inland Revenue) and the Health and Water Authorities are all examples of such devolution of power. So too are the Boards which are responsible for the management of nationalized industries which are considered later. First we shall consider some regional authorities in Britain.

Regional authorities

As a result of reorganization in 1973, the National Health Service in England is administered by fourteen Regional Health Authorities responsible for the design and construction of new buildings and for planning in general. (In Scotland and Wales, the Health Service is administered by the Scottish and Welsh offices respectively.) Each RHA is further divided into 190 District Health Authorities responsible for the day-to-day running of the service. None of these bodies is elected. The RHAs are administered by boards chosen by the Secretary of State for the Environment, while the District Health Authorities consist of persons nominated by the RHAs and the local authorities. In addition, within each district are Community Health Councils to represent the users of the Health Service. These councils also have a nominated membership. They are not genuinely independent and not directly accountable to those whom they serve. There is a similar lack of accountability in the Water Service and the Regional Economic Planning Councils. England is divided into nine Regional Water Authorities. Most of the members of the RWAs are appointed by the Secretary of State for the Environment and the remainder by the local authorities. In Wales responsibility is exercised by a single authority responsible to the Welsh Office, while in Scotland the system is administered through the regional councils.

The eight Regional Economic Planning Councils were established as advisory bodies in the 1960s. Their members — usually people prominent in the locality — are again appointed by the Secretary of State. Although the Councils could make a genuinely important contribution to regional planning through co-ordinating the work of different local councils, they lack real authority. They have no power base and, while they can make recommendations, they cannot force local authorities to adopt them.

Regionalism and the future

It is quite clear that some form of regional organization already exists in Britain. It is needed to provide services which could not be usefully administered on a smaller scale or to develop broad planning strategies of concern to a number of different authorities.

The current pattern of regional organization, however, suffers from two major defects. In the first place, it is not systematic. In no case do the boundaries of one regionally provided service correspond to those of another. Moreover, in many instances they do not correspond to the boundaries of local authorities. This is particularly true of Regional Water Authorities. The second weakness is that these authorities are relatively free from parliamentary control (ministerial control being very remote) and not directly accountable to the local electorate. In a sense they are a law unto themselves when, given the importance of the functions they perform, some form of democratic control over them would clearly be desirable.

Over the past decade the case for some form of regional government in Britain has been widely canvassed. In 1969 the Redcliffe-Maud report recommended the establishment of eight Provincial Councils covering areas similar to those of the current Regional Economic Planning Councils (see also page 156), and the cause of regionalism received further encouragement from the Royal Commission on the Constitution which reported in 1973. The Commission had been set up in 1969 in response to the growing strength of nationalist movements in Wales and Scotland but its two reports — majority and minority — had a much broader significance. The majority report recommended the establishment of elected assemblies in Scotland and Wales, together with co-ordinating and advisory councils for England and Wales consisting of local authority representatives and other co-opted members, and based on the existing economic planning regions.

The memorandum of dissent written by Lord Crowther-Hunt and Alan Peacock went much further. This suggested that Scotland, Wales and the English regions should be treated uniformly through establishing elected assemblies for Scotland, Wales and five English regions. The assemblies were to be directly elected through a form of proportional representation, and they were to administer services rather than determine policy. Their function was to co-ordinate the work of all existing regional authorities, including the regional departments of central Government. They were not to be legislative bodies. Lord Crowther-Hunt believed strongly that if major administrative functions could be devolved to the regions, then central Government would be able to address itself to its main concern — general policy-making.

Finally, in December 1976 the Labour Government published a consultative document, 'Devolution: The English Dimension', which set out very clearly the case for a greater measure of regional devolution while drawing attention to some of the difficulties. It recognized the danger of central Government becoming over-burdened with administrative details and the possibility of the Government becoming too remote from the people. It also acknowledged the case for making the regional Health and Water Authorities subject to democratic control and for establishing a new tier of government, smaller than the whole country but larger than the existing local authorities.

But the document was also conscious of the problems of regionalism. If regional assemblies were given executive and legislative powers, then considerable regional inequalities could develop. Even if they were to be purely administrative bodies, there would be difficulty in defining precisely the areas in which they should operate (in that boundaries suitable for one function are not necessarily suitable for another). Finally, as the document pointed out, consideration must also be given to the desirability of a further measure of reorganization coming so soon after the other major change in the 1970s.

Just as the rise of nationalism was a major theme in British politics in the 1970s, so the devolution of power from Westminster will probably continue to be an important issue during the 1980s. Hopefully it will be seen not as a measure to appease nationalist or even regional opinion, but as a genuine contribution towards improving the government of the United Kingdom and taking it towards the people.

Questions
2 Drawing on the evidence in the whole of the chapter, make a case for and against devolving more power to the various regions of Britain.
3 If a further measure of devolution *was* to be introduced, ought it to be 'administrative' or 'legislative' or both? Why?

The nationalized industries

Most nationalized industries, such as the National Coal Board, British Rail, the British Steel Corporation and the Post Office, have been set up since World War 2, although others, such as the Central Electricity Board (now the Central Electricity Generating Board), were established in the 1920s. The nationalized industries operate through the administrative device of the Public Corporation but not all Public Corporations are publicly owned. The Independent Broadcasting Authority, for example, is administered by a Public Corporation but is a private organization.

Because Parliament often supports nationalized industries from public funds, the nationalized industries are, ultimately, accountable to Parliament through the appropriate minister and through the work of the new Departmental Select Committees (see pages 77–8). The minister may, for example, answer questions in Parliament of a general nature on the coal industry but he would not be expected to respond in detail on issues such as specific pits.

The powers of the minister in relation to the Corporation or Board are considerable. In the first place he appoints the Board for a fixed period and has the power to dismiss its members. The contracts of the Chairmen of British Steel (1976) and the Central Electricity Generating Board (1977) were not renewed. The minister is also entitled to call for accounts and information; he may take an interest in plans for development and, perhaps most importantly, he is able to give general directions to the Board. The approval of the minister, for example, is generally needed for large schemes of capital investment and, in recent years, frequent interruptions of investment in the industries as a result of ministerial intervention have created friction between the Boards and ministers. In 1980, Sir Francis Tombs, Chairman of the Electricity Council, argued that there was a need for Government to agree on a medium/long-term plan for the industry so that an investment strategy could be devised and implemented without interruption. Other recent Chairmen such as Sir Monty Finniston (British Steel) and Sir Richard Marsh (British Rail) have complained about ministerial intervention to restrain price increases. Ministers have interfered with the commercial freedom of Boards in other ways too. The CEGB, for example, has been made to buy British coal for its power stations and British Airways has been required to buy planes other than those they would have chosen on commercial grounds. The sharpest disagreements have come where the commercial interests of the Board have conflicted with the minister's understanding of the national interest.

These disagreements raise the question of whether the present organization of the nationalized industries is adequate. The National Economic Development Office (NEDO) in a Report in 1976 argued that relations between Government and industry were unsatisfactory and that new Policy Councils should be created for each industry. The Councils were to have an independent Chairman and they — not the minister — were to appoint the Board for the industry. The minister would have the right to attend Board meetings but would be more remote — intentionally — than at present.

The Labour Government responded to the NEDO Report in a White Paper in 1978. This rejected the idea of Policy Councils (because they would diminish ministerial control) and suggested instead 'performance indicators' (such as international comparisons, growth, productivity and quality of service) to measure the achievements of each industry.

Despite the debate on the structure of the nationalized industries in the late seventies little change emerged. Where change has been much more apparent is over the size of the public sector. To this we now turn.

Question

4 Why has the structure of nationalized industries often been criticized and why has it remained unchanged?

Privatization

The policy of Conservative Governments after 1979 towards the nationalized industries was markedly different from the attitude of previous post-war Governments both Labour and Conservative. Throughout the post-war years, until 1979, both major parties accepted the 'mixed economy' — the balance between the 'public' and the 'private' sectors in industry. Mrs Thatcher's Governments after 1979 had a markedly different attitude. They sought, through a policy of 'privatization', to alter the balance between the public and private sector decisively in favour of the latter. Many industries (see Figure 27) were transferred to private ownership and by 1983 £1.7 billion had been raised in revenue. By the end of Mrs Thatcher's second term in office the privatization policy will have yielded about £11 billion. The change has been remarkable and it has aroused strong feelings. Some of the arguments surrounding the policy are considered below.

Figure 27 *The privatization programme*

Date	Company	% sold	Sold for (£ million)
October 1979	British Petroleum	5.6	276
February 1981	British Aerospace	51.6	148.6
October 1981	Cable and Wireless	49.36	224
February 1982	Amersham International	100	71
February 1982	National Freight Consortium	100	53
November 1982	Britoil	51	548.8
February 1983	Associated British Ports	51.5	46
May 1984	Wytch Farm Oilfield	100	215
June 1984	Enterprise Oil	100	392
July 1984	Sealink	100	65.7
August 1984	Jaguar	100	294
November 1984	British Telecom	50.2	3,900
June 1985	British Aerospace	48.4	364.0
August 1985	Britoil	49	450.0
December 1985	Cable and Wireless	50.7	593.0

The case for privatization

(i) By diminishing the role of the state in industry, companies have been left freer to invest, to expand, to respond to commercial pressures and to meet international competition. No longer are ministers interfering in matters which are best left to private initiative, private enterprise and private judgement.

(ii) Nationalized industries have been 'inefficient' and, far from being profitable, often in debt. This has increased public borrowing and made them a burden on the tax-payer. Moreover, dependence on the tax-payer had become a habit and the nationalized industries, in many cases, were no longer even expected to be profitable.

(iii) Privatization has given many workers the opportunity to own shares in the company in which they work. This in turn may increase their awareness of business considerations such as profitability, encourage realistic wage settlements and give both workers and employers a common interest in industrial success.

(iv) Just as many people have wanted Britain to be a 'property owning democracy' (a policy furthered by the selling of council houses) so the spread of share ownership, which privatization has encouraged, has helped to make Britain a share-owning democracy. Both these developments have increased the wealth and financial independence of many people.

(v) Public opinion has favoured the policy. Opinion polls show that a clear majority of the electorate favour privatization and the public's readiness to buy shares was well illustrated when, in November 1984, two million applications were made for shares in British Telecom.

The case against

(i) It is untrue to say that all nationalized industries are inefficient. Privatization has involved selling off only the efficient and profitable industries while leaving others, such as British Rail, in the public sector but without the capital to modernize.

(ii) The policy of privatization, while providing short-term revenue for the Government, has denied the nation some of its most important assets.

(iii) The Government's approach to the issue has been too doctrinaire. They have failed to see that there is good and bad in both the public and the private sectors. British Leyland, for example, failed as a private company but has since partially recovered under public ownership. The Government has also failed to recognize that there are many other criteria by which industries can be judged as well as profitability. For example, they can be judged by the quality of the service they offer. If British Rail were to operate purely with a view to profit, many local commuter services would be withdrawn. Equally, the postal service in remote areas would have to be reappraised.

(iv) The Government has undervalued many of the state assets it has sold in order to ensure a successful sale. This has meant a loss to the nation of revenue which could have been used for needed capital projects and a considerable gain to the private speculators who bought the shares. British Telecom Shares, for example, were offered to the public at 50p partly paid. Very quickly the shares were worth over £1. On this view, privatization has accentuated the gulf between rich and poor in Britain.

Questions

5 Follow the development of the Conservative Government's privatization policy and the reaction of the Labour Party.
6 Consider the merits and demerits of the policy from the viewpoint of (a) the Government, (b) the industries which have been privatized, (c) the shareholders, (d) the general public.

10 Crime and the legal system

The meaning of law

In the first chapter of this book we discussed the importance of the rule of law and its meaning. We saw that even in the simplest form of society, some system of rules or laws is necessary for civilized living. We may also say that the more complex the society, the greater the need for law to regulate the relationships between individuals. Law is not the enemy of liberty but a very necessary condition of it.

But what is the law? It is the body of rules which gives the state legitimate authority over its members. It is, in Lord Hailsham's words, 'the whole framework which dictates the relationship between man and man'. Law is related to politics in that much (but not all) law is passed by Parliament and is the product of argument and debate between the major parties. Law is also similar to politics in that both are alternatives to the use of force in the settlement of disputes. And yet law is different from politics in that, although it often comes from politics, it is superior to it. Politics is in part a process by which laws are made, and yet, once made, laws have a majesty and importance greater than any political party. Law is binding on the members of society. It is supposed to be neutral and just, whereas politics, as we have seen, is a process involving conflict among different interests, principles and ideals.

We have introduced here the concept of justice which is often regarded as being synonymous with law. Yet the idea needs to be used carefully. When we speak of justice, we may mean simply formal justice — ensuring that laws which are known are properly and impartially applied to a case. Most people would agree that in Britain efforts are made in various ways to ensure that court proceedings are formally just (see pages 199–204). But although proceedings may be honest and the law fairly applied, that offers no assurance that a particular law itself is just. Justice in this second sense is far more difficult to achieve because although those responsible for making laws, whether politicians or judges, would claim to be seeking justice, they interpret it in very different ways. What is justice for the Conservative Party is not justice for the Labour Party. What is justice for a trade union is not justice for an employer. Here we come back again to politics in that it is through political argument and debate that different conceptions of justice in concrete rather than purely formal terms are expressed.

The law is also linked very frequently to morality. To a degree they have common characteristics. Both are concerned with regulating human conduct. Moreover, moral beliefs frequently reinforce law, such as the law relating to violence against another person. Indeed if there were no relationship between laws and generally accepted moral values, much law would become difficult if not impossible to enforce. But law and morality are really quite distinct. First, laws must be observed and those who break them punished, whereas moral principles may be broken without any such consequences. Second, if a law is not observed it will very quickly fall into disrepute and probably have to be repealed. This happened, for example, to the Industrial Relations Act of 1971 which was repealed in 1974. A moral principle, on the other hand, may continue to be valid whether it is observed or not, such as the idea that we should love our neighbours as ourselves. Third, it is quite possible for something to be illegal without being immoral or to be immoral without being illegal. Parking a car for one hour on a meter allowing only forty minutes would be a good example of the first, and adultery of the second. Finally, as many examples from the twentieth century remind us, there are occasions when the law and morality are in distinct conflict. In Nazi Germany, for example, anti-Semitism was lawful and actively encouraged, but few would regard it as morally acceptable. In Britain too laws have been passed which some people have felt themselves unable to obey. Thus during both World Wars, a number of pacifists refused to take up arms because they felt that in no circumstances was the taking of a human life justifiable.

This raises the first general question which we need to consider of whether it is ever permissible to break the law. The example of Nazi Germany makes it clear that to obey the law can never be an absolute principle. There are circumstances in which Governments may pursue policies which are such an affront to human dignity as to make resistance to them the only honourable course. And yet before we do break the law we need to weigh a number of considerations very carefully. First, the fact that not all law is acceptable to us does not mean that we have a right to ignore it. If we simply obeyed law with which we agreed, there would not be much point in having law at all. Second, in Britain, the highest form of law is that made by Parliament, and such law can be and very frequently is changed. It is far more sensible and constructive to seek to change laws one disagrees with than it is to break them, for if you claim the right to ignore laws you find offensive, then you must grant a similar right to those who disagree with you. Finally, a distinction ought to be made between collective acts of disobedience and those involving one person. The latter acts usually win respect, for when an individual breaks the law, he does it in the knowledge that he will have to face the consequences. Conscientious objectors to military service in both World Wars fall into this category. Defiance by groups of people, however, is a different matter for this can very easily amount to intimidation and make the law itself, because of sheer weight of numbers, impossible to apply.

Questions
1 Distinguish between law, justice and morality.
2 Can you find any current examples of (a) individuals, and (b) groups deliberately defying the law? Why are they doing it? Are they justified?

People in the law

The English legal profession has many branches. There are those engaged professionally in the practice of law: barristers, solicitors and judges. There are others such as magistrates and jurors whose contributions, while important, form only a part of their work and who are not paid for their services. Finally, there are the various legal officers and court officials, some of whom are also politicians or civil servants.

Barristers
There are about 4000 barristers in practice in England and Wales. In court they are known as 'counsel' and refer to each other as 'my learned friend'. They have an exclusive right of audience in the higher courts, but they may also appear in the lower courts at their discretion. They do not communicate directly with the general public but are briefed about cases by a solicitor — a custom which tends to increase costs for the client. Groups of barristers share a building known as 'chambers' and collectively employ a clerk to negotiate their fees.

Barristers are specialist advocates and are equally proficient in prosecution and defence. To gain entry into the profession one must have passed the Bar examinations and be a member of one of the four Inns of Court: Inner Temple, Middle Temple, Lincoln's Inn and Gray's Inn. Inns are under the direction of senior barristers known as 'masters of the bench' and new members are admitted by a 'call to the bar'. The Senate of the Inns of Court controls the admission of students and exercises disciplinary powers over barristers. It has the power to prevent a barrister from practising. The General Council of the Bar exists to represent and promote the interests of all members of the profession.

A barrister of ten years' standing may, on the invitation of the Lord

Chancellor's Office, apply to 'take silk' and become a senior barrister or Queen's Counsel (QC). There are about 400 QCs in England and Wales of whom about 250 are in practice. High Court judges are generally appointed from their ranks.

Solicitors

Solicitors qualify by completing the examinations of the Law Society and a period of about two years as a trainee solicitor within a particular practice. There are about 30,000 solicitors in England and Wales, and it is common for many of them to work in partnerships (of which there are about 8000). These enable solicitors to specialize in certain aspects of the law, such as conveyancing (the buying and selling of property), probate (obtaining the legal title to a deceased person's estate), crime, divorce, tax law and company law. Lord Hailsham has described the differences between barristers and solicitors as follows: '. . . the solicitor must be at his desk, deploying his staff, interviewing clients, dictating letters . . . throughout the day. The barrister must hold himself free to appear in court whenever he is needed, to be consulted, to research his opinions, and to keep very much up to date with the increasing flow of new law. The one is a man of business, the other, to some extent, an artist and a scholar.' But of course they are not completely separate. Solicitors appear in magistrates courts, county courts and, for some cases, crown courts. They also brief barristers for cases in court where they themselves have no right of audience.

The governing body of solicitors is the Law Society. It has an elected council, a president and a disciplinary tribunal which handles cases of professional misconduct. From 1980, entrance to the student ranks of the profession has been limited to graduates or to those with special professional qualifications.

Some people would like to go further than this and create a unified profession, arguing that it might help to end some of the restrictive practices such as the expensive convention that barristers can only be approached through solicitors. Resistance from within the profession (and especially from barristers), together with the fact that barristers and solicitors do very different work, makes any immediate change unlikely.

Question

3 What qualities would you expect to find in (a) a good barrister and (b) a good solicitor?

Judges

The responsibility of a judge is to see that each case is properly conducted in court. He must follow the evidence closely, give rulings on points of law, sum up the factual evidence fairly for the jury at the end of the trial (in cases where a jury is sitting) and pass sentence or, in civil cases, deliver judgement. Here, precedents are usually followed (see page 198).

High Court judges, circuit judges (those who work in both the crown courts and county courts and move around 'on circuit'), recorders (who serve in the crown courts as part-time judges), and lay and stipendiary magistrates are appointed by or on the advice of the Lord Chancellor. No judge appointed since 1959 may sit indefinitely. Those in the higher courts must retire at 75, circuit judges at 72 and magistrates at 70.

The independence of the judiciary is protected in a number of ways. In the first place, the choices are not arbitrary. Judges are chosen from the ranks of experienced barristers (those with at least ten years' experience and very frequently much longer). Their years in advocacy, together with membership of the Bar, usually give them strong independence of mind. They are also appointed until the age of retirement. Although the Lord Chancellor is able to remove judges in the lower courts for incapacity or misbehaviour (and magistrates without giving a reason), High Court judges can only be removed by an address to the Crown from both Houses of Parliament. Since being introduced by the Act of Settlement in 1701, this power has only been exercised once.

Judges are also protected by their salary structure. It would clearly be undesirable for them to try to win favour with the Government to secure promotion. The possibility of this is unlikely because although salaries are good, the rewards for advancement are small. Also salaries are charged on the Consolidated Fund and not authorized annually by Parliament. They are therefore not the subject of political argument. Moreover, judges are disqualified from membership of the House of Commons and are expected to refrain from partisan political activities. They cannot be criticized in Parliament for their judgements, and they (like lawyers, jurors and witnesses) are protected from liability in damages for any remarks made during a hearing. These provisions give judges their reputation for independence and impartiality.

A number of senior judges in the high courts wield particular influence. The *Lord Chief Justice* is the head of the Queen's Bench Division of the High Court but also presides over the Criminal Division of the Court of Appeal and the Divisional Court of the Queen's Bench Division. The *Master of the Rolls* (the senior judge in the Civil Division of the Court of Appeal) ranks second to the Lord Chief Justice in status. He is also responsible for the rules of the Law Society and for admitting solicitors into practice. The *Lords of Appeal in Ordinary* (of whom there are eleven) are the Law Lords who sit in the House of Lords and from whom the Lord

Chancellor will usually select a bench of five when the House of Lords has to hear a case in its capacity as the final court of appeal. Below them are the sixteen *Lord Justices of Appeal* in the Court of Appeal. The relationship between the various courts is set out in Figures 28 and 31.

A large proportion of judges are drawn from the public schools and the universities of Oxford and Cambridge. They also tend to be middle-aged (if not elderly), middle class and conservative in outlook and temperament. But the conclusion (which is often drawn) that judges are hostile to and lack understanding of the working class is unjustified. Just as each individual has his own beliefs and attitudes, so no judge can be neutral in an absolute sense. But that is not to deny that English judges generally dispense justice of high quality and inspire considerable public trust, respect and confidence.

Magistrates

There are about 26,000 lay magistrates (or Justices of the Peace) in England and Wales who are responsible for dispensing justice in the magistrates' courts. They are appointed by the Crown on the advice of the Lord Chancellor, who is in turn guided by about 190 local advisory committees. Although any person or body may make recommendations for appointment, it is an unfortunate truth that most JPs are drawn from people active in public life in the locality. This tends to produce 'political' appointments and prevents suitable people in other fields from having the opportunity to serve.

JPs receive no salary but draw allowances and are reimbursed for loss of earnings. They have no formal legal qualifications, but since 1966 all new JPs have been obliged to take an initial training course before service. They also attend refresher courses and are kept informed on sentencing policy by the Home Office.

In their work they are assisted by a much smaller group of about fifty stipendiary magistrates (barristers or solicitors of at least seven years' standing) who are paid for their services and who are concentrated in London.

Juries

Juries are rare in civil cases but essential in criminal cases except in magistrates' courts. Under the Juries Act of 1974 most people between the age of eighteen and sixty-five who are on the electoral register are liable for service. Peers, judges, barristers, solicitors and clergymen are, however, exempt. Moreover, those convicted of a recent criminal offence occasioning more than three months' imprisonment may be disqualified, while those who have received prison sentences exceeding five years are permanently disqualified. Juries consist of twelve persons (except in the county court where the number may be between seven and eleven) unknown to the accused. Jurors receive allowances for travel and subsistence and are reimbursed for loss of earnings. They cannot be punished for any verdict they might bring and, once sworn, are expected not to communicate with anyone outside the jury about the case under consideration. In the most serious cases they may be protected by the police as they leave and make their way to the courts.

Juries, like magistrates, bring law closer to the people and prevent it from becoming a purely professional concern divorced from the feeling of the ordinary citizen. Moreover, since 1974 they have represented a genuine cross-section of the community for the old property qualification has been abolished. Lord Denning, the Master of the Rolls, has described the system as 'the bulwark of our liberties'.

And yet criticisms of the jury system are frequently made. Doubt is often expressed about the ability of laymen with no special training to follow closely, and very often over several days, arguments and evidence which can be exceedingly complex. There is also the feeling that jurors might have prejudices of which they are unaware and yet which affect their judgement on a case. Moreover, when charged with responsibility for assessing damages, consistency is difficult to achieve. After the Telly Savalas case (see page 24) the foreman of the jury wrote a letter to *The Times* saying how difficult it had been for the jury to settle the figure for compensation. Finally, when the jury retires at the end of a trial to consider its verdict, there is the possibility that one or two articulate and persuasive members may have an exaggerated influence on the rest. This last point illustrates very well one of the main characteristics of juries — public ignorance of them. We know how the courts operate for we can visit them and see magistrates, judges, barristers and solicitors at work. Juries are different. Their proceedings are secret and exactly how verdicts are reached is not known. The strengths and weaknesses of the jury system are given further consideration below.

Documents: The jury system

Below are extracts from a lengthy correspondence in *The Times* in January 1977 on the strengths and weaknesses of the jury system. The correspondence was occasioned by the Criminal Law Bill which, among other proposals, contained a provision for making theft and similar offences involving amounts of less than £20 triable only in magistrates' courts. *The Times* had criticized this proposal in a leading article on 6 January 1977.

1 From the Chairman of the Bar, Mr Peter Webster

Sir, All sections of the Bar with which I have been in touch would agree with your leader of January 6: they had already expressed to me almost identical views. One point, however, although touched upon seems to me not to have been made with sufficient emphasis: you express it as 'the belief that justice for the innocent defendant is more certain before a jury . . .' In my view it is more than a belief: it is an inevitable inference from certain facts.

Those facts are: that before a jury, the prosecution have to satisfy twelve, or after two hours, ten, persons of the accused's guilt: before magistrates they only have to satisfy between one and three; that most prosecutions rely to a considerable extent upon the evidence of police officers: few jurymen, if any of them, will ever have heard any police officer give evidence — often magistrates have heard the same officer giving evidence before; and that at every trial juries are specifically reminded by the judge of the burden of proof.

The inevitable inference from these facts is that, all other things being equal, and however fairly proceedings are conducted, it must be inherently less likely that the prosecution will establish the guilt of an accused person before a jury than before magistrates . . .

2 From Mrs Joyce Purser

Sir . . . There is no doubt that the quality and efficiency of magistrates varies considerably, both from bench to bench, and within the membership of each petty sessional division. A similar criticism could be made of the professional judiciary (why else do counsel manoeuvre to have their cases heard by one judge rather than another?).

It is at least arguable that magistrates, who are experienced in weighing the value of evidence presented to them and in assessing the credibility of witnesses and defendants, and who moreover are accustomed to court procedure may be a little more likely to arrive at the truth than a group of citizens with no experience, qualification or training for the task; who may also be bewildered and puzzled by the unfamiliar procedure of the crown court . . .

3 From the President of the Law Society, Sir David Napley

Sir . . . Those tried before magistrates, as the Law Society has repeatedly pointed out, are denied the right vouchsafed in a higher court, of knowing in advance the case they have to meet . . . I have long applauded the valuable contribution which the magistracy makes to the administration of justice. Forty years' experience of the operation of the criminal courts, however, has convinced me and the Council of The Law Society, that lay magistrates in general, and stipendiaries in particular, should not be given an exclusive jurisdiction in all charges of petty theft such as shoplifting . . . Whilst a number of such cases might safely be left to them, there are a significant number in which, because justices tend unlike juries, to be case hardened and more legalistic, justice is denied . . .

4 From His Honour Judge Starforth Hill, QC

Sir, While appreciating the argument . . . that 12 good citizens may come to a more just decision (where the issues are delicately balanced) than a smaller number of trained and experienced magistrates, this has never been proved to be so, and I doubt if it is.

There is, however, a powerful argument against allowing such a right of trial, namely, that jurors (who are not to be regarded as just pawns in the game) including hard-working and busy men and women are finding themselves more and more summoned away from their work for jury service only to find that it entails deciding whether a fellow citizen stole a bar of soap or two lemons . . .

Furthermore, consider the cost to the taxpayer of trial by jury where the issue is the theft of two lemons — the jury must be paid, the solicitor must be paid, and the counsel (who is obligatory) must be paid. The total cost is staggering.

Finally, it seems to be forgotten that there is always the right of appeal from conviction at the hands of magistrates to the Crown Court which takes the form of a complete rehearing of all the evidence and any additional evidence sought to be called . . .

Question

4 Having read pages 190–96 and the documents carefully, make separate lists of the arguments for and against trial by jury. Which of the arguments used in *The Times* correspondence do you regard as the most persuasive? Why?

The Lord Chancellor, officers and officials

The Lord Chancellor has both political and judicial responsibilities. He is a member of the Cabinet and presides over the House of Lords (see page 122). He is also head of the judiciary with responsibility for a wide range of judicial appointments and for the full machinery of the courts. Although he seldom sits as a judge himself, he arranges who shall sit to hear cases in the House of Lords and the Judicial Committee of the Privy Council (see page 115). He superintends the legal aid and advice scheme in civil cases (legal aid in criminal cases being the responsibility of the Home Office), and he is the minister responsible for law reform in which capacity he is advised by the Law Commission, whose members he also appoints. His duties are wide-ranging and through them the legislative, executive and judicial branches of Government are linked.

The *Attorney-General* is the main legal adviser to the Government. He represents the Crown in court cases. He is a barrister, an MP and a member of the Government. His leave or consent is required before certain kinds of criminal proceedings can be instituted (for example, concerning the Official Secrets Act). This gives him very wide discretionary powers which could be abused for political purposes. It has been suggested that the office of Attorney-General be made entirely non-political in order to protect the Attorney from accusations of political bias. Deputy to the Attorney-General is the *Solicitor-General*, who also is a barrister, an MP and a minister. The Attorney-General is answerable for, and may give directions to, the *Director of Public Prosecutions (DPP)*. He is a civil servant and a solicitor (or barrister) of ten years' standing. He undertakes about 3000 prosecutions each year in serious criminal cases or in cases put to him by Government departments.

Proceedings in civil and criminal law

English law can be of two kinds, civil and criminal. Criminal offences are those where the person accused may be felt to have offended against the community as a whole and where his action might encourage a general disregard for the rights of other people. In such cases the purpose of proceedings is to determine the innocence or guilt of the accused. If a person is found innocent he is acquitted, but if he is found guilty he may be punished, put on probation or given treatment to enable him once more to play a responsible role in society. In criminal cases prosecutions are brought in the name of the Sovereign (for example, Regina *v.* Smith) and the cost of the trial is generally borne by the state. For some crimes any member of the public may initiate criminal proceedings, but others require the consent of the Attorney General.

Civil cases are different. They arise from disputes between one individual or body and another, and the purpose of court action is not to punish either party, but to decide whether the plaintiff (the person making the complaint) should gain redress or compensation. In most, but not all, civil cases the state is involved only to the extent that it acts as arbiter in the dispute. Contract, tort and family law are among the most important branches of civil law. Contract is concerned with the enforcement of legally binding agreements between parties and tort with the awarding of damages where one person causes harm or loss to another. Good illustrations are the offences of defamation (the use in speech or writing of untrue statements about another person which might tend to lower his reputation), nuisance, trespass and negligence. Family law relates to a wide range of issues such as divorce, maintenance and children. In a civil action the usual practice is for the successful party to be awarded costs.

In many cases the person wronged has to choose between civil and criminal action; he has to decide whether to seek to punish the accused or to obtain compensation from him. Once a criminal prosecution has been started it cannot be withdrawn, except by the Attorney General, but many civil cases are withdrawn with the consent of both parties before proceedings begin and matters are settled out of court.

Sources of English law

English law comes not from any one document but from four main sources.

Common law

Before the development of a centralized system of Government, law was based mainly on custom and tradition. Gradually more uniformity evolved and 'precedents' (decisions of judges in higher courts which were binding on other judges) began to be accepted as part of national law. Today common law (or judge-made law) is still very important. There are now over 300,000 case decisions.

Although the common law system produces great complexity in each branch of the law and therefore makes specialization within the legal profession generally necessary, it has a number of distinct advantages. The doctrine of judicial precedent — which is at the heart of the common law system — has encouraged consistency in the application and development of law. It has enabled people to foresee the legal consequences of their actions and lawyers to predict with a fair degree of certainty the attitudes of the courts. Thus their advice to clients is more assured.

The doctrine of judicial precedent means quite simply that when a judge tries a case, he looks back to see how similar cases were dealt with and tries to make a judgement which is consistent with past principles. Now if this was all judges did at common law, then except where a case arose for which there was no obvious parallel, consistency might have been achieved only at the cost of flexibility. Fortunately the common law system is remarkably flexibile, for it combines the principle of respect for the judgements of higher courts with the possibility of judicial review. For example, decisions of the House of Lords (the highest court in the country) are binding on lower courts, whereas the judgements of circuit judges are not at all binding. High Court judges regard precedents from other High Court cases as persuasive but not binding. Similarly the two divisions of the Court of Appeal, though binding all lower courts, do not in practice bind themselves for the future. Finally, the House of Lords decided in 1966 that 'too rigid an adherence to precedent may lead to injustice' and that in future it would not be bound by its own pronouncements.

Question

5 Why is the idea of judicial precedent important and why are precedents sometimes changed?

Statute law
Statute law is law passed by Parliament. During the twentieth century the importance of statute law has increased greatly as the involvement of the Government in the social and economic life of the nation has grown. Statute law prevails over common law where the two conflict, but on some questions it is subordinate to international law arising from Britain's membership of the European Economic Community.

Delegated legislation
As we saw in Chapter 4, Parliament may delegate to other bodies (usually ministers or local authorities) the power to make law in certain circumstances. This is known as delegated legislation.

European Community Law
On 1st January 1973 Britain joined the European Economic Community. One of the most important effects of this (as critics of British membership very frequently point out) is that community law has become a source of law in Britain and that moreover, it prevails over British law where the two come into conflict. Of course the Treaty of Accession signed by Britain concerns only those questions which are of interest to other members of the community, but here the impact of the treaty is, in Lord Denning's words, 'like an incoming tide', and the final authority on the interpretation of the treaty is not the English courts but the European Court of Justice.

Criminal courts and proceedings

The nature of proceedings
Criminal offences in England and Wales may be either summary or indictable. Summary offences, such as speeding or parking offences under the Road Traffic Act and minor theft, are the least serious. These are tried in the local magistrates' court. In 1981 there were over 1,600,000 convictions for summary offences, of which 71 per cent were driving offences. Indictable offences (such as murder or robbery) are more serious and are tried by a different procedure. In 1983 there were 461,000 indictable offences in England and Wales. It is Parliament itself which decides, in the legislation it passes, whether an offence is summary or indictable.

In all criminal cases the burden of proof is upon the prosecution to satisfy the court 'beyond reasonable doubt' of the guilt of the accused. In various ways efforts are made to ensure that the accused has a fair trial — that the principle of formal justice defined in the introduction to this chapter is respected. On his arrest the accused is protected by the 'Judges' Rules' — rules for the guidance of the police in their interrogation procedures. These are designed to ensure that the interrogation shall not be oppressive, that statements given to the police shall be voluntary and that the person shall be notified that he is not obliged to say anything in response to police questions. The person must also be allowed access to a solicitor. At his trial the accused is again protected. He may, for example, choose not to enter the witness box. Hearsay evidence (evidence relating to what someone not before the court once said) and attempts by the prosecution to strengthen its case by casting doubt on the character of the accused are both inadmissible. Moreover, the accused is protected by the laws relating to contempt of court. Any action which may create a risk that the course of justice will be seriously impeded or prejudiced constitutes a contempt and in criminal cases the risk of contempt starts from the moment of arrest. For example, any past criminal record is kept from the court, and the publishing during the trial of anything which might prejudice the minds of the judge and jury is also unlawful. Both provisions are intended to encourage the court to concentrate on the facts of the case. The intimidation of witnesses also constitutes a contempt. Last, justice is seen to be done; court proceedings are open to the public. What the accused may not do, however, is to plead ignorance of the law. In England, although the law is very complex and at times unclear, everyone is presumed to know it.

Summary offences and magistrates' courts

Summary offences are tried in magistrates' courts of which there are about 900 in England and Wales. Usually between two and seven magistrates hear cases. They are known as the 'bench' and referred to as 'Your Worships'. Stipendiary magistrates have the power to hear cases alone as do JPs for some offences such as drunkenness. During the course of a trial, a magistrate may seek legal advice from the Clerk to the Justices — usually a barrister or solicitor of at least five years' standing.

Prosecutions are usually brought by the police, who lay information about the offence before the magistrate. If the magistrate is satisfied, he issues a summons to the accused. (It is because of the important role of the police within them that magistrates' courts are sometimes known as police courts.) A solicitor retained by the police conducts the case on their behalf. The accused may have legal representation or he may conduct his own defence. Both the prosecution and the defence have the right to summon witnesses to support their case. Alternatively (and most frequently) the accused may plead guilty, in which case the purpose of the hearing is to determine the punishment. For some offences, such as those under the Road Traffic Acts, the accused is not even obliged to appear in court. Two or more magistrates have the power to award sentences of up to six months in jail or fines of up to £1000. In cases where they believe a harsher sentence than is within their power would be appropriate, they have the right to transfer the case to a higher court. Appeal procedure is illustrated in Figure 28.

Magistrates are also responsible for the preliminary hearings of indictable offences and for trying offences of those under the age of seventeen in the juvenile courts. The public is not admitted to these hearings, and the names of those appearing before juvenile courts are not revealed in the press. Procedure is less formal.

Magistrates' courts are often criticized because of the way in which JPs are appointed, because of occasional inconsistencies which arise in sentencing, because of the possibility that magistrates, hearing so many similar cases, may become 'case-hardened' and because of the belief that some magistrates may be too inclined to accept police evidence. On the other hand, they provide justice which is both swift and cheap. They also keep the judicial system in touch with the local community and prevent it from becoming a purely professional concern. Most importantly of all, they carry public confidence.

Indictable offences in the higher courts

For indictable cases the procedure is different. If arrested, the accused has to be brought before a magistrate within twenty-four hours, after which he is granted bail (usually with conditions attached) or remanded in custody for a maximum of eight days. During this time committal proceedings begin. Two magistrates hear the prosecution evidence to decide if there is a case to answer. If they decide that there is such a case, the accused is sent for trial to the Crown Court. The period between committal proceedings and the actual trial may be considerable, and for the 30 per cent of defendants refused bail, this can mean a loss of liberty at times for months without compensation. In 1984 in London 51 per cent of those in custody had to wait more than twenty weeks for trial, and 89 per cent had to wait at least eight weeks. It should be pointed out, however, that comparable figures for the whole country were 22 per cent and 60 per cent respectively. The Bail Act of 1978 does, however, make the granting of bail customary unless there are very strong reasons for refusing it. In future years this may significantly reduce the number of people being detained before trial.

At the Crown Court the accused is first asked to plead. If he pleads guilty, the judge delivers sentence following a plea in mitigation from defence counsel. If the plea is not guilty, then a jury is sworn in. The accused has the right to replace three jurors without explanation and others also if an explanation is given to the court. In the famous

Figure 28   *The criminal courts*

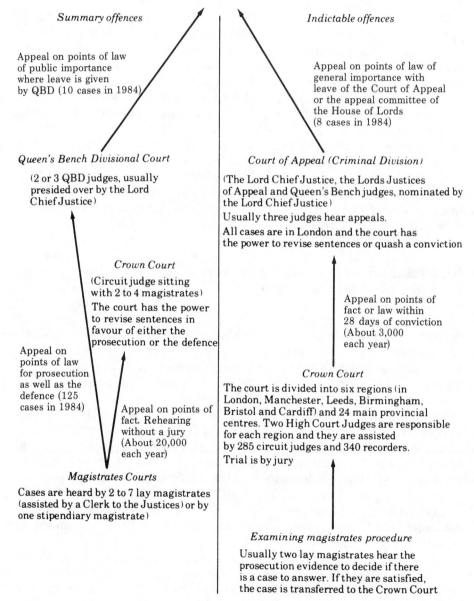

House of Lords

(The Lord Chancellor and 11 Law Lords)
Usually five Law Lords hear appeals

Summary offences

Appeal on points of law
of public importance
where leave is given
by QBD (10 cases in 1984)

Indictable offences

Appeal on points of law of
general importance with
leave of the Court of Appeal
or the appeal committee of
the House of Lords
(8 cases in 1984)

Queen's Bench Divisional Court

(2 or 3 QBD judges, usually
presided over by the Lord
Chief Justice)

Court of Appeal (Criminal Division)

(The Lord Chief Justice, the Lords Justices
of Appeal and Queen's Bench judges, nominated by
the Lord Chief Justice)

Usually three judges hear appeals.

All cases are in London and the court has
the power to revise sentences or quash a conviction

Crown Court

(Circuit judge sitting
with 2 to 4 magistrates)

The court has the power
to revise sentences in
favour of either the
prosecution or the defence

Appeal on
points of law
for prosecution
as well as the
defence (125
cases in 1984)

Appeal on points of
fact. Rehearing
without a jury
(About 20,000
each year)

Appeal on points of
fact or law within
28 days of conviction
(About 3,000
each year)

Crown Court

The court is divided into six regions (in
London, Manchester, Leeds, Birmingham,
Bristol and Cardiff) and 24 main provincial
centres. Two High Court Judges are responsible
for each region and they are assisted
by 285 circuit judges and 340 recorders.
Trial is by jury

Magistrates Courts

Cases are heard by 2 to 7 lay magistrates
(assisted by a Clerk to the Justices) or by
one stipendiary magistrate)

Examining magistrates procedure

Usually two lay magistrates hear the
prosecution evidence to decide if there
is a case to answer. If they are satisfied,
the case is transferred to the Crown Court

Source: Adapted from K.J. Eddey, *The English Legal System* (Sweet and Maxwell
1977) pages 55 and 61.

Figure 29 *Circuit, High Court and Crown Court Centres*

High Court and Circuit Judges

● Civil and criminal work

● Criminal work

Circuit Judges

• Criminal work

⁓⁓ Circuit boundaries

blasphemy trial at the Old Bailey in 1977, the defence had fourteen jurors changed. This was, however, exceptional.

The trial opens with the prosecution presenting its case and calling witnesses in support. These in turn are cross-examined by the defence, after which the defence too has the opportunity to state and support its case. The court has the authority to compel witnesses to attend, although it is unusual for a close relative to be called to give evidence against another. If the defence intends to try to prove innocence through the use of an alibi, it must first give notice to the prosecution before the trial. During a trial the judge may ask the jury to withdraw from the court to enable him to hear certain evidence and decide whether it may be put before the court as a whole. When all the evidence has been heard, closing speeches are given by the prosecution and the defence. The judge then sums up the evidence for the benefit of the jury, drawing its attention to the main issues of the case and offering guidance to them on points of law. He is usually careful not to reveal his own attitude. The jury then leaves the courtroom to consider the facts of the case and to reach a verdict. Its first duty is to elect a foreman to chair its discussions. Until 1967 the verdict of a jury had to be unanimous, but the Criminal Justice Act of that year made it possible for judges to accept verdicts by a majority of not less than 10–2 provided that the jury had deliberated for at least two hours. If the jury finds the accused innocent he is immediately discharged, but if he is found guilty, the judge, having heard in court the past criminal record of the accused, delivers sentence. If the jury is unable to reach agreement by the necessary majority, the judge orders a retrial.

Appeal against sentence may be made on the grounds of either fact or law. If, for example, the jury was felt to have ignored certain evidence or if new evidence became available, an appeal might be made on the facts of the case. If, on the other hand, it was felt that the law had been misinterpreted or that the trial had been unfairly conducted, an appeal could be made on the grounds of law. The procedure for both cases is illustrated in Figure 28.

Question

6 What efforts are made to ensure that justice is done to the defendant in indictable cases? Read pages 199–204 carefully before answering.

Civil courts and proceedings

The County Court

Although magistrates' courts do have a limited civil jurisdiction, their main concern is with criminal law. The burden of work in civil cases falls on the County Court. County Courts are curiously named for their work bears no relation to existing county boundaries. They deal mainly with claims of up to £5000. In a typical year about two million cases may be started in the County Courts. Fortunately the vast majority of claims are settled without trial, and in 1983 only 7 per cent of cases started actually came to court. Were this not so, the courts would be unable to cope with the sheer volume of work.

In civil cases the burden of proof rests with the plaintiff, who files a request for a summons at the county court giving details of the claim. The court then issues a summons to the defendant for a specified day at least three weeks later. If the matter is settled within the period to the satisfaction of the plaintiff (by the defendant paying either the full amount claimed or a compromise figure), the case is dropped. If the defendant ignores the summons, then judgement is usually given in favour of the plaintiff. If the case is defended, then after the three weeks the court registrar (a solicitor of seven years' standing responsible for the administration of the courts together with minor cases) fixes a date for the trial. This entails the judge (very occasionally assisted by a jury of eight) hearing first the case of the plaintiff, then that of the defendant. Both parties may call witnesses, and they either may conduct their own defence or have legal representation. At the end of the hearing, judgement is given. The process is quick and relatively inexpensive. An alternative procedure for small claims of less than £300 is that of arbitration before either a judge or the registrar, although arbitration cannot take place without the consent of both parties.

The High Court of Justice
If the claim is above £5000, the action is taken directly to the High Court of Justice. Within this court there were, in 1983, seventy-seven judges distributed among three divisions (see Figure 30). Judges may serve in all three divisions but tend to remain in the division to which they are appointed.

Proceedings are initiated as in the County Court, although the statement of claim is prepared by counsel. If the case is defended, then a counter-claim is filed by defence counsel and all the written evidence and documents laid before the judge at the trial. Judgement is given and the unsuccessful party is usually required to pay costs. Appeal procedure is shown in Figure 31.

Question
7 Why are the majority of civil cases heard before judges alone rather than juries?

Figure 30 *The jurisdiction of civil courts*

Court	Jurisdiction
Magistrates Court	Matrimonial proceedings, custody of children, licensing of public houses and clubs
County Court	Contract and tort (for claims not exceeding £5000 and excluding libel and slander), land, trusts, mortgages, bankruptcy, probate, divorce, adoption, guardianship, racial discrimination
The High Court of Justice Queen's Bench Division	Contract and tort, accidents on the road or at work, claims under commercial or admiralty law. QBD also has responsibility for cases in the Restrictive Practices Court and those before the Employment Appeal Tribunal. QBD provides judges who try criminal cases in the Crown Court. The Divisional Court hears criminal appeals and applications for the writ of *habeas corpus*
Chancery Division	Bankruptcy, probate, conveyancing, company law. The Divisional Court hears income tax appeals, together with appeals from the County Court on bankruptcy and land registration
Family Division	All questions relating to family law. The Divisional Court hears appeals on family law matters from the magistrates' courts and the County Court

Other courts

A number of courts do not fit easily into the main structure. One of these is the *Coroner's Court*, presided over by either a barrister, a solicitor or a doctor, whose responsibility it is to inquire into deaths which are unexplained and which may have been brought about by other than natural causes. In certain cases the coroner may be assisted by a jury of between seven and eleven people. If a crime is suspected, proceedings are initiated in the normal manner.

Another important court is the *Employment Appeal Tribunal*, set up in 1975 to hear appeals from decisions of industrial tribunals and especially those relating to unfair dismissal, redundancy and equal pay. The court consists of two laymen with knowledge of industrial relations and a High Court judge. Appeals go directly to the Court of Appeal.

Figure 31 *The civil courts*

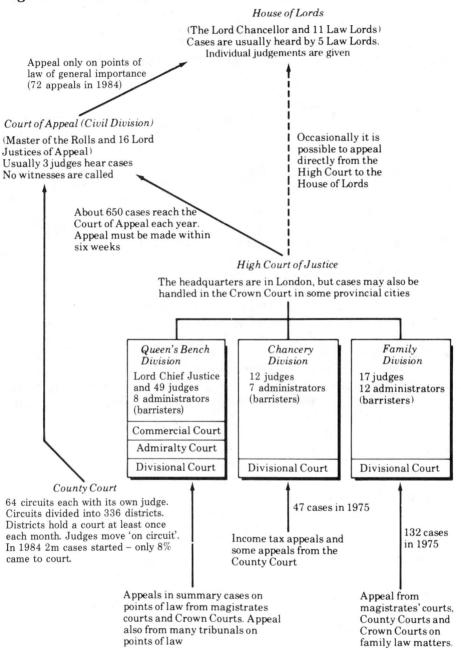

Source: Adapted from K.J. Eddey, *The English Legal System* (Sweet and Maxwell 1977), p. 46.

The work of the Judicial Committee of the Privy Council has already been referred to (see page 115), while the *European Court of Justice* has responsibility for interpreting the various treaties directly concerning members of the European Economic Community. The judgements of the court on EEC matters are binding in this country.

Legal aid and advice

The equality of each citizen before the law is one of the cardinal principles of British justice. Unfortunately the simple cost of litigation can place justice beyond the reach of many people. In civil cases legal aid has been possible since 1949 under the Legal Aid Scheme administered by the Law Society. Each applicant for aid must put his claim to one of 112 local committees. If the committee refuses aid, it is possible to appeal to one of twelve area committees. Aid is granted according to means. Once an offer of aid has been made and accepted, the applicant chooses a solicitor or barrister ready to act in legal aid cases.

As well as offering aid in court cases, current legislation also provides for legal advice. Oral advice to those receiving social security benefits is available from solicitors free of charge for an interview not exceeding thirty minutes. Others may have the service for a small charge. Since 1972 solicitors have been able to give advice up to the value of £25 at the expense of the legal aid fund if their client qualifies for help.

Because legal aid is so clearly important, a great deal of disquiet is often expressed about the working of the system. First, its provisions are not generous and have failed to keep pace with inflation. Second, its benefits are somewhat unevenly distributed. It brings genuine help to the very poorest people but does little for the person with even a modest income. Third, there are certain cases, such as libel and slander (and the majority of cases before administrative tribunals) for which aid is not available. We have not yet reached a position in which all have equal access to the law.

In criminal cases too the position is far from satisfactory. Since 1903 it has been possible for poor people to have aid, and today the courts have the power to grant aid to any applicant. In 1983, 95 per cent of defendants in trials at the Crown Court were legally aided. However, the accused may be required, even if acquitted, to contribute to costs following assessment after the trial. In 1973, for example, a woman acquitted of stealing a sweater was refused costs and confronted with a bill for £808. Where this does happen, it is often felt not only to impose an unjust financial penalty on an innocent person, but to leave a stain on his character as well.

Question
8 Consider the arguments for and against the legal aid system.

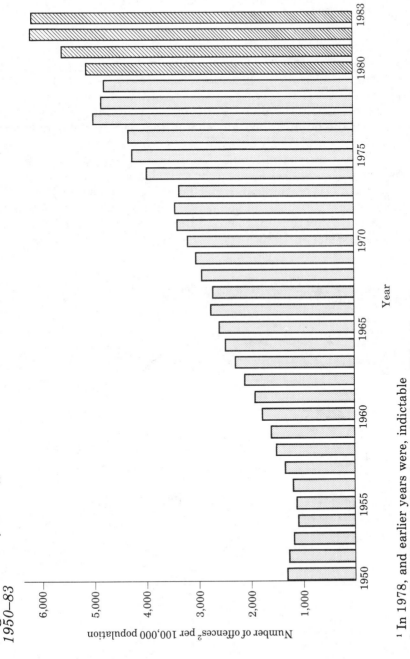

Figure 32 *Notifiable[1] offences recorded by the police in England and Wales per 100,000 population 1950–83*

Number of offences[2] per 100,000 population

Year

[1] In 1978, and earlier years were, indictable
[2] Excluding 'other criminal damage' of value £20 and under
Source: Criminal Statistics 1984.

Crime

One of the major issues in British politics over the past decade has been that of law and order. There has been a feeling that Britain has become a more violent and less law-abiding society, and the Conservative victory in the General Election of 1979 can probably be explained in part by the emphasis they gave in their manifesto to fighting crime. Unfortunately, little has changed. The number of notifiable offences recorded by the police has increased steadily since the mid-fifties (see Figure 32) and the Conservative Government has been unable to reverse the trend. Moreover, as the British Crime Survey of 1982 demonstrated, the number of offences recorded by the police is probably only a small proportion of the offences actually committed. For example, only about 50 per cent of burglaries and even fewer rape offences are recorded because many of the victims do not report them. Equally, many offences, especially in the metropolitan areas, are not cleared up. This is especially true of burglaries (two-thirds of which do not lead to charges) but is less true of violence against the person, where, in the great majority of cases, the offences are cleared up. Figure 33 analyses offences committed in England and Wales in 1983.

Figure 33 *Notifiable offences recorded by the police in England and Wales 1983*

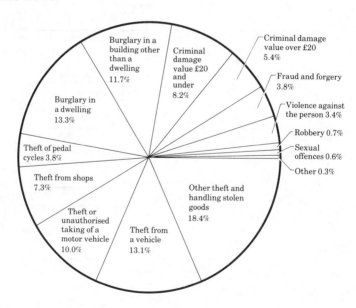

Source: Criminal Statistics 1984.

Another aspect of the law and order problem has been rioting by football hooligans or by some of those in our inner cities. The first serious wave came in 1981 in Brixton, Moss Side in Manchester, and Toxteth in Liverpool. In 1985, there was further rioting in Tottenham and the Handsworth district of Birmingham. Shops were looted, windows smashed, cars set on fire and barricades erected. In Tottenham a policeman was killed and the police had to use riot gear to contain the unrest. The seriousness of the violence was brought to millions through television.

The upward trend in general crime together with mob rioting has encouraged widespread public debate about why Britain appears to be becoming a more violent society. Two fundamentally different interpretations have emerged. Those on the right, politically (although not all members of the Conservative Party) have tended to place the emphasis on a decline in moral values, an erosion of the idea of individual responsibility, and a weakening of the traditional centres of authority — parents, schools and the church. They have argued that it is important to try to inculcate in young people a respect for property, people and the law and that violence has grown because those who ought to be responsible for the transmission of civilized values from one generation to the next have neglected their responsibilities.

Those on the left politically offer a very different explanation. They argue that violence is a natural by-product of a capitalist, acquisitive society which places emphasis upon competition, which distributes rewards unequally and which leaves many feeling rejected and alienated. They argue that violence arises from the circumstances in which many underprivileged elements in our society are expected to live — from poverty, bad housing, squalor, and above all from unemployment. If people have no job — and levels of unemployment in inner city areas and among ethnic minorities are considerably higher than in the country as a whole — then they can every easily lose their self-respect. For them, violence becomes a means by which their frustration is expressed or by which they seek to acquire goods that they cannot afford but which a materialist society encourages them to want. Three-quarters of all crimes in England and Wales are crimes of gain.

Both explanations — of the left and of the right — are inadequate by themselves. Neither does justice to the complex and interlocking factors which have made the issue of law and order one of the central points on the agenda of British politics in the eighties. But with it has come another issue — that of policing, to which we now turn.

Question

9 Make a list of the reasons why, in your view, it is difficult to be certain about what is at the root of crime.

The police

The growth in violence on the streets of Britain has given the police a higher public profile than they have had for many years. They have often been in the front line and policing has become a more hazardous occupation. The growing demands on the force have been reflected in their pay which increased by 30 per cent between 1979 and 1983 and in the size of the forces which has increased by 9 per cent. To many the police have performed a remarkable job in difficult circumstances defending life and property and, for the most part, remaining a disciplined and restrained force despite, at times, serious provocation. To others the police have, either through insensitivity or through prejudice, been responsible for provoking some of the violence themselves. It is not uncommon in inner city areas to hear references to police 'harrassment' as a source of conflict and, very often, it is the ethnic minorities who claim to be subject to such unfair treatment. What is certainly true is that over the past twenty years both the nature and the powers of the police in Britain have changed. Many of these changes the police have regarded as necessary in the fight against crime, but concern has been expressed about the threats to the liberty of the citizen that some of the changes, especially in police powers, pose.

First, the number of forces in Britain fell, through reorganization, from 117 in 1963 to 43 in 1973. Today, no force has fewer than 800 officers and the Metropolitan Force has over 20,000. The desirability of further amalgamations has been suggested by James Anderton, Chief Constable of Greater Manchester. We may be moving towards having a national force. Second, the work of the police has become more specialized. New squads have been created to handle issues such as drugs, fraud and terrorism. Third, the police, understandably, have tried to use resources of modern technology in the fight against crime. The Police National Computer Centre now handles information for the whole country on missing persons, fingerprinting and stolen cars, and the policeman in his panda car has become more prominent than the policeman on the beat. There is a feeling that the police have become detached from the communities they are intended to serve. Fourth, police spokesmen have often commented in a partisan manner on social and political issues. Sir Robert Mark, for example, a former Commissioner of the Metropolitan Police, campaigned successfully for the introduction of majority verdicts in trials and James Anderton, Kenneth Oxford and John Alderson, Chief Constables of Manchester, Liverpool and Devon respectively, have often given their views on a wide range of issues. Most significantly of all, during the 1979 General Election the Police Federation published an open letter asking voters to support 'law and order' candidates. The invitation to vote for the Conservative Party was thinly veiled. Finally, the Police and

Criminal Evidence Act of 1984 has given new powers to the police to assist them in the fight against crime — powers of stop and search, power to search premises and power to detain suspects for questioning for up to ninety-six hours. The police have welcomed these provisions but others have seen in them a threat to civil liberties, and argue that the new powers of detention threaten the long-established principle of *habeas corpus* — that no person can be held without trial or charge. The issue of the police and police powers has become a political one, with the views of the Labour and Conservative Parties often sharply polarized. This too has caused concern. Increasingly the Conservative Party has become strongly identified with the police, while the Labour Party has often been critical of the police especially in its relationship with trade unionists and ethnic minorities.

Question
10 Why is it not helpful for the police to become aligned with any one particular political party?

The organization of the police
The organization of the police in Britain is complex. They like to consider themselves independent of political control, not subject to the direction of politicians, and free to carry on in their own way the business of protecting the citizen and maintaining law and order. Others feel that since the power of the police is potentially considerable, they ought to be subject to the control of those who are themselves accountable to the people. In practice, a balance is struck between the two positions.

Chief Constables are responsible for the direction and control of the force. On issues of policy and operations (for example, responding to inner city violence) decisions are theirs alone. The Police Authorities (see pages 160–6) are responsible for the maintenance of the force. They appoint the Chief Constable, his Deputy and the Assistant Chief Constable and are jointly responsible (with the Home Office) for funding the forces. Each authority receives an Annual Report from its own Chief Constable. The Home Office exercises many responsibilities. In general terms it is responsible for the efficiency of the force. The Home Secretary may require a Chief Constable to retire or to offer a Report on the work of his force. The Home Office is also responsible for the Chief Inspector of Constabulary who inspects and reports upon each force (except the Metropolitan Force), for the endorsement of senior appointments and for the maintenance of the Police College. In addition, the Home Secretary is the Police Authority for the Metropolitan Force.

Complaints against the police

Accusations of police prejudice and brutality, especially against coloured citizens, have become increasingly common in recent years and the procedures for investigating these complaints have often been regarded as inadequate. At the root of the problem has been the fact that, at least initially, the police have had responsibility for investigating complaints against themselves. The Chief Officer of Police (in practice any officer above the rank of Superintendent but from another force) is the first to look into accusations which are made. A Report is prepared for the Deputy Chief Constable who may, if he feels there has been criminal misconduct, report the issue to the Director of Public Prosecutions. If he does not feel there has been an offence, he may take no further action. In effect, the procedures have often tended to make the police judge and jury in their own cause.

In 1976 the opportunity for greater independent scrutiny was made available with the creation of the Police Complaints Board. This consists of non-police personnel who receive reports from Chief Officers of Police and determine the action to be taken. In the event of disagreement between the police and the Board, two Board members, together with the Chief Constable of the force, reach a decision. It was a modest reform which satisfied neither party but was followed by a bolder reform in 1984 (much resented by the police) creating an independent authority to investigate complaints against the police. How effective this will be remains to be seen.

Question

11 What kind of political interference in the work of the police is acceptable? Is any form of interference unacceptable?

Administrative tribunals

What are tribunals?

During the twentieth century the involvement of the state in the social and economic life of the country has increased enormously. Through nationalization the state now controls certain industries. It provides services such as health and education and provides benefits to the old, the sick and the unemployed. It may be involved either directly or indirectly in redundancy payments, in claims for industrial injuries and in planning decisions concerning transport, redevelopment or the compulsory purchase of land. In addition local authorities have considerable powers relating to, for example, rating and council house rents. One of the consequences of this growth in the power and influence of Government has been the possibility of citizens coming into conflict with ministers and their departments or with local authorities and public corporations on questions of an administrative kind.

Of course, as we have seen, the ordinary courts do have jurisdiction over some administrative questions such as licensing, but for reasons discussed below, the courts are for the most part unsuitable for handling the majority of administrative questions. In response to this, a pattern of administrative justice based on tribunals has developed in the twentieth century. The bulk of administrative law derives from Acts of Parliament and delegated legislation (see page 75). Its growth has been haphazard rather than planned. Each new tribunal has been a response to a specific problem. Today there are over 2000 tribunals handling over 150,000 cases each year (see Figure 34).

Figure 34 *Cases before some important tribunals 1971–81*

Tribunal	Thousands			
	1971	*1976*	*1979*	*1981*
1 (a) Rent Tribunals	16.1	6.6	5.7	20.3
(b) Rent Assessment Committees	4.3	13.9	8.1	
2 Rates: Local Valuation Courts	24.9	60.6	100.5	36.3
3 Social Security	49.2	50.8	54.3	57.2
4 Pension Appeal Tribunals	3.8	2.4	2.5	2.9
5 Supplementary Benefit Appeal Tribunals	29.6	54.4	51.4	51.3
6 Mental Health Review Tribunals	1.0	0.8	0.8	0.7
7 Industry and employment	10.0	44.2	42.3	46.4

Source: Adapted from *Social Trends* (HMSO 1983).

But if the main function of tribunals is to hear disputes between the citizen and some branch of Government, it is not the only one. Some tribunals help resolve disputes between two individuals or parties. For example, although rent tribunals handle many cases involving local authorities, they also hear private disputes between a landlord and his tenants. Finally, there is a third category of tribunal, of little concern to the general public, the main purpose of which is to enforce professional discipline. The Disciplinary Committee of the General Medical Council and the Law Society are two such examples. They arrange their own procedures.

How tribunals operate

The working and organization of tribunals today is based largely on the report of the Franks Committee in 1957. Franks recommended that tribunals should operate openly and impartially and that they should follow the rules of natural justice (that no man should be judge in his own cause and that in a dispute both sides should be heard). Franks also recommended that citizens should be made aware of their right to appeal to a tribunal, that those appearing should generally be entitled to legal aid and that the procedure should be orderly but informal. The committee felt that a citizen should know in good time the case he had to meet and that both sides in a dispute should be fully informed of the reasons for the tribunal's decision. It also urged that there should be a right of appeal and that statutory rules of procedure for each tribunal should be established with the guidance of a Council for Tribunals. Moreover, the councils should appoint members of tribunals although the chairman, Franks recommended, should be appointed by the Lord Chancellor.

The Franks Report became the subject of the Tribunals and Inquiries Act of 1958 by which the greater part of the recommendations were implemented. But tribunals today do not operate precisely as Franks suggested, and a number of important weaknesses persist. First, although the Lord Chancellor has the right to appoint the chairman (who is usually legally qualified) and although the consent of the Lord Chancellor is needed before any tribunal member can be dismissed, the two other members of tribunals are appointed not by the Council but by the minister most directly concerned. This goes very close to granting legislative, executive and judicial power to ministers or officials and thus challenges the idea of the separation of powers discussed in Chapter 1. Second, contrary to Franks' proposal, except in the case of the Lands Tribunal and the Employment Appeals Tribunal, legal aid is unavailable. Third, the rules of procedure follow no clear pattern for there is no *system* of administrative justice. In some cases details are set out in a statutory instrument (see page 75), but in others, tribunals are left to formulate their own procedure. Invariably the procedure is less formal than before the courts, and some would say that this in itself is an obstacle to justice. Fourth, there is no common appeal procedure. Appeals on law are usually referred to the Divisional Court of the Queen's Bench Division. They may be referred to the minister or to a superior tribunal. In some cases there is no right of appeal on a point of fact at all.

Tribunals are, however, subject to two controls designed to prevent abuses. If they exceed the limits of their jurisdiction or do not observe the rules of natural justice, their judgements may be set aside by the courts. In addition, their work is supervised by the Council on Tribunals, which consists of up to fifteen members appointed by the Lord Chancellor and the Secretary of State for Scotland and which meets each month. The Council submits an annual report to the Lord Chancellor, investigates complaints and is usually consulted by the minister responsible about membership and any rules of procedure for particular tribunals which may be thought desirable. In 1976 it considered twenty-nine sets of draft rules of procedure for tribunals and inquiries.

But the Council too has been subjected to criticism. Its role is purely advisory. It does not have the power to propose new tribunals in areas where they may be useful — for example, in education, or appeals against the police. Furthermore, it is relatively uknown to the public. Finally, to carry out its responsibilities thoroughly, it would require a full-time inspectorate. At the moment only its chairman is a full-time salaried official. The Council helps to bring a degree of coherence and uniformity to the pattern of administrative justice, but it has weaknesses which are characteristic of the system as a whole.

Why tribunals are necessary

Despite the criticisms we have made of the working of tribunals today, a strong case for administrative justice can be made out. First, on purely practical grounds, without tribunals the additional burden on the normal courts would be unmanageable. Second, the kind of issue handled by tribunals is really unsuitable for the normal courts. Precisely because the issues are as much administrative as judicial, there is a need for flexibility in decision-making which the normal common law procedures might inhibit. Third, proceedings before tribunals are usually not only informal but also short, quick and cheap. No court fees are payable and no legal representation is necessary. Finally, the use of tribunals enables specialists to be involved in settling disputes. Very quickly those on tribunals develop a deep understanding of their field and a wide knowledge of cases relating to it. This kind of knowledge (concerning, for example, rents, industrial injuries or supplementary benefits) the ordinary courts cannot be expected to have.

Tribunals may operate imperfectly and require closer co-ordination and supervision, but few would deny that they make an important and necessary contribution to the legal system.

Questions

12 Drawing on the whole of this chapter, consider the main differences between courts and tribunals.
13 How might the pattern of administrative justice be improved?

Ministerial inquiries

A second kind of procedure for settling disputes between a citizen and central or local government (though not between two individuals) is that of the ministerial inquiry. The most frequent and best known cases concern town and country planning. If the minister of transport, for example, wanted to build a motorway and was resisted by a group of residents affected by the decision, he might appoint an inspector to hold a local public inquiry. Each side in the dispute would be allowed to present its case with the help of witnesses, and very frequently the inspector might be able to settle the dispute himself. In other cases he would forward the results of the inquiry to the minister concerned, who would then make the decision. The minister must explain his decision, but he cannot be bound by the inquiry, nor can there be an appeal against his decision. Ministers are bound by the findings of tribunals but not by inquiries.

This, of course, raises the obvious question of what the purpose of an inquiry is. It is threefold. It allows ministers to have access to all information relating to a particular case before reaching a decision. It enables them to consult and inform local opinion. And it allows those affected by a decision to state their case publicly. Inquiries cannot prevent ministers or local authorities acting within the law from doing what they believe to be necessary in the interests of the community as a whole, but they do help to make the process of decision-making seem less arbitrary.

Law reform

English law is in a state of perpetual change and reform. Much of this is due to the sheer volume of legislation — and accompanying statutory instruments — passed by Parliament each year. Other changes come from decisions by the judges in the courts or from the suggestions from bodies directly concerned with law reform such as the Law Commission, the Law Reform Committee and the Criminal Law Revision Committee. Last, changes might come through the influence of pressure groups such as the Howard League for Penal Reform, the Law Society and the Bar Association. All of these bodies are usually responding to or trying to encourage some broader change in public feeling, and each would claim to be seeking to make the law more just. It is because justice is not a static concept that the law must be subjected to constant and critical review.

11 Political attitudes, behaviour and communications

Attitudes and behaviour

The role of public opinion

The phrase 'public opinion' is one frequently used in political discussions and yet it is difficult to say precisely what it means. In a sense, of course, it is meaningless for there is no such thing as a single and united public opinion; there are only public opinions — individuals and groups holding different attitudes on a wide range of questions. nor is there a constant public opinion. Public attitudes towards political questions change and the political public itself changes. Each year thousands die and as many come of age. Public opinion is in a state of constant flux.

A further difficulty is that not all expressions of public concern are equally powerful or important. Some opinions carry greater weight because those holding them are in positions of influence, such as trade union leaders or businessmen. Other types of opinion matter because they are effectively organized. A good example of this might be the Child Poverty Action Group, which is discussed in Chapter 12 (see page 246).

And yet the phrase 'public opinion', meaning what the majority of people feel on any issue, is useful in political discussion. Today it is often said that 'public opinion is hostile to trade unions', or 'public opinion would support a stricter attitude to football hooliganism'. This does not mean that every person in the country takes these attitudes but that the general feeling is disposed towards them.

The importance of 'public opinion' is that through it a dialogue can be established between the Government and the governed. The feelings and attitudes of individuals communicated through groups, through public opinion polls, through demonstrations and election results become one source of opinion a Government will wish to consider in framing its policies. But, of course, Governments cannot govern simply by relating their policies to what they perceive public feeling to be. In the first place, it is difficult to say precisely what the majority of people do feel on any particular question and, second, a slavish attachment to the whims of the public would make it impossible for Governments to develop coherent policies at all.

But there is a limited yet important sense in which the public is sovereign — it has the power to overthrow Governments. To lose public confidence is to face the prospect of electoral defeat. Of course Governments do follow policies which cause them to lose public support in the short term. Over the past twenty years both major parties when in power have been responsible for trying to control wage increases, and both have lost popularity because of their efforts. But it is equally true that they have sought to make such controls temporary.

The opinions of the public expressed through various channels can never actually determine Government policy, but they can both provide Governments with useful sources of information and in the last analysis remove them.

How interested and informed is the public?

Although over half the electorate claims to be 'interested' in politics, the number closely involved in political work is very small and is probably declining. The political élite which is closely involved in politics is probably less than 2 per cent. Evidence relating to the extent of political knowledge is equally revealing. In 1978 a survey conducted by Opinion Research Centre (ORC) showed that only 46 per cent of 1092 people questioned were able to identify their MP. A public opinion poll by MORI in May 1983 (less than three weeks before polling day) revealed that although 97 per cent of respondents were able to identify photographs of the Prime Minister and the Leader of the Opposition, only 40 per cent could identify Mr Norman Tebbitt, then Secretary of State for Employment, and only 33 per cent could identify Mr Roy Hattersley, then Shadow Home Secretary. Ignorance of issues is as general as of personnel. In 1963, ten years before we actually joined, several million electors, according to Gallup Poll, thought that Britain was already in the EEC and an opinion poll in 1977 revealed that 8 per cent of the electorate (about three million people) believed that the Conservative Party favoured a wealth tax and 4 per cent that it wanted to nationalize the banks.

Recently a good deal of concern has been expressed about political ignorance in young people. A report for the Hansard Society in 1977 on the political awareness of the young school leaver revealed that less than half of 4000 young people co-operating in the survey could name the Foreign Secretary, less than half knew the name of their MP, 44 per cent thought the IRA was a protestant organization and 25 per cent believed that the Conservative Party favoured a policy of nationalization. There is little evidence to suggest that either voters or prospective voters have an adequate understanding of political issues.

Question

1 Do the low levels of political interest and involvement in Britain matter? Consider carefully their probable consequences.

How public opinion is measured

Public opinion can be measured in many ways, of which the most obvious are general elections, local elections and by-elections. But it may also be assessed by, for example, public demonstrations, the correspondence columns of newspapers, the post-bags of MPs and by public opinion polls, the influence of which has increased greatly in recent years and whose findings are published by the newspapers that commission them.

The purpose of the polls is to assess public attitudes towards the major parties and towards general political questions. This is done by taking a sample of between 1000 and 3000 electors, the size of which is less important than its representative nature. Two methods are used to try to ensure accuracy. The first, the random method, consists of interviewing, for example, every one-hundredth or five-hundredth person on the electoral register. The second, the 'quota' method, involves interviewing a representative proportion within each sex, age grouping and occupation, etc. Of the two, random sampling is the more reliable, but with either method there are problems. A poll of 2000 people can never be completely representative of the feeling of a nation. Also it is very difficult (although allowances are made) for polls to assess factors such as the turnout. Last, and perhaps most important, because of the time involved in sampling, assessing and publishing findings, polls are always out of date, if only by a few days. This makes it difficult for them to assess the movement of opinion during an election campaign which, although small, can have a very significant effect on the result. In 1970, for example, all the polls except ORC pointed to a Labour victory, and what probably enabled ORC to make a correct final assessment was substantial re-interviewing during the last week of the campaign to allow for late shifts of opinion. Gallup, which did not re-interview, indicated that Labour had a 7 per cent lead over the Conservatives. The example of 1970 is often cited to demonstrate the futility of the polls. This is unfair because both before and since, polls have been reasonably accurate in gauging public feeling.

But polls have their critics. It is often suggested that they not only measure opinion, but help to create it in that they may lull the supporters of a party with a large lead into complacency and therefore abstention. Alternatively they may create a bandwagon effect in favour of the party which appears to be leading. These critics argue that polls should be banned (as in West Germany) in the weeks immediately preceding a general election. So far no political party has sought to make this an issue.

The value of polls between Parliaments when no election is pending may also be questioned. Polls are an important source of information for Governments on the way in which their policies are being received and a valuable opportunity for public feeling to express itself. But they offer no guide to good Government. And there is one further reason for concern. Polls strengthen the already considerable power the Prime Minister enjoys in being able to decide the election date. It would be folly for Prime Ministers to regard the evidence of polls as conclusive, but it cannot be denied that they are a most useful guide and that they help Prime Ministers to choose the moment of maximum advantage to themselves and their party.

The 'volatility' of public opinion

While it is possible, after research, to try to explain political attitudes, it should always be remembered that general statements, although useful, are also dangerous. People react differently to the circumstances of their lives, and what follows is not intended to suggest that *all* attitudes may be attributed to one or even to a group of factors. What is clear, however, is that voting behaviour is in a state of flux. Allegiances to parties are less powerful than twenty or thirty years ago and shifts of opinion can be very marked even over a relatively short period. For example, between the two elections of February and October 1974, 31 per cent of the electorate switched party allegiance. The strength of commitment to parties is also less intense. Thus, whereas in 1964, 40 per cent of the electorate claimed to 'identify strongly' with either the Labour or Conservative Parties, by 1979, that proportion had fallen to 20 per cent.

This degree of 'volatility' has a number of explanations. It has arisen from many of the factors which have also brought a challenge to the two-party system itself (see pages 49–51), from the emergence of major political issues which cut across the traditional left/right divide, from the failure of successive governments to resolve Britain's economic problems, and from the growing importance of television as the principal source of political information for the majority of people — a development which has probably encouraged the electorate to see politics in other than simple right or wrong, black or white terms. Other factors weakening traditional allegiances relate to the parties themselves. Labour voters have become increasingly out of sympathy with many of Labour's traditional policies (see page 50) and the Conservatives have lost the image which helped them, probably up to about 1960, of being 'born to rule' or of being 'the natural party of Government'. Both parties (but more especially Labour) have appeared to the electorate as divided, and lastly, and probably most importantly, there has been a marked trend away from voting on class lines. It is because of these changes that many of the old assumptions about voting behaviour need to be questioned.

Traditional explanations of voting behaviour

Traditional explanations of voting behaviour in Britain have given considerable emphasis to general social factors and, in particular, to the issue of social class. One such factor, important in the nineteenth century, was religion, but today its influence is declining. It remains true, however, that Catholics and non-conformists tend to be Labour sympathizers, whereas members of the Church of England tend to be Conservative. Moreover, religion is a more powerful influence on voting behaviour in Wales and Northern Ireland than it is in England.

Education is also significant. Generally speaking, those who leave school at the earliest opportunity are more likely to be Labour sympathizers than the more educated, who tend to be strongly Conservative. But it should also be remembered that the majority of those going into higher education tend to be 'middle class'. This factor may well be a stronger influence on attitudes than education.

The effect of the mass media on attitudes is also complex. Television is certainly the major source of political information for the majority of people — probably for as much as 80 per cent of the electorate. But while television has done much to widen political knowledge, it has done little to change attitudes or even to form them. In this, the press appears more important. Readers tend to share the political views of their newspaper. A MORI survey in 1975, for example, showed that 70 per cent of readers of the *Daily Telegraph* were Conservative voters, while 57 per cent of *Daily Mirror* readers were Labour voters. Again, it is difficult to say whether readers choose papers because of their views or whether their views are moulded by papers. It is probably the case that newspapers do more to reinforce views already held by readers than to make political converts. It should also be remembered that many readers are either unconscious of their paper's bias or indifferent to it.

Age is another factor about which it would be dangerous to be too dogmatic. In the period between 1945 and 1964 the 21–29 age group showed a consistent preference for Labour while those between 50 and 64 were predominantly Conservative. In the 1983 election, however, all age groups showed a bias to the Conservatives. What may be more important than age is the generation to which one belongs. Labour, for example, appears to have been strongly and consistently supported by that generation which first voted in 1945. The fading of the pre-1940–50 electorate, and its replacement by a new electorate conditioned by years of relative post-war prosperity, may well work to the disadvantage of Labour in future.

Sex, trade union influence and nationality have also been linked to voting behaviour (see Figure 35). Men, trade unionists, coloured people and the unemployed have all, generally, shown a bias to Labour. But again, caution is important. Differences between men and women could be influenced by the working environment and coloured support for Labour may well reflect the influence of class. Equally, many of these generalizations do not hold for the 1983 General Election in which both sexes showed a bias to the Conservatives, and Labour's support from trade unionists suffered an appreciable decline.

Figure 35 *Aspects of voting behaviour 1983*

%	Class				Trade Union member	Sex	
	AB	C1	C2	D		Men	Women
Con.	62	55	39	29	32	46	43
Lab.	12	21	35	44	39	30	28
Lib./SDP	27	24	27	28	28	24	28

AB   Higher and intermediate professional and managerial
C1   Supervisory clerical, routine non-manual
C2   Skilled manual
D   Semi-skilled, unskilled, casual workers, pensioners

Source: Adapted from Ivor Crewe's survey in *The Guardian*, 13 June 1983.

There are also important local and regional variations in party support. The Conservative Party is stronger in England than in Scotland and Wales, while with Labour the converse is the case. Alliance support is much more equally distributed throughout Britain (see Figure 36).

Important local variations have also been noticed. In mining towns Labour has taken as much as 91 per cent of the working-class vote and 36 per cent of the middle-class vote, whereas in seaside resorts the comparable figures are 48 per cent and 7 per cent. Finally, communities having one predominant industry show greater cohesiveness in political attitudes than those having many industries and occupations.

But of all the social factors emphasized in traditional explanations of voting behaviour two have always been paramount: the family and social class.

The process of socialization, through which an individual acquires a view of society and of himself, begins very early in life. Most young people derive from their home an attitude to authority, a sense of their place in the social structure and a natural loyalty, which have a marked effect upon political attitudes. Many people form their basic attitudes in their youth and remain attached to them. As well as influencing voting habits, the family appears to have an impact on attitudes to and interest in politics. Where there is a tradition of political interest within a family, the likelihood of children becoming politically concerned is much greater. In

Figure 36 *Regional distribution of party support 1983*

	Con.	Lab.	Alliance	Nat.[a]	Other	Total
England	46.0	26.9	26.4	–	0.7	100.0
North	34.6	40.2	25.0	–	0.1	100.0
Yorks. & Humberside	38.7	35.3	25.5	–	0.5	100.0
East Midlands	47.2	28.0	24.1	–	0.8	100.0
East Anglia	51.0	20.5	28.2	–	0.3	100.0
South East[b]	50.5	21.1	27.4	–	1.0	100.0
South West	51.4	14.7	33.2	–	0.8	100.0
West Midlands	45.0	31.2	23.4	–	0.4	100.0
North West	40.0	36.0	23.4	–	0.7	100.0
Wales	31.0	37.5	23.2	7.8	0.4	100.0
Scotland	28.4	35.1	24.5	11.8	0.3	100.0
Northern Ireland	–	–	–	–	100.0	100.0
United Kingdom	42.4	27.6	25.4	1.5	3.1	100.0

[a] Plaid Cymru and SNP only.
[b] Of which, in Greater London the Conservatives gained 44.6 per cent; Labour 30.3 per cent; and the Alliance 25.1 per cent.

Source: House of Commons Factsheet

many cases an interest in politics is passed from father to son. Equally, a family tradition of political apathy or indifference can be self-perpetuating. In some working-class families the view that politics is of little concern to ordinary people is strong and continuing.

For many years, social class was regarded, in the words of Peter Pulzer, as 'the basis of British Party politics'. All else, he said was 'embellishment and detail'.

Class may be defined either objectively (using factors such as education, occupation, income or style of life) or subjectively (accepting a person's own judgement of his social class). The Registrar General has objective information on social class from the national census, which uses occupation as the main basis for classification. Various market research organizations have adopted his classification to establish a relationship between class and voting behaviour. Figure 35 relates to the General Election of 1983.

The diagram illustrates clearly the importance of class as a basis of support for the Conservative and Labour Parties although not for the Liberal/SDP Alliance. The lower a person's social class, the more likely he is to vote Labour. The higher his class, the more likely he is to vote

Conservative. But this simple and obvious statement needs qualification. The Conservative Party wins a bigger proportion of the vote in AB and C1 than the Labour Party wins in C2 and D. Also the support for the Conservative Party among the working class (without which it could never win a general election) is far higher than the support for the Labour Party among professional and managerial people.

What has become clear in recent years is that both the family and class are declining in importance as explanations of voting behaviour. Possibly a general weakening of authority has eroded the influence of the family, and class attitudes too have become more complex. In 1983, more skilled workers voted Conservative than voted Labour and the ratio of support for the Labour and Conservative parties among manual workers C2 and D shifted from being 68:32 in 1964 to 56:44 in 1979. By 1983, less than half the voters identified with their natural class party.

Two social groups not voting in accordance with class have received particular attention. The first, middle-class supporters of the Labour Party, are statistically of lesser importance. It appears to consist for the most part of those who, having received higher education, have gone into a service such as education or welfare rather than into industry. The second, the working-class Conservatives, comprise two distinct types, 'deferentials' and 'seculars'. The former support the Conservative Party because they see it as the natural party of Government and its leaders as simply 'better' people. The importance of the 'deferentials', however, appears to be declining. In their place a newer and younger group of working-class Conservatives who support the Conservative Party out of self interest has grown in importance. They may be better paid, anti-trade union, anti-immigration, in favour of 'law and order', private sector workers and owner-occupiers — many perhaps buying their own council home. In 1983, 59 per cent of Labour voters in 1979 who were buying their own council home switched their support to the Conservative Party. Class attitudes are changing as the nature of the working class itself changes. The old manual working class in the traditional industries of coal, cotton, steel and shipbuilding, with strong community loyalties, has been replaced by a newer, often non-manual working class in, for example, chemicals and electronics. Traditional lines of class demarcation have become blurred such that whereas in the past many people shared a group of characteristics which made them self-evidently working-class, today such class 'stereotypes' are rare. And people's perception of themselves has changed. In 1964, 32 per cent of the electorate considered themselves to be 'working class'. By 1981, that figure had fallen to 15 per cent.

The social changes described here have worked to the particular disadvantage of the Labour Party. Labour has continued to be seen by much of the electorate as a working-class party at a time when such an image was no longer helpful. Equally, Labour's attachment to nationalization, high social spending and the trade unions has been far less in tune with public feeling than the Conservative emphasis upon privatization, controlling trade union power and reducing taxation. This brings us to the last of the influences we need to consider on voting behaviour — images and issues.

Images and issues

The image of a party is important. Labour, as we have seen, has not been helped by its continuing image as a working-class party. Neither has it been helped by its image as a divided party. The image of a leader can also be influential. It is quite possible for the most popular party leader to lose an election, as happened to Sir Harold Wilson in 1970 and Mr Callaghan in 1979, but this simply emphasizes that few decide on this issue alone. Mrs Thatcher's image in 1983 as 'firm' and 'resolute' undoubtedly worked to the advantage of her party. The image of the Labour leader, Mr Foot, was less helpful.

A separate but related factor is that of issues which have probably become more important as social factors have become less prominent. Housing, as we have seen, was an influential factor for many people in 1983 and, at a more general level, the electorate's sense of well-being and its confidence (or lack of it) in the politics of the respective parties also counts. Thus, although there were over three million people unemployed at the time of the 1983 election, the Conservative Government was able to win. Unemployment was recognized as a major issue and the policies of the Conservatives carried greater credibility than those of the Labour Opposition.

Specific issues may also count. The rise in Mrs Thatcher's personal popularity came after her handling of the Falklands War in 1982, whereas the last Labour Government never really recovered from a period of prolonged industrial strife and unrest in 'the winter of discontent' of 1978–9. Labour was defeated in the General Election of May 1979. Today, as Vernon Bogdanor has observed, it is often the case that 'the vote is a verdict on the past'.

Questions

2 How would you explain the differences in voting habits shown in Figures 35 and 36?

3 Why is it impossible to reach firm conclusions about voting behaviour?

4 Why is the relationship between class and voting behaviour less close than it used to be?

5 What is the state of public opinion in Britain at the moment? What factors, in your view, are influencing opinion?

Communications — the mass media

The role of the mass media

The press, radio and television, known collectively as the mass media, constitute the major source of political information for the British public. About 75 per cent of people over the age of sixteen read a daily and nearly 85 per cent read a Sunday newspaper. Virtually every home has a radio and over 97 per cent have television. The press has a much longer history than radio and television, and although it is no longer the principal source of political knowledge for the majority of British people, it continues to play a vital role (as the Royal Commission on the Press acknowledged in its report in 1977) in helping 'to advance public interest by publishing facts and opinions without which a democractic electorate cannot make responsible judgments'. Its role (or rather the role of the 'serious' press) is to disclose what the Government may wish to conceal, to encourage the public to see issues in ways different from those in which they are presented by the Government and, through exposing Government policy to sustained and critical commentary and debate, to make a vital contribution to the political process.

The role of television and radio is less obviously political. Like popular newspapers, both are primarily sources of amusement and entertainment rather than channels for political information. There are regular news and current affairs programmes, but it has seldom been possible to bring to television and radio sufficient depth of fact and analysis to promote genuine political understanding. Television's involvement in politics has, however, grown steadily over the years, and it has been particularly important during election campaigns. Up to 1955 no campaign speeches were reported in news bulletins, but in 1958 Granada Television gave extensive coverage to the Rochdale by-election, and the 1959 General Election was the first in which television played a central role. In the same year the State Opening of Parliament was also televised for the first time. In the summer of 1975 there was an experimental four-week period of radio broadcasting of Parliament. In 1978 regular transmissions began. Here the media will be discussed from the point of view of their contribution to the political life of this country. The role of the media in popular entertainment lies outside the scope of this book.

The press today

Ownership and control

The ownership of newspapers in Britain is concentrated in the hands of a small number of large organizations (see page 230), some of which control more than one paper. By 1985, only *The Guardian* and *The Daily Telegraph* among the national daily and Sunday newspapers were still private concerns. It is often said that the organization of the press gives enormous power to a very small number of people whose political sympathies tend to be predominantly conservative and whose papers in turn support the Conservative Party. Only the *Daily Mirror*, for example, of mass daily newspapers is aligned with the Labour Party, and the bias to the Conservatives has been accentuated in recent years by the emergence of the *Sun* as a strongly Conservative paper.

The position is, however, more complex than is often appreciated. First, the power of the press lords has been diminished through the advent of radio and television. Newspapers are no longer the only, or even the most important, source of political information for the majority of people. Second, the present degree of bias to the Conservative Party in daily papers only really emerged after 1974. In the 1970 Election, for example, the total Conservative circulation was 55 per cent against Labour's 44 per cent, but this distribution changed to 64 per cent — 34 per cent in 1974 with the *Sun*'s switch to the Conservatives. Interestingly, the national support for the Conservative Party in February 1974 (36 per cent of the total vote) was the lowest it had recorded at any general election since the war, at exactly the moment when its support in the press had never been stronger. That the press has a bias towards the Conservative Party few would deny; that this has a decisive impact on election results is far more open to question.

Third, it is equally easy to exaggerate the degree to which newspapers today are under the control of one man or a small group. From the time of Lord Beaverbrook's death in 1964, for example, the proprietors no longer played a decisive role at editorial conferences at the *Daily Express*. The whole structure became more democratic and many important decisions were left to journalists. But not only is the proprietor becoming less important — except of course as a source of revenue — journalists are becoming more important. The recent Royal Commission affirmed the principle that 'journalists ... should be involved in the appointment of editors', and when between 1972 and 1978, the editorships of the *New Statesman* (twice), the *Guardian* and the *Observer* changed, journalists were closely involved in each new appointment. The whole question of the the distribution of power in the press today is also affected by the growing influence of trade unions (see also page 250).

The 'Lobby'

Journalists use many official sources of information in their work. They may draw, for example, on proceedings in Parliament, on Government publications and on press conferences. But a great deal of the knowledge they acquire is gained unofficially through the 'Lobby'. This is the system whereby a group of about 130 parliamentary journalists, known as the Lobby, exchange opinions and ideas freely with back-benchers, ministers,

Figure 37 *Newspapers in Britain 1985*

Paper	Founded	Ownership	Circulation 1985 Thousands	Policy	Nature
The Times	1785	Times Newspapers Ltd (Rupert Murdoch)	480	Conservative	Serious
The Guardian	1821	Guardian Newspapers Ltd (Scott Trust)	487	Independent	Serious
Daily Telegraph	1855	Daily Telegraph Ltd (Conrad Black)	1,221	Conservative	Serious
Financial Times	1888	Financial Times Ltd (Pearson Longman Group)	229	Independent	Serious
Daily Mail	1896	Associated Newspapers Ltd	1,828	Conservative	Popular
Daily Express	1900	Express Newspapers Ltd	1,875	Conservative	Popular
Daily Mirror	1903	Reed International	3,272	Labour	Popular
Sun*	1964	News Group Newspapers Ltd	4,066	Conservative	Popular
Daily Star	1980	Express Newspapers Ltd	1,434	Conservative	Popular
Morning Star†	1966	Morning Star Co-op. Society	uncertified	Communist	Popular
Sunday newspapers					
Observer	1791	Observer Ltd (Lonhro)	746	Independent	Serious
Sunday Times	1822	Times Newspapers Ltd (Rupert Murdoch)	1,258	Conservative	Serious
News of the World	1843	News Group Newspapers Ltd	4,787	Conservative	Popular
Sunday People	1881	Reed International	3,090	Labour	Popular
Sunday Express	1918	Express Newspapers Ltd	2,405	Conservative	Popular
Sunday Telegraph	1961	Sunday Telegraph Ltd (Conrad Black)	690	Conservative	Serious
Sunday Mirror	1963	Reed International Group	3,211	Labour	Popular
Mail on Sunday	1982	Associated Newspapers Ltd	1,605	Conservative	Popular
Political weeklies					
Spectator	1828	Spectator Ltd	23	Conservative	Serious
Economist	1843	Economist Newspaper Ltd	278	Independent	Serious
New Statesman	1913	Statesman & Nation Publishing Company	29	Socialist	Serious

*Replaced the *Daily Herald* which was published from 1912 to 1964.
†Replaced the *Daily Worker* which was published from 1930 to 1966.
In addition there are 19 provincial morning daily papers, 6 provincial Sunday papers, 77 provincial evening papers, 1072 provincial weekly papers.

Source: Adapted from *British Rate and Data,* July 1985

opposition spokesmen and press officers either in Whitehall or on the Prime Minister's staff. In this way journalists obtain a great amount of 'inside' information but use it without naming a source. Politicians like the system because it allows them to 'float' ideas in public without being held directly responsible for them, and journalists like it because it gives them much information they would not otherwise have. However, the system has its critics. It is widely felt that much information passed on through the Lobby could be given officially and with less danger of misunderstanding than at present. It has also been argued that the Lobby system makes journalists far too dependent upon official sources for their information and that, because of this, the system introduces an 'HMV (His Masters'/Mistresses' Voice) effect into political reporting as it enables Downing Street to dominate the agenda of mainstream political discussion week by week' (Peter Hennessy).

Information comes to journalists packaged from the official source. It relieves them of the need to research their articles and makes them lazy. In Peter Hennessy's view, the whole system has 'underachievement built into it'. The view is being increasingly widely held that some political decisions (such as the building of Concorde) might not have been taken had there been rather fewer official statements and rather wider genuine public discussion.

Question
6 Why are both Governments and journalists happy with the Lobby system? Why are aspects of the Lobby system not healthy for a democracy?

The law and press freedom
The law touches the activities of journalists at many levels. The importance of the laws relating to libel and race relations have already been considered (see page 24), but there are many other constraints as well, such as the doctrine of parliamentary privilege (see page 68). Contempt of court (see page 200) is a more serious offence. It has led to heavy fines and even in 1949 to imprisonment for a newspaper editor. Moreover, it is no defence in such cases for a journalist to appeal to the 'public interest'.

Government is also protected by the Official Secrets Act 1911 (see page 146). A revision of Section 2 of that Act (which makes the unauthorized giving or receiving of official information an offence) is overdue. A number of recent examples illustrate how powerful a constraint on journalists the Act can be. In 1970, towards the end of the Nigerian Civil War, the *Sunday Telegraph* published a private report by a British diplomat showing how Britain had given more arms to the federal side than had been disclosed. A prosecution was brought (unsuccessfully) under the Official Secrets Act. Again in 1972 the *Sunday Times* revealed that the Government was thinking of large reductions in the railway network. The police, on the instructions of the Director of Public Prosecutions, cautioned the editor of the *Sunday Times*. The paper was involved in a further dispute in 1974 when, following the death of the former Labour Cabinet Minister, Richard Crossman, it announced its intention to publish extracts from his Diaries on the 1964–70 administration. The Cabinet Secretary and the Prime Minister (Mr Wilson) tried to prevent the *Sunday Times* from publishing the extracts on the grounds that if they went ahead, frank and open discussion in Cabinet would never again be possible. In January 1975, however, the *Sunday Times* began serialization and shortly afterwards the Diaries appeared in book form, after a High Court ruling. Finally in 1976 *New Society* published an account of a Cabinet dispute over a new child benefit system. No prosecution was brought on this occasion, although the possibility was considered. A great deal of uncertainty remains about where the line between the public's right to know and the Government's right to conduct its business in confidence should be drawn. This makes the task of the journalist a hazardous one. Tension between politicians and the press will persist because, whereas newspapers live by disclosure, politicians are often by nature more secretive. They will continue to invoke the law on their behalf.

The Press Council
The General Council of the Press was set up in 1953 but reconstituted in 1963 as the Press Council. It has a lay chairman and a lay membership amounting to one-third of the full council and half of the complaints committee. The council has many purposes, the most important of which are to preserve the freedom of the press, to maintain the highest standards, to consider complaints, to watch for restrictions on the supply of information (in which capacity it has recently been highly critical of trade unions in Fleet Street) and to bring public attention to any developments pointing towards greater concentration of power in the press. The Royal Commission of 1977 claimed that the council played a vital role in maintaining public confidence in the press but insisted that it should continue to be an independent body.

Some problems
Fleet Street today is confronted with a number of serious problems of which one of the most obvious is financial. Other than income from proprietors, press income derives from two main sources, advertising and

sales. Quality newspapers are dependent upon advertising for about 60 per cent of their income, whereas the populars receive about 70 per cent of their income from sales. Indeed, given the cost of newsprint and labour, advertising in the popular press probably represents a net loss to the paper. Moreover, in the serious press advertising goes to papers which need it least. Where two papers (such as the *Sunday Times* and the *Observer*) serve a common audience, an advertiser will always choose the one with the larger circulation. This was one of the reasons why the *Observer* found itself in acute financial difficulty in 1975, prior to being taken over by Atlantic Richfield. The financial weakness of newspapers has caused the question of subsidies to be raised in the Royal Commissions of 1961 and 1977. Both rejected the idea, but neither was able to propose a solution to the financial problem.

The problem of finance has been intensifed by that of labour relations. Fleet Street is overmanned and inefficient. In 1975 the *Observer* was able to win the consent of the unions for a 30 per cent reduction in staffing, and in 1979 *The Times*, after suspending publication for almost twelve months, was able to secure a reduction in manning levels and other agreements but only through conceding substantial wage increases. Agreements on reducing manning levels are unusual because the anxiety of management to reduce labour costs (which are about 40 per cent of total costs) conflicts with the anxiety of unions to maintain employment. Moreover, in an industry which is constantly working to deadlines, good labour relations are essential. The Royal Commission of 1977 made some very severe references to unofficial strike action by unions and said that if the 'suicidal behaviour' persisted it would inevitably cause the collapse of some papers.

Equally serious has been recent interference by the unions with the supply of information. In 1971 pressure from the Society of Graphical and Allied Trades (SOGAT) caused a letter on overmanning to be withdrawn from the *Observer*. The *Evening Standard* had been stopped because print workers objected to a cartoon about a power workers' dispute, and in 1977 the National Graphical Association (NGA) prevented the apperance of *The Times* because of the paper's intention to publish an article on industrial problems at the *Observer* by that paper's former editor. Finally, there is the very serious threat to editorial freedom from the 'closed shop'. This is given separate consideration in Chapter 12.

Questions
7 How free is the British press? Compare the ways in which proprietors, unions, the law and the method of political reporting each restrict press freedom.

8 Consider the arguments for and against state subsidies to newspapers.

The media's coverage of politics
Television and radio

Although both major parties have complained about the ways their views have been represented on radio and television, broadcasting has generally maintained a high standard of political impartiality in conformity with regulations imposed upon it by statute (see Figure 38). Of course, not everything which appears on television or is heard on the radio is neutral. Specialist correspondents employed by the BBC and the IBA frequently, if discreetly, give their own views in reports, and this also happens very often when a major public figure is being interviewed. Moreover, television has recently shown a number of plays, such as 'Days of Hope' and 'The Spongers', which have had clear political messages.

Television and radio are seldom criticized, however, for conscious bias in news programmes but more frequently for the way in which they handle issues. Some doubt whether television can ever be a suitable medium for political discussion because pictures convey impressions more easily than sustained argument or thought. In 1958 the late Richard Crossman drew attention to the 'gladiatorial' approach and the 'trivialization' effect as being two of the main dangers in the coverage of politics by television. By the first, Mr Crossman referred to the tendency of television to present politics as little more than a conflict of personalities between whom there was little understanding or mutual sympathy. By the second, Mr Crossman meant the attempt by television, in search of mass audiences, to treat important issues as 'an inferior form of entertainment'. It is certainly true that television tends to dramatize its news coverage such that news can easily become another of the evening's entertainment programmes to which neither more or less importance is attached than to the comedy which preceded it. Moreover, frequently what determines the amount of time given to a news item is not the worth of the item itself but the extent to which it lends itself to picture presentation.

Others have echoed Mr Crossman's criticisms. John Birt and Peter Jay have argued that there is a 'bias against understanding in television journalism', and Sir Robin Day, himself a celebrated television journalist, has complained about 'overcrowding' (meaning the tendency to include too many issues or too many people in one short discussion programme) and the craving for pace in an attempt to retain a large audience. He has also pointed out that such programmes as do offer reasoned argument and serious analysis are transmitted at a very late hour when audiences are much smaller.

All three critics feel that major changes are needed in television's treatment of news and current affairs. They have suggested an hour-long news programme, to be screened at about ten o'clock, which would make it possible to explain the context of events rather than simply film the latest incident. Birt and Jay have also suggested that '... it is not

Figure 38 *Broadcasting authorities*

Authority	Services		Organization	Finance	Influence of state
British Broadcasting Corporation (BBC)	1926	Sound Broadcasting began with the National Programme	Controlled by a board of 12 Governors appointed by the state for a fixed term	Financed by fees from licences for use of a television (£18 for a black and white television and £58 for a colour television in 1985). The licence fee is determined by the Government.	1 Both receive the right to broadcast from the state 2 Both are responsible for their programmes but are expected to give balanced treatment to controversial questions in news programmes. 3 The Home Secretary has the power to withhold any programme 4 Both are obliged to broadcast any Government announcement as requested and to refrain from
	1936	BBC Television started			
	1939	National Programme became the Home Service			
	1945	Light Programme started			
	1946	Third Programme			
	1951	BBC TV developed national coverage			
	1964	BBC TV started a second channel			expressing their own opinions 'on current affairs or on matters of public policy' 5 The BBC must broadcast an impartial account of the daily proceedings in Parliament. It is also required to maintain the External Services to other countries.
	1967	Radio 1 introduced. Light Programme became Radio 2. Third Programme became Radio 3. Home Service: Radio 4			
Independent Television Authority (ITA), set up in 1954, was renamed Independent Broadcasting Authority in 1972	1955	One television channel began	Privately owned. Arranges contracts with 15 programme companies, e.g. Granada TV and Thames TV. Independent Television News (ITN) offers a common news service. IBA appoints a board of Directors of the Channel Four Company.	Revenue from advertising. Channel Four is financed from the ITV companies through an additional subscription payable to the IBA. ITV companies receive an income from the sale of advertising on Channel Four.	
	1973	Local sound broadcasting started			
	1982	Channel Four Television Company (an IBA subsidiary) started. The schedule of programmes is required to be complementary to those on ITV. Channel Four commissions and acquires programmes; it does not make them.			

the public's taste which is becoming more frivolous but that of the programme makers', and they have argued that far from being unsuitable as a medium for serious communication, 'television's ability to match picture to sound often makes difficult ideas easier to follow than they are in print'.

Television's coverage of politics could obviously be improved, but it should not be forgotten that some current affairs programmes, such as Panorama or Weekend World, have been able to explore and analyse the major issues in a way which has enabled them to make a genuine contribution to political understanding. We might hope for more of them.

Question

9 Consider the various criticisms made here of the treatment of politics on television in the light of your own experience.

The press

If television is deficient in its coverage of politics, the press is generally more so. The Royal Commission on the Press in 1949 reported, 'In our opinion, newspapers, with a very few exceptions, fail to supply the electorate with adequate materials for sound political judgement'. This remains true today, although the exceptions to which the Royal Commission referred are important.

The 'quality' newspapers (see page 230) do offer detailed coverage of political, economic, social and cultural issues both at home and abroad. They support this with leading articles (in which the paper sets out its own view on a particular question) and other articles which, while expressing a distinct viewpoint, do not necessarily follow the paper's official line. Some newspapers, of which *The Times* is the most obvious example, have correspondence columns in which an issue may be developed over a period of weeks. (Extracts from letters to *The Times* are included on pages 195–6.)

The extent to which newspapers do offer serious coverage of the major international and domestic issues may be gauged from an analysis of the main front page reports in the daily newspapers. A distinction between the serious press, whose main concern is to report political news at home and abroad, and the popular press, which gives greater emphasis to non-political stories of general interest, emerges very clearly. As Cecil King, a former controller of the *Daily Mirror*, once said, 'We do not sell any copies on our politics'.

Question

10 Keep a record of the main front page shown in your own newspaper for
a period and then analyse the stories under three headings: (a) foreign
news, (b) serious domestic news, (c) general interest. Does your
newspaper contribute to political understanding?

The quality newspapers are expected to maintain a clear distinction
between 'news' and 'opinion' by making news reports as objective as
possible and by placing the 'opinion' section clearly apart in the middle
pages. But this distinction can never be absolute for the selection of news
items, and the reporting of them, involves editors and journalists in
judgements about what they think is important.

In the 'popular' press little effort is made at times even to pretend that
'news' and 'opinion' are separate, and very frequently the front page news
story will include the paper's own highly partial attitude towards it,
inviting the reader to identify himself with the paper's stance. Thus at the
start of the general election campaign in February 1974, the front page of
the *Daily Mirror* consisted simply of a photograph of Mr Heath and the
words, 'And now he has the nerve to ask for a vote of confidence'. Similar
bias in the populars could be seen in the reporting of the opinion polls. Thus
on 23rd February 1974, although the polls indicated a fall in Conservative
support, the main story in the *Daily Express* began, 'The Tories are
roaring ahead, Labour are floundering badly'. The *Daily Mail* too gave the
impression that the Conservatives were heading for an easy victory.

The press reports of the Ilford by-election, which the Conservatives
won from Labour in March 1978, also illustrate clearly the political
leanings of newspapers as well as the instinct for sensationalism in the
popular press. The *Daily Mail*'s headline was 'Smash hit for Maggie!' and
the front page report went on to refer to the 'spectacular and shattering
defeat of the Labour Government'. The *Daily Express* was equally
jubilant and referred to Labour being 'swept out by the unstoppable Tory
chariot'. A similar bias was evident, if to a lesser extent, in the reports of
the more serious newspapers. The *Daily Telegraph* spoke of a 'morale-
bruising blow' to the Government, while the *Guardian*, in a significant
switch of emphasis, pointed to the fact that although the Conservatives
had won, 'the swing from Labour . . . was the lowest in any by-election for
two years . . .'

But if the press is politically partisan, how influential is it in creating
opinion? Its influence on the ordinary voter is very doubtful (see page
223), but on politicians and civil servants the influence of the serious
press is probably considerable. For them the press is an important source
of information, and it helps to shape the general climate in which political
debate takes place. Once the press has managed to make something an
issue, politicians cannot simply ignore it.

But, of course, many popular papers do not exist primarily to engage in political discussion. They exist to make money. The *Daily Herald* tried to interest its readers in politics and its circulation declined. In 1969 its successor, the *Sun*, adopted a more popular approach with the result that between 1970 and 1976 its sales went up by over two million. Newspapers are commercial undertakings which exist to satisfy the needs of their readers. For a minority of the population, the needs are political and cultural and the 'serious' press satisfies them, but for the majority the popular press serves a different purpose. In Britain we have the press we deserve.

Question
11 Try to detect bias in (a) news reporting and (b) leading articles in your
   own daily newspaper.

12 Pressure groups and the trade unions

The nature of pressure groups

In Chapters 2 and 3 we considered two ways in which public opinion can be expressed — through the electoral system and through political parties. In this chapter we shall consider a third and increasingly important channel for the expression of public feeling, pressure groups. But it would be wrong to think of the three as distinct and separate. At times groups operate through formal or informal links with parties, and parties operate through the electoral system. The amount of interaction is considerable.

For much of the nineteenth century, interests were directly represented in Parliament. Up to 1846, for example, the Conservative Party was seen as the spokesman of the landed interest and throughout the century it retained strong connections with the brewing interest, while the Liberal Party was closely identified with the temperance movement. Today interests are less directly represented in the House of Commons than before, with the result that pressure brought upon Parliament from the outside assumes a greater importance.

But what exactly is a pressure group? It is an organization which attempts to advance a cause or causes by exerting pressure on the public, on private bodies, parties and local and central government with a view to influencing decision-making. It is to be distinguished from an interest group, such as a youth club, a football club or a photography club, in that these generally have no need for political activity. Pressure groups act as channels through which ideas can be transmitted and influence brought to bear on those in authority.

Of course political parties are also important vehicles for the transmission of ideas and the promotion of causes, but parties differ from groups in five important senses. First, although not all pressure groups are concerned purely with one objective, their aims are generally limited, whereas a political party must concern itself with all areas of national policy. Second, groups, unlike parties, aim to exert influence but not to take power. Third, in pursuit of power, parties tend to mould and adapt their principles and policies in response to forces outside the party system, while pressure groups, if they are to be faithful to their cause, have rather less room for manoeuvre. Fourth, parties and groups have different memberships. The appeal of a party is to the whole of the social spectrum and each party is a coalition. In contrast a group has a much more restricted appeal to those with common interests. Finally, unlike political parties, all activities of which are related directly or indirectly to the pursuit of political power, pressure groups may have many non-political activities. The Royal Insitute of British Architects (RIBA), for example, administers entrance qualifications into the profession, while other groups, such as the British Medical Association (BMA) and the National Union of Teachers (NUT), help to advance knowledge and understanding on matters of professional importance. Similarly, for many the services offered by bodies such as the Automobile Association or the Ramblers Association, rather than the opportunity for political influence, cause people to join them.

Types of pressure groups

Pressure groups today

There are a vast number of pressure groups in Britain differing in size, purpose, membership, resources, solidarity and importance. Pressure groups first became prominent in the nineteenth century. The BMA was founded in 1832, the Trade Union Congress (TUC) in 1868, the NUT in 1870, the National Farmers Association in 1908 and the Federation of British Industries in 1916, to name only a few examples. But it is only since the end of World War 2 that pressure groups have begun to play a major role in British politics and to command much greater attention from Parliament. In part this is because of their number (there are, for example, 25,000 employers' associations alone), but it is also part of a more general movement towards participation. Many people now are reluctant to think of democracy purely in terms of the right to exercise a periodic choice between parties. They want to have a more direct impact on matters which affect their lives. Indeed pressure groups represent two important themes in democratic theory, the right to participate in policy-making and the right to seek redress of grievances.

Two kinds of pressure group may be distinguished — protective or sectional groups and promotional or cause groups. It is not always easy to make clear distinctions between them, but broadly speaking protective groups exist to protect their members, to further their interests, to enhance their status and to promote services on their behalf. Promotional groups, in contrast, seek to advance a particular cause. The power and influence of these groups differ greatly and are not always directly related to their size. For example, the Automobile Association (AA) has about

3,000,000 members, but it is not as influential a body as the BMA with about 70,000 members. Some groups, such as the AA and the Royal Automobile Club (RAC), compete for members, while others, such as the Abortion Law Reform Committee and the Society for the Protection of the Unborn Child, serve interests which are in total conflict.

Most protective groups and all promotional groups claim to be non-political in the sense of not being affiliated to a political party. The obvious exceptions are the trade unions and the co-operative societies which have strong links with the Labour Party (see page 255), and business interests, which are often identified with — but not affiliated to — the Conservative Party (see page 56).

Some promotional groups too may feel that their interests are more likely to be advanced by one party rather than another. Thus, the Campaign for Nuclear Disarmament (CND) has always been more closely identified with the Labour Party than with the Conservatives. Other groups, such as the Council for the Preservation of Rural England, Alcoholics Anonymous and the RSPCA, are, however, genuinely non-political.

Differences between pressure groups

Although both types of group are similar in that they operate through organized pressure, they are also very different. In the first place, although promotional groups, precisely because they are concerned to advance a cause other than defend a particular interest, have a potentially wider appeal than protective groups, the latter, because they are based on self-interest, have a larger actual membership. Second, whereas many join protective groups through custom or convention, joining a promotional group involves an element of conscious choice. This usually means that the members's commitment to the group is stronger. Third, the membership of promotional groups tends to be drawn from the middle and upper classes, whereas protective groups draw their membership from all classes. Fourth, promotional groups, for reasons discussed below, have a much more difficult task in winning recognition. Finally, while all the activity of a promotional group is concerned directly or indirectly with the advance of the particular cause, some protective groups, as we have seen, do more than simply provide in a general sense for their members' interests (see page 240).

Question

1 Look at a recent newspaper and find as many examples as you can of pressure groups in action. Try to classify them using Figure 39.

Figure 39 *Some pressure groups today*

Examples of protective groups

Type	Examples
Organized labour	Trade Union Congress (TUC)
	All other unions, such as National Union of Railwaymen (NUR)
Business	Confederation of British Industry (CBI)
	Specialized associations usually affiliated to the CBI
	Association of British Chambers of Commerce
Professions	Royal Institution of Chartered Surveyors
	British Medical Association (BMA)
	Society of Civil Servants
Local government	Association of Metropolitan Authorities
	Association of County Councils
Welfare	National Federation of Old Age Pensioners
Recreational	The Ramblers' Association

Examples of promotional groups

Type	Examples
Welfare	Child Poverty Action Group
	Alcoholics Anonymous
	Shelter
	Help the Aged
Environmental	Conservation Society
	Friends of the Earth Society
	Council for the Protection of Rural England
Political	Electoral Reform Society
	Campaign for Nuclear Disarmament
	Hansard Society
Education	Council for the Advancement of State Education
	National Education Association
Penal	Howard League for Penal Reform
Animals	RSPCA
	League Against Cruel Sports

How pressure groups work

Pressure groups exert influence at two levels — indirectly on the general public and directly on MPs, parties and local and central government.

Indirect pressure: the general public

Pressure groups operate upon the general public through advertising, through their own publications, through writing letters to or being reported in the press and through public demonstrations and appeals.

These activites are important for a number of reasons. They help to win financial support and increase membership. They spread knowledge and give the group the chance to establish something which is very important — a favourable public image. They help to create in the group's membership a sense of purpose, a feeling that something is actually being done. Without this, morale and confidence could easily dwindle.

But pressure on the public is of only secondary importance for most groups. Indeed when a group gives unusual emphasis to its public activity through, for example, demonstrations, this may well indicate its failure to command the attention of the Government. It should also be remembered that attempts to influence the general public are essentially attempts to increase the bargaining power of the group with the Government, if by more indirect methods.

Direct pressure: Westminster and Whitehall

Pressure groups have a wide range of political and administrative connections. Some groups have influence with particular MPs. Thus the NUT sponsors candidates from all three main parties with a view to having spokesmen in the House of Commons. Others may ask an MP to take up a particular case as need arises. Others may give an Honorary Vice-Presidency to an MP or offer a company directorship. Interestingly, the business connections of most MPs are associated with smaller firms or with those (such as property and advertising companies) which are concerned to develop a favourable image. To have an MP on the board (or with a declared interest) can help to improve the image of a company. The bigger organizations, such as Unilever, ICI or the large insurance companies, carry sufficient influence by themselves to make parliamentary connections less important.

MPs can be of use to interest groups in a number of ways. They can lobby other MPs and ministers informally, as well as using Question Time to obtain information, and adjournment debates or Private Members' Bills to give an issue publicity. And yet the influence which a group can have over a single MP should not be exaggerated. No MP can be obliged to support a group; nor will an MP offer support if the interests of the group conflict with those of his or her party. For this reason, although individual contacts are useful, they are not as important as those with parties, Government and the Civil Service, which very frequently are even more anxious to establish links than groups themselves.

Influence on political parties may be exercised in a number of ways. Groups supply advice, facts and statistics to parties to try to influence their strategy (for a good illustration of this see page 246). Alternatively, and far less frequently, groups operate from within parties, although no group wishes to become dominated by a party to the point where it loses its independence.

Government and the Civil Service also approach pressure groups to broaden the process of consultation, to gain information and to win consent for their policies and co-operation in carrying them out. Groups also help Government to estimate the impact of policies on public opinion. It is now understood that Governments will, as a matter of course, seek wide consultation with organized groups. As Mr Wilson said in 1966, 'It is our duty to consult with the CBI, the TUC and others'. Where legislation is involved, ideas are usually exchanged before a Bill is introduced into Parliament, and amendments may be made in committee if a group presses a point which commands general support in the House. Moreover, in some cases the power of groups can be considerable. Lord Boyle, a former Conservative Minister of Education, has acknowledged the influence of various pressure groups on educational policy-making.

There is also a wide range of contacts with the Government which are less obvious and less well known. Pressure groups are generally represented on Royal Commissions, Committees of Inquiry and advisory committees. There are over 500 advisory committees attached to departments and public boards. Group involvement in them is widespread. Finally, it should be remembered that many groups are concerned with local activities, and their success or failure depends not upon the Government but upon their relationship with local authorities.

Factors explaining the success of pressure groups

Protective groups

It is extremely difficult to generalize about the circumstances in which groups are likely to be successful. In the case of protective groups, one important factor is the degree of support they obtain from the Government. But that is not the only or even the most significant consideration. Techniques also matter. A case which is thoroughly researched and fairly presented will usually make a bigger impression than one for which no sound evidence is produced. Much too depends upon the moment at which a group is pressing a claim and upon factors such as general public feeling. The position of the miners, for example, in their major strikes of 1972 and 1974 was considerably strengthened by the widespread public sympathy they enjoyed. In their year-long strike of 1984–5 public opinion was very different and the miners were defeated. In addition, the bargaining power of a group in terms of its strategic importance in the economy, its capacity to cause inconvenience or hardship and its readiness to use the strength it has, may be decisive. This has, on occasions, made the power of some trade unions self-evident, whereas other bodies such as the National Federation of Old Age Pensioners clearly have far less bargaining power.

Promotional groups

The fortunes of promotional groups are even more difficult to explain precisely, although here too the attitude of the Government is important. For example, a group such as the CND, advocating a policy totally at variance with the Government's intentions, stands little chance of success, while one seeking to amend or develop an existing policy, such as the Child Poverty Action Group (CPAG), has far better prospects. The role of the Government can also be crucial for groups trying to advance their cause through a Private Member's Bill. Unless the Government is prepared to allow parliamentary time, the chances of the Bill reaching the statute book are remote. Governments are also mindful of electoral considerations. No cause, however worthwhile, will be enthusiastically endorsed if it would undermine the Government's popularity. Finally, much depends on the distribution of support within Parliament. If the group is opposed by the whole of the party in power, its prospects are negligible, but if it can command some support from all sides of the House, its chances are better. No Government wants to resist all outside pressure all the time.

But it is not only the Government which can determine the success of a promotional group. Parties too can help to create a climate of opinion in which success is more likely, and general public feeling can be decisive in strengthening the position of groups such as the RSPCA. When public attitudes change over generations, then groups such as the Lord's Day Observance Society can find their task much more difficult.

Two further points should be mentioned briefly. First, a pressure group is helped considerably if it receives attention from the mass media, for then it can project both its image and its objectives to a wide public at no cost to itself. Second, if it can convey through the media the impression that its private concerns are also in the public interest, it will be less easy for the Government to dismiss it as a minority concern.

Question

2 Compare the factors affecting the success of protective and promotional groups. Are the differences more impressive than the similarities?

Pressure groups: some areas for concern

Although pressure groups are now an accepted part of the political process in Britain, aspects of their work have given rise to concern. For example, how far do groups actually represent their memberships? This question is most frequently discussed in relation to trade unions (see page 252), but they are not the only groups which might fail to represent the views of their members. The danger exists with promotional groups as well, and it may in fact be more acute. A group with few, if any, branches could easily fall under the control of an articulate minority and become virtually independent of its members.

And there is a further issue. If public policy ever reflected directly the degree of pressure brought by groups, then the weak and poorly organized could expect to see their interests, however just, being neglected. Pensioners or consumers, for example, have legitimate interests but little bargaining power. Now this is precisely where the role of the Government is important. A strong pressure group may be a help to the Government, but it may also be a threat. Almost by definition, groups have no overall political perspective. They exist to further their own private enthusiasm, which may make little or no contribution to the good of the country as a whole. It is the responsibility of the Government to consider policy issues in a much broader context than most pressure groups would wish to. As J. D. Stewart has pointed out, party or government policy must derive 'from a view of society, not merely from the view of a group in society'. Moreover, once Government has reached a decision, it must have the will to enforce it. It cannot afford to be coerced by a minority, for that would be a challenge not only to its own authority but to parliamentary sovereignty. Pressure groups have an important role to play in bringing influence to bear on Parliament from without, but they cannot take over from the Government the burden of decision.

A promotional group in action: Child Poverty Action Group (CPAG)

The Child Poverty Action Group, set up in October 1965, is a good example of a promotional group. Its aim is to promote 'action for the relief, directly or indirectly, of poverty among children and families with children'. It seeks to realize this aim by bringing influence to bear upon the main political parties.

By the end of 1966 CPAG had 454 members, but ten years later that figure had risen to 2500, by which time it had an annual budget of £60,000 and a full-time staff of eleven. One-fifth of its income is drawn from individual subscriptions, publications and lecture fees, but it has also received money from trusts and the Voluntary Services Unit which is supported by the Government. Its policy is determined by a National Executive Committee elected by the membership. In 1974 nine of the fourteen members of the Executive were in academic life. The group has local branches which work on particular cases and try to develop public understanding about welfare rights. It also has close contact with the trade unions. In 1970 CPAG and the TUC agreed to advance the claims of the lower income groups, and in 1974 the group created the post of trade union officer to further mutual co-operation.

CPAG has relied almost entirely on a clear presentation of the facts to parties and Government. It has faith in reasoned argument and since 1966 has published a quarterly journal, *Poverty*, and more recently, four pamphlets a year. It has submitted memoranda to Governments and to House of Commons committees of enquiry. All its work is carefully researched and prepared. Surprisingly CPAG is not officially consulted by Government departments to which its work might be of concern, but it has managed to use the knowledge of the Civil Service to further its programme. In 1974 MPs of all parties asked 300 questions on behalf of CPAG and this gave the group much detailed information. It has also been able to promote its ideas through the mass media.

CPAG's general policy has been to try to encourage political parties to develop a comprehensive plan to abolish poverty. It has campaigned for increases in the family allowance, for a more equal distribution of wealth, higher welfare benefits, an extension of legal aid and a national minimum wage. Probably its biggest achievement has been to identify the 'poverty trap' — the tendency for low wage-earners to lose all special benefits following a small increase in earnings and therefore to be worse off. It has also helped to further understanding on the inter-relationship of wages, taxation and welfare benefits and drawn attention to the public's ignorance of benefits to which they are entitled. Whether it has had a decisive impact on public attitudes to poverty at a time when the vast majority of British people enjoy a fairly high degree of affluence may, however, be doubted.

Questions
3 Why has CPAG been a relatively influential and successful pressure group? Consider pages 245–7 before answering.
4 Does this brief study of CPAG reveal any of the 'areas of concern' over the work of pressure groups which were discussed in pages 245–6?

Trade unions and their role

Types of unions
During the 1970s, trade unions became a major power in the land. One opinion poll in 1976 revealed that in the opinion of the majority of people, Mr Jack Jones, then General Secretary of the Transport and General Workers Union (TGWU), was more powerful than the Prime Minister. It is because of the power of the trade union movement that its position needs consideration. Here we shall give particular attention to the growth in the political influence of trade unions during the 1970s.

In 1985 there were over ten million people in Britain (about half the total work-force) in over 400 trade unions. Of these, ninety-eight were affiliated to the TUC. Moreover, as Figure 40 shows, membership is concentrated in the larger unions. In 1980, the eight largest unions, each with a membership of more than 400,000, claimed 60 per cent of the total membership of unions affiliated to the TUC.

Figure 40 *Membership of principal trade unions affiliated to the Trades Union Congress and to the Labour Party 1980*

Trade Union	Membership	Affiliation to Labour Party	
		Number	Percentage
Transport and General Workers Union (TGWU)	1,887,000	1,250,000	66%
Amalgamated Union of Engineering Workers (AUEW)	1,381,000	1,009,000	73%
National Union of General and Municipal Workers (GMWU)	916,000	650,000	71%
National and Local Government Officers Association (NALGO)	782,000	Not affiliated to Labour	
National Union of Public Employees (NUPE)	699,000	600,000	86%
Association of Scientific, Technical and Managerial Staffs (ASTMS)	491,000	147,000	30%
Union of Shop, Distributive and Allied Workers (USDAW)	450,000	436,000	97%
Electrical, Electronic, Telecommunication and Plumbing Union (EETPU)	405,000	227,500	56%
Union of Construction, Allied Trades and Technicians (UCATT)	312,000	200,000	64%
National Union of Mineworkers (NUM)	257,000	243,000	94%
National Union of Teachers (NUT)	232,000	Not affiliated to Labour	
Civil and Public Servants Association (CPSA)	216,000	Not affiliated to Labour	
Confederation of Health Service Employees (COHSE)	216,000	135,000	62%
Union of Communications Workers (UCW)	202,000	192,000	95%
Society of Graphical and Allied Trades (SOGAT)	197,000	50,000	25%
National Union of Railwaymen (NUR)	170,000	180,000	106%*
Banking, Insurance and Finance Union (BIFU)	141,000	Not affiliated to Labour	
Association of Professional, Executive, Clerical and Computer Staff (APEX)	140,000	109,000	78%
Post Office Engineering Union (POEU)	131,000	78,500	60%
National Association of Schoolmasters and Union of Women Teachers (NAS/UWT)	124,000	Not affiliated to Labour	

*The NUR had more 'members' affiliated to Labour than there were in the union.

Source: Adapted from *Trades Union Congress Report*, 1981, and the Labour Party Conference Report, 1981.

Broadly speaking, unions are of four types. Of these, craft unions are the oldest and today the least important. Their membership is usually very small — being restricted to those with a particular skill — although one, the Associated Society of Locomotive Engineers and Fireman (ASLEF), has a membership of 27,000. Industrial unions, such as the National Union of Railwaymen (NUR) and the National Union of Mineworkers (NUM), consist of both skilled and unskilled workers. The general unions such as the TGWU and the GMWU, after expanding rapidly in membership in the 1970s, have recently contracted, while white-collar unions, such as the National Union of Teachers (NUT), the Civil and Public Servants Association (CPSA), and the Association of Scientific, Technical and Managerial Staffs (ASTMS), have, after a period of rapid growth, again suffered from a general decline in trade unionism in the 1980s.

Development and role

Organizations of working people have existed for centuries, but modern trade unions only began to emerge following the development of the industrial revolution in Britain in the late eighteenth and early nineteenth centuries. They were legalized by Act of Parliament in 1824, and the attitudes of trade unionists today are often more easily understood when considered in the light of the history of the movement. In 1834, for example, six labourers from the village of Tolpuddle in Dorset (the 'Tolpuddle Martyrs') were sentenced to transportation for the offence of swearing men into a union. In 1901, in the famous Taff Vale Case, unions were made responsible for losses brought on employers by strike action. In 1926 a General Strike called by the TUC in defence of the miners was easily defeated by the Government, and in the 1930s the trade unions appeared helpless as the level of unemployment in Britain rose during the depression to over three million. It is against this background of struggle and defeat that modern trade unionism must be seen.

But what is it that trade unions exist to do? According to the late Victor Feather, a former General Secretary of the TUC, 'the object of a union is to get the best possible living standard and working conditions for its members'. Trade unions make their own contribution to this end in providing benefits for disputes, unemployment, sickness and accidents for their members, as well as death and retirement grants and legal representation before various tribunals (see page 214). But this forms only a very small part of their work and amounts to an annual expenditure of less than £10 per member. Much more important are their relations with employers and with the Government. With the former, unions are involved in collective bargaining, the procedure by which management and unions negotiate to settle wage levels. They are also involved in discussions about hours and conditions of work, manning levels, redundancies, the introduction of new technology, security of employment and a whole range of other issues affecting their members. In some instances unions are being drawn more fully into management (see page 258). The involvement of unions with Government has declined in significance since the return of a Conservative Government in 1979, but was particularly important in the period of the Labour Governments of 1974–9 and will be considered separately (see page 253–5).

The organization of trade unions

The branch and the shop steward

Most trade unions are organized at four levels — national, regional, district and branch. The basic unit is the branch, consisting of between 50 and 1000 members, paying an average annual subscription of about £16 (1985). Branch meetings are usually held monthly, but the average attendance is only about 4 per cent. Branches rely heavily on voluntary work. Officials are part-timers, generally elected by a show of hands and without opposition. The most important official is the secretary, who handles correspondence and prepares the agenda and minutes for meetings.

For the vast majority of trade unionists (though not for members of 'white-collar' unions), the official with whom they are most frequently brought into contact is the shop steward. There are about 300,000 shop stewards in Britain. They represent trade unionists at their place of work, help to recruit new members, collect contributions to union funds, deal with grievances and negotiate with management on behalf of their members. They may also negotiate productivity agreements (arrangements whereby increases in production, perhaps through the introduction of new technology, are rewarded by wage increases). Shop stewards are unpaid and spend about seven hours a week on their union duties at their place of employment. This time is allowed for by management. In large plants where many unions are represented, a group of stewards often elect a convener to handle questions of common interest with management.

The essential role of the shop steward is that of conciliator. His duty is not to cause disputes but to prevent them and, if they occur, to settle them. During the last fifteen years his power has increased because of the growing tendency for bargaining to take place at plant level rather than at national level. It is an arrangement which generally satisfies both shop stewards and management, but it has decreased the influence of union national leadership and increased the possibility of unofficial disputes being started by the shop steward without national support.

Union leadership

The most obvious characteristic of the organization and structure of unions at national level is its complete lack of uniformity. Each union has its own rule book and each handles its internal affairs in its own way. The leader of most unions is the General Secretary (although in the NUM and the Amalgamated Union of Engineering Workers (AUEW) it is the President). All unions claim to be 'democratic' but see democracy in very different ways. For example, the General Secretary of the TGWU is elected by branch ballot. In 1977, 39 per cent of the membership voted to elect Mr Mostyn Evans. In the NUM, in contrast, the President and General Secretary are elected by pithead ballot. This makes voting easier for members, and on the last occasion it was used, it brought a turnout of over 75 per cent. The President of the AUEW is elected nationally by postal vote, while the General Secretary of the National and Local Government Officers' Association (NALGO) is appointed by the National Executive Council — a body of seventy elected by individual ballot.

Similar contrasts can be seen in the election of union executives which, subject to Annual Conference, decide the general policy of the union. The GMWU, the NUR and the National Union of Public Employees (NUPE), use 'block' votes in the election of their respective executive committees. This means that although only 10 per cent of the branch membership may vote in the election, the *whole* of the branch vote goes to the candidate obtaining a majority. In contrast, the executives of the AUEW and the Electrical, Electronic, Telecommunications and Plumbing Union (EETPU) are elected by postal vote, while the executive of the Union of Post Office Workers (UPW) is elected by the union's Annual Conference.

There are further differences in union organization to which it is useful to draw attention. The national elections of the NUM, EEPTU, NUPE, NUR, NUT and the National Union of Seamen (NUS) are supervised by the independent Electoral Reform Society. Others are not. Only the AUEW, EEPTU and the Union of Construction, Allied Trades and Technicians (UCATT) arrange for General Secretaries to be re-elected. In the AUEW, for example, the President and all other full-time officers have to be re-elected first after three years and subsequently every five years. In the TGWU, although industrially the power of the branches and of the shop stewards is considerable, political power is concentrated in the hands of the General Secretary. The union's executive meets only four times each year, and there is a full union conference only every other year. All the union's 500 full-time officials are appointed by the General Secretary.

Finally, in many union elections, even when a General Secretary is being elected for life, the views of the candidates are not brought out clearly. In the TGWU election addressed are forbidden, and even in other unions, when postal votes are used, members will have only the vaguest idea of the political leanings of candidates. The internal procedures of many unions do not inspire confidence, and in many cases they hold out the possibility of abuse.

Question

5 The internal organization of trade unions differs greatly. Which of the unions mentioned above appears to have the most 'democratic' structure?

The closed shop

The device of the 'closed shop' (an arrangement whereby the right to work in a particular industry is, unless a person has deep and genuine conscientious objections, dependent upon union membership) is one of the most divisive aspects of trade unionism. Unions wishing to establish closed shops received encouragement from the Trade Union and Labour Relations Acts of 1974 and 1976, and today about four million workers are in closed shops. The advantages of such arrangements from the unions' point of view are easy to see. They increase the membership and influence of unions in the place of work. They discourage the development of multi-unionism (something welcomed also by management because it enables negotiations to be conducted more easily). They enable unions to exclude those not regarded as suitable for the work being done and they guarantee that, just as all workers are supposed to benefit from negotiations conducted with management by unions, so all shall contribute to union funds.

But closed shops can also be abused very easily. By making eligibility for jobs dependent upon union membership, the closed shop can erode the freedom of individuals not to join a trade union. In 1979 the only lawful reason for refusing to enter a closed shop was that of religious conviction. In 1980–81 however the Conservative Government enacted legislation to broaden the conscience clause and to increase compensation to those losing their jobs through refusing to join a trade union (see pages 254–5).

The closed shop has particularly serious implications in the newspaper industry. If the NUJ sought to establish a closed shop (as it has not yet done), it could not only prevent anybody outside the union from contributing to newspapers, but compel the editor to join as well. The Royal Commission on the Press in 1971 recognized that the present position was unsatisfactory because of 'the potential capacity of the NUJ to influence or control editorial policies', and it urged that a press charter should guarantee the right of journalists and editors to write without union interference. No such charter has been produced.

Question

6 Consider (a) the usefulness, and (b) the morality of closed shops.

The Trades Union Congress (TUC)

Leadership of the trade union movement in Britain is vested in the TUC, whose headquarters is at Congress House in London. It has a full-time staff of only thirty, and much of its work is concerned with research and the provision of services for affiliated unions. It has the authority to investigate disputes between affiliated unions, to expel unions and to intervene in industrial disputes (although not to impose a settlement). Its own training college offers residential and correspondence courses to union officials.

The main decision-making body of the TUC is the General Council. Its thirty-eight members are elected by the Annual Congress. Affiliated unions are divided into eighteen trade groups, and seats on the General Council are allocated in proportion to members. The General Council meets monthly, and its function is to carry out the decisions of Annual Congress and to formulate policy on matters arising between Congresses. Much of its work is done through committees, of which the most important and influential in recent years has been the economic committee. This has been responsible for shaping the policy of the TUC on issues such as prices, wages and employment. The most prominent member of the General Council is the General Secretary, who is elected for life by Congress.

Responsibility for policy-making within the TUC rests with Annual Congress. Each affiliated union is entitled to send one delegate for every 5000 members. Delegates are chosen by a variety of practices, and some are mandated by their branch or district to support or oppose a particular policy. Voting at Congress is by 'block'. General Secretaries consult with their delegations and then cast a single vote on behalf of their entire membership. Thus, in 1980, Mr Moss Evans cast, on behalf of the TGWU, nearly two million votes.

The main functions of Annual Congress are to debate the Report of the General Council, to elect a new Council and to determine the general policy of the TUC. Any union is entitled to submit a motion for debate although many are 'composited' (grouped together). About sixty motions are debated each year, the majority being carried, often after a single speech. In 1976, for example, sixty-two motions were carried and only four defeated — a reality which tends to leave the General Council with considerable flexibility in implementing policy.

The influence of the TUC

It would be dangerous to exaggerate the power of the TUC within the trade union movement as a whole. The General Council is not an executive body. It can recommend and it can influence, but it cannot bind other unions to any of its resolutions. This was most clearly demonstrated between the years 1974–5 when, after the TUC had arranged a 'social contract' with the Labour Government and undertaken to link wage claims to the level of price increases, the contract was clearly broken by a number of powerful unions with the TUC unable to do anything about it.

It is also important to remember that although individual trade unions are affiliated to the Labour Party, the TUC itself is politically independent. No member of the General Council is entitled to sit on the Labour Party's National Executive Committee and General Secretaries of the TUC tend to stay away from Labour Party Conferences. This political neutrality is important because the TUC, like other pressure groups, must be ready to deal with whichever party is in power. The formation of the TUC–Labour Party Liaison Committee in 1972 suggested that the TUC was becoming more closely attached to Labour, but after Labour's election defeat in 1983 some trade unionists expressed misgivings about having so close a relationship.

The power of trade unions

Throughout the 1970s there was fairly general agreement on the fact that the power of the trade unions was increasing. Trade unions often appeared as the 'new barons' with a power and authority greater than that of Government itself. In 1969 Mr Wilson's Government abandoned its efforts to introduce new legislation on industrial relations because of trade union opposition. In 1971 Mr Heath's Government introduced its own Industrial Relations Act, but this was repealed by Labour in 1974, having been made all but unworkable because of union opposition. In 1972 five East London dockers sentenced to imprisonment under the 1971 Act by the National Industrial Relations Court were released from prison after the General Council of the TUC had called a general strike to free them. Moreover, between 1970 and 1975, with the principal exception of the postmen's strike in 1971, unions developed a sense of their own power through successful strike action. The miners' strikes of 1972 and 1974 were both triumphs for the NUM and humiliations for Mr Heath's Government. Other unions had similar, if less dramatic, successes.

After 1974 the Labour Government deliberately furthered the power and privileges of unions through the Trade Union and Labour Relations Acts of 1974 and 1976 and the Employment Protection Act of 1975. The first gave trade unions legal immunity for any breach of contract, protection against unfair dismissal and the right to set up a closed shop. The second guaranteed compensation for lay-offs and provided other benefits. Between 1975 and 1978 the Labour Government was able to win the support of the trade unions for a policy of pay restraint, but the winter of 1978–9 saw a return to free collective bargaining and considerable industrial unrest. It was widely believed that this contributed to Labour's defeat in the General Election of May 1979.

Since 1979, however, there has been a decisive change in the mood and the power of trade unions. This has two main causes. First, the great increase in the level of unemployment to over three million has reduced both the size and the bargaining power of unions. Second, Conservative Governments after 1979 pursued a policy of cautious, gradual and modest trade union reform. The Employment Act of 1980 made public money available for unions wishing to have postal ballots in their own elections, provided compensation for employees unfairly dismissed for refusing to join a 'closed shop', and confined picketing to an employee's place of work or near to it. A further Employment Act in 1982 provided a £2000 minimum award for dismissal in closed shop cases and established the principle that, if a trade union had not held a ballot within the preceding five years in which 80 per cent of the work-force had expressed their support for a closed shop, then any worker dismissed for refusing to join that closed shop could claim unfair dismissal. Further legislation in 1984 provided for the wider use of secret ballots in union elections, before strike action and for the purpose of authorizing a political levy (see page 256).

The legislation, together with the general economic climate, has helped to temper the industrial militancy of many unions. In 1982 and again in 1983, the miners voted against strike action first over pay and then over pit closures. When they did strike in 1984 over the issue of pit closures (but without a ballot), the union was comprehensively defeated after a twelve-month struggle. Within a decade much had changed.

Question
7 How useful does this section on the power of trade unions suggest that the law can be in industrial relations?

Trade unions and the Labour Party

Although about one-third of trade unionists in Britain are Conservative Party supporters the trade unions themselves have a strong political allegiance to Labour. The roots of this are historical. As Ernest Bevin, a former General Secretary of the TGWU and Labour Foreign Secretary, once said, 'The Labour Party grew out of the bowels of the TUC'. This allegiance is reflected both in the influence exercised within the Labour Party by the trade unions and in the amount of money they contribute to it. We have seen that the TUC itself is not affiliated to the Labour Party but individual unions are. In 1984, of the 104 unions affiliated to the TUC, 46 were also affiliated to the Labour Party. They accounted for 90 per cent of Labour's total membership of 6,802,000 and controlled a similar percentage of votes at Annual Conference, the party's main policy-making instrument (see page 53).

The trade unions also provide Labour with a substantial proportion of its finances through the 'political levy', the arrangement whereby members of affiliated unions pay, unless they specifically 'contract out', a small weekly contribution to Labour Party funds. In some unions, such as ASTMS, the number contracting out is very high (see Figure 40). In many other instances, however, the levy is paid out of ignorance rather than conscious choice. A recent study of postal workers showed that although 95 per cent of union members paid the levy, only 51 per cent realized that they did so. The unions are also responsible for about 95 per cent of the money raised by the Labour Party in special election appeals, and some trade unions sponsor parliamentary candidates (see page 56).

Understandably, the unions expect some return. They obtain this through the use of the 'block vote' at Labour's Annual Conference, where it is quite possible for a handful of union leaders to commit the party to a particular policy independently of the views of the party's political leadership. The 'block vote' also controls the election of eighteen of the twenty-nine seats on the Labour Party's National Executive Committee (twelve trade unionists, five women and one young socialist).

The most interesting recent development in relations between the unions and the Labour Party was the setting up of the TUC–Labour Party Liaison Committee in 1972. The committee has twenty-one members drawn equally from the General Council of the TUC, the NEC of the Labour Party and the Parliamentary Committee or, if the party is in Government, the Cabinet. The Committee has helped to promote mutual understanding which resulted not only in co-operation between the Labour Government and the unions between 1974 and 1978 over wages, but also in a much wider political influence for the unions than they have ever experienced before. To this we now turn.

Question
8 Is it desirable for the trade unions to be so closely identified with one political party?

The political influence of trade unions

Trade unions have for long been involved in politics, in the sense that tax policy and legislation relating to employment are of direct interest to their members. During the seventies, however, the scope of their political activities markedly increased.

In 1931 the TUC was represented on only one Government committee. In 1948 it sat on sixty. The setting up in 1962 of the National Economic Development Council (a body in which trade union leaders, industrialists and ministers discuss questions of common interest) marked a further stage in the expansion of union influence. Today trade unionists are prominent on a wide range of public boards, corporations and commissions, and acquire their positions through the patronage of ministers. In 1974 alone fourteen members of the General Council of the TUC received such appointments.

But the political influence of trade unions recently has gone much deeper than this, and during the period of Labour Government between 1974 and 1979 it acquired a new dimension. Then in exchange for encouraging wage restraint, union leaders were given the opportunity for regular consultations with ministers covering a far wider area than that of immediate interest to their members. One writer, Stephen Milligan, has pointed out that in 1974 the TUC gave advice to the Government on issues such as industrial and employment law, wages, prices, food subsidies, income distribution, energy, education, the social services, pensions, sex discrimination, race relations, pollution, the arts, tourism, the European Economic Community and other issues of foreign policy. In June 1976 the TUC–Labour party Liaison Committee published a list of the achievements brought about by co-operation between the unions and the Labour Government. These included improved pensions, the repeal of two pieces of legislation (the Industrial Relations Act and the Housing Finance Act) passed by the previous Conservative administration, legislation to bring development land into public ownership and the introduction of Capital Transfer Tax. Moreover, union influence on other aspects of Government policy was considerable. The agreement in the summer of 1975 to limit wage increases for twelve months to £6 per week came from a proposal by Jack Jones, and unions were also closely involved in the preparation of legislation on industrial relations and the docks. In April 1976 they were given the opportunity to influence the annual budget when Mr Healey, the Chancellor of the Exchequer, agreed to barter tax cuts for wage restraint.

All of this amounted to a considerable influence, and it helped to build up within the trade union movement the expectation that it would be consulted even about issues which would previously have been regarded as being of only secondary concern to it.

Some people suggested that there was a threat to the sovereignty of Parliament in these procedures, because very important decisions were being taken outside Parliament in private conversations between the Government and TUC. Others have said that the involvement of the TUC has broadened the process of consultation and enabled important groups to influence decision-making. Either way, the development was significant, although it was noticeable that Mrs Thatcher showed no wish to continue such extensive consultations when the Conservatives returned to power in 1979. During her administrations the political influence of trade unions appeared minimal. No longer were they invited to Downing Street for frequent consultation on economic and industrial issues. By 1985, the political influence of the trade unions, outside the Labour Party's own affairs, was negligible.

Questions
9 Are agreements such as that between the Labour Government and the unions between 1974 and 1978 desirable? Consider carefully the benefits and dangers of such partnerships.
10 Look again at pages 252–4. Is the TUC in a position to be able to honour any agreements it might make with the Government?

Industrial democracy

The last major issue is worth separate consideration. The case for industrial democracy (in which the last Labour Government showed considerable interest) is based on the view that what bedevils industrial relations in Britain is the tendency for relations between employers and employees to be characterized by conflict rather than co-operation. It is a problem most clearly reflected in the phrase, 'the two sides of industry'. Some (on both sides of industry) may prefer to see industrial relations in these terms. For example, when in 1973 the TUC produced a report in favour of industrial reform, the response from many unions was lukewarm.

Since then attitudes have gradually changed, and the arguments that partnership in industry will produce greater efficiency, that workers should be able to participate in decision-making in companies and that responsibility for the success of an enterprise should be shared between employers and employees have begun to gain ground.

Precedents for worker participation already exist in Britain and elsewhere. The National Dock Labour Board, for example, has had equal representation for unions and management since 1946. British Steel has fourteen worker directors. The TGWU has a seat on the Mersey Docks and Harbour Board, and in 1978 the Industry Secretary, Mr Varley, named seven trade union directors to serve on the Post Office Board for an experimental two-year period. Moreover, in West Germany, Holland, Norway, Sweden and Denmark, participation in management and decision-making already exists.

In view of all these considerations, the Labour Government introduced its own White Paper on Industrial Democracy in 1978. Its main proposals were:
1 Companies employing more than 500 people should be required by law

to discuss all major proposals with representatives of employees before decisions were made.

2 Joint Representation Committees (JRCs) representative of all employees should be set up to convey feelings on the shop floor to management and to open discussions on company strategy.

3 Employees should have a right to representation on company boards. In the case of companies employing more than 2000 people, employees should have a legal entitlement to representation on the *policy* board. In the first instance it is expected that one-third of directors would be employee representatives.

4 The policy board would be responsible for formulating company policy and setting objectives but not for day-to-day company management. The policy board would elect a management board of company executives on which there would be no employee representation.

Any movement towards industrial democracy clearly has its attendant difficulties. There is the danger that conflict on the shop floor could be taken into the boardroom, that attitudes would not change and that fairly prolonged educational and training programmes might be needed to equip trade unionists for their new responsibilities. But despite this, the idea of industrial democracy is a hopeful one. It offers participation and it expects responsibility. If it ever materializes, it may help to ease some of the problems which have often bedevilled industrial relations in Britain. The interest of the Conservative Government since 1979 has not been in the kind of industrial democracy discussed here. Its concern, as we have seen, has been to introduce greater 'democracy' into the internal affairs of unions themselves. That may well be desirable but some would question whether, by itself, the reform goes far enough.

Question
11 What effect might the development of industrial democracy have on
   (a) trade unions, and (b) employers?

Appendix: Britain and Europe

The background to British membership

About a hundred years ago Britain was one of the most powerful countries in the world. It owed its supremacy to the fact that it had been the first country to industrialize and had become a great trading nation, to its navy which provided security from attack, and to its Empire which offered not only markets, manpower and raw materials, but important strategical bases as well.

This supremacy made Britain distrustful of continental commitments. It wanted to trade with Europe and kept a watchful eye on developments which might threaten British interests. Otherwise, its policy was one of detachment. By the beginning of the present century, these attitudes were beginning to change. The emergence of new, powerful and often provocative states such as Germany appeared to be a threat to Britain and encouraged it to develop closer understandings with France and Russia, Britain's allies in the First World War.

After 1919, Britain played an important part in setting up the League of Nations — a clear recognition that isolation was no longer practicable. By 1945, the position had changed even more dramatically. Two great 'superpowers', the United States and Russia, had emerged and Britain, like the other states of Europe, seemed weak and insignificant in comparison. In addition, countries within the British Empire were moving rapidly towards independence. Britain clearly needed new sources of trade and a new basis for security.

In part, trading outlets were found in the Commonwealth (which emerged from the old Empire and which is a much looser organization) and in the European Free Trade Area (EFTA) set up in 1959 to promote trade between its members, Britain, Denmark, Norway, Sweden, Portugal, Austria and Switzerland. Security for Britain and eleven other countries in the 'free world' was provided through the North Atlantic Treaty Organization (NATO). This was set up in 1949 to protect Western Europe from the threat of Communist expansion which was acute in the immediate post-war years. NATO remains the cornerstone of defence policy for Western Europe.

But while Britain was involved in NATO from the start and has remained committed to it, she took no immediate part in more ambitious movements towards European co-operation which were developing in the post-war period. These were intended to promote prosperity and solidarity between the states of Western Europe so recently at war with each other. The first major achievement was the setting up in 1952 of the European Coal and Steel Community (ECSC) between France, the German Federal Republic, Italy, Belgium, Holland and Luxemburg. The treaty abolished duties on trade in coal and steel between member states and made provision for future capital investment, expansion, modernization and improved conditions in the industries.

In 1957, the six nations extended the agreement. By the Treaty of Rome they set up the European Economic Community (EEC), committing themselves to a progressive abolition of restrictions on trade between member states, the pursuit of better living and working conditions and the development of the prosperity of overseas countries. More significant, they confirmed their desire to lay the foundation for greater unity among the peoples of Europe. The following year, the six set up the European Atomic Energy Commission (Euratom) to promote the development of nuclear power for peaceful purposes. In 1967, the ECSC, EEC and Euratom treaties were merged.

Britain played no part in these developments. It was reluctant to accept the relative decline in its power and viewed with distrust the idea of close treaty obligations with other European states. Of political parties, only the Liberals gave firm support to the idea of European unity in the 1950s.

By the early 1960s, opinion was changing. The arguments in favour of entering the Community were both economic and political. On the one hand membership would give Britain access to a market of over 250 million people, which was far more conveniently situated and much larger than the market offered by her EFTA partners. The potential stimulus this could offer to British industry and trade was considerable. On the other hand, EEC membership would enable Britain to speak with a louder voice in the councils of the world; it would give it international influence which, as a small off-shore island, it could not claim for itself. And it would also help Britain to contribute to the development of 'Third World' countries.

In 1961, Britain made its first attempt to join the Communities. That application was vetoed by France in 1963 and a further British application in 1967 met with similar opposition. Not until 1 January 1973 did Britain (together with Ireland and Denmark) become members of the Community. This third application was initiated by the Conservative Prime Minister, Edward Heath, but the terms his Government negotiated were regarded as unacceptable by the Labour Opposition. When Labour returned to power in March 1974, the terms of British membership were renegotiated and the issue presented to the British people in a referendum, in June 1975. Two-thirds of those who voted in the referendum supported continued British membership. Britain remains a member of the Community, if a rather doubting and critical member. The process of integration into a Community which already existed has not been straightforward. Britain played no part in the Community during the first sixteen years of its life at a time when its institutions and policies were being developed. The Community we joined was one which had been shaped to suit the interests of its founder members and it has been less than enthusiastic about adapting itself to Britain's very different needs. For this reason Britain's membership of the EEC remains an issue. The Labour Party has favoured withdrawal, and even the most enthusiastic Europeans have acknowledged that the Community has many weaknesses and that the task of reform is a very urgent one. Critics of the Community often direct themselves at two issues — the structure and institutions of the Community and the policies it pursues. These issues are considered below.

The Community today

The Council of Ministers

The Council is the most important law-making body in the Community. Each member state has one representative on the Council — usually the foreign minister — although other ministers may serve according to circumstances. The role of ministers on the Council is to represent their own countries. They are not obliged or expected to subordinate national interests to those of the Community as a whole. The presidency of the Council changes at six-month intervals and voting is weighted. Britain, France, Germany and Italy each cast ten of the fifty-eight votes.

The Council receives and considers proposals from the Commission. Many but not all its decisions are reached by a majority. Where the vital interests of a country are at stake, decisions must be unanimous.

The Commission

This serves a different purpose from the Council. It has thirteen members — one from each of the smaller states and two from the larger ones. Commissioners are appointed by the Council of Ministers and each has responsibility for a particular area of policy. The Commission as a whole is the largest of the institutions of the Community, employing about 10,000 people at its headquarters in Brussels. They are concerned with reconciling the often conflicting viewpoints of member states and mediating between states, with initiating Community legislation by putting proposals to the Council of Ministers, and with implementing policy agreed by the Council of Ministers. In the course of this work the

Commission is often drawn into extensive consultations with, for example, the Community's Economic and Social Committee — a body representing employers, trade unions and other interest groups.

The European Parliament

It is through the European Parliament that the people of Europe are represented. The function of the Parliament is to supervise and question both the Commission and the Council of Ministers. It is a forum for debate, consultation and investigation but it has no law-making powers. It does, however, examine draft legislation and it can both suggest amendments and initiate proposals of its own. Much of its work is carried out through eighteen specialist committees.

The negative powers of the Parliament are, in principle, considerable. By a majority of two-thirds it is able to dismiss the Commission as a whole and, while it agrees the Community's annual budget jointly with the Council of Ministers, it has the power to amend or reject it entirely as it did in December 1979 and December 1984.

It was felt that when the European Parliament ceased to be a nominated body and became a directly-elected assembly, as it did in June 1979, pressure would develop for it to be given legislative powers. The demand has often been made but power remains firmly with the Commission and the Council of Ministers. The pattern of voting in the elections is varied. For example, elections do not even take place on the same day and, because in some member states voting is mandatory, levels of 'turnout' do fluctuate markedly. Finally, different voting systems are used. All states, with the exception of Britian, use some form of proportional representation and — to confuse matters further — proportional representation is used in elections in Northern Ireland. The use of the first-past-the-post systems for 78 of the 81 European constituencies in Britain has caused predictable criticism from the Alliance parties. In the second direct elections of June 1984, the Alliance parties obtained 20 per cent of the poll but failed to gain a single MEP.

The European Court of Justice

Any experiment in international co-operation such as the Common Market is bound to involve occasional friction and conflict between member states. In part, these conflicts are reconciled through the European Court, which consists of eleven judges appointed by agreement among the member states. The court exists to interpret the meaning of the treaties which form the basis of the Community, to determine the validity of actions taken by the Council of Ministers, and to hear appeals against Community institutions, member states and individuals. The rulings of the European Court are by majority and are binding on national courts and, as we have already seen (page 16), community law prevails over the national law of member states where the two conflict.

Finance

One of the most contentious issues within the Community since Britain joined in 1973 has been the issue of the budget to which all member states are required to contribute. In 1974 Britain's contribution was 10 per cent but this rose steadily to over 20 per cent in 1980. About 70 per cent of the budget is used for the purpose of agricultural support (through the Common Agricultural Policy) and from this the French benefit dispropor-tionately while Britain gains not at all. Whereas 7.7 per cent of the population of the Community as a whole is engaged in agriculture, only 2.7 per cent of Britain's population is in agriculture. But the CAP has been criticized for reasons other than that it is to Britain's financial disadvantage. Its basic purpose — to establish common prices throughout the community in order to guarantee a suitable income for farmers — has been derided as a protectionist tactic whose consequences are thoroughly objectionable. It has led, for example, to the deliberate confiscation of surplus food capacity and the sale of surplus butter to the Soviet Union at massively discounted prices. Its reform has long been on the agenda of European debate but its structure remains, in essence, unchanged.

But while Britain remains a substantial net contributor to the Community, the financial balance sheet shows some elements of gain. Money is directed by the Community to the European Social Fund (to finance, for example, occupational training and to encourage labour mobility) and to the Regional Development Fund for the provision of aid to the least prosperous areas of the Community. From both Britain has gained. Britain has also, after much persistence, managed to negotiate a reduction in the size of her contributions to the Community budget. The Fontainebleau Agreement of June 1984 settled what had been a difficult and divisive issue. It was agreed to refund to Britain some element of her contributions for 1983 and 1984 and to lower the rate of contributions for future years.

The development of the Community

As we have seen, the political arguments in favour of going into Europe figured prominently at the time of Britain's accession in 1973. Many thought the Community would give us a new voice in the world and, while these expectations have not been fully realized, the Community is still entitled to claim that its role on international questions has been constructive. Heads of government of the member states now meet (as the

European Council) three times each year. Over the past ten years, issues such as Rhodesia and the Middle East have been considered by the Community and ministers have also drawn up a code of conduct on employment practices for companies of member states operating in South Africa. In 1978, the Community began to develop an energy policy recognizing the need to cut dependence on imported energy to 50 per cent. In the same year the Community signed a trade agreement with China, and negotiations directed towards gaining better access to Japanese markets also made progress. One of the most important international agreements concerning members of the Community was the Lome Convention of 1975 — an agreement on trade and mutual co-operation with forty-six developing countries.

The Community has also taken steps in recent years towards the realization of its broad economic objectives. Between 1973 and 1977 tariffs on industrial products were eliminated and in 1978 heads of government meeting at Bremen decided on a common approach to economic problems. Advocates of the European cause hope that the next decade may see further developments towards integration and co-operation.

Acknowledgements

Thanks are due to the following publishers and authors for permission kindly granted to reproduce from copyright works:

Mr Frank Allaun MP for an extract from a letter to *The Times*, 8 July 1975.

BBC, Radio Three and The Right Honourable Edward Heath MBE, MP for an extract from a broadcast, 'How Cabinet Government Works', 12 March 1976.

B.T. Batsford Ltd: Geoffrey Alderman, *British Elections* (1978).

Lord Boyd-Carpenter for an extract from a letter to *The Times*, 1 July 1977.

Jonathan Cape Ltd: the Richard Crossman Estate, *Inside View: Three Lectures on Prime Ministerial Government* (1972); Patrick Gordon-Walker, *The Cabinet* (1971).

Wm Collins Sons & Co. Ltd: R.H.S. Crossman, 'Introduction' to Bagehot's *English Constitution* (Fontana 1963); Lord Hailsham, *The Door Wherein I Went* (1975); Roy Jenkins, *Essays and Speeches* (1967).

Dod's Parliamentary Companion Ltd for an extract from *Dod's Parliamentary Companion* (1980).

Gallup Social Surveys (Gallup Poll) Ltd for an extract from the *Daily Telegraph*, February 1978.

The *Guardian* for an extract from an article by Mr Paul Rose, 23 February 1979.

HMSO: *A Guide for Visitors to the House of Commons*; Central Statistical Office (1979); *Social Trends (1979 and 1983); Local Government in Britain* (1975); *Annual Abstracts of Statistics* (1979 and 1983); all extracts reproduced with permission of the Controller of Her Majesty's Stationery Office.

Hamish Hamilton Ltd: R.H.S. Crossman, *The Crossman Diaries* (1975).

Hutchinson & Co. (Publishers) Ltd: Sir Ian Gilmour, *Inside Right* (1977).

Longman Group Ltd: Cross and Mullen, *Local Government and Politics* (1978); Enid Russell Smith, *The Home Civil Service: Modern Bureaucracy* (1974).

Macmillan, London and Basingstoke: Butler and Kavanagh, *The British General Election of October 1974* (1975); Butler and Stokes, *Political Change in Britain* (1969).

Sir David Napley for an extract from a letter to *The Times*, January 1977.

The *Observer* for an extract from a letter by C.A.R. Crosland, 23 November 1975; and for an extract from a letter by Sir Keith Joseph, 28 May 1978.

Oxford University Press: Redcliffe-Maud and Wood, *English Local Government Reformed*, Oxford University Press 1974.

Penguin Books Ltd: Edward Boyle, Anthony Crosland, Maurice Kogan 1971, *The Politics of Education* (Penguin Education Special 1971), pp. 177–9 and 182–4; Maurice Kogan and William van der Eyken, Dan Cook, Claire Pratt, George Taylor 1973, *County Hall: The Role of the Chief Education Officer*, pp. 34–5; both reprinted by permission of Penguin Books Ltd.

The Political Quarterly for an extract from an article by Patrick Seyd on the Child Poverty Action Group.

Mrs Joyce Purser for an extract from a letter to *The Times*, January 1977.

The Right Honourable Lord Shawcross GBE, QC for an extract from a letter to *The Times*, 10 July 1975.

The Spectator for an extract from an article by Mr J. Enoch Powell MP, 11 December 1976.

Spokesman (the publishing imprint of the Bertrand Russell Foundation): Frances Morrell, Spokesman pamphlet No. 57 (1977).

His Honour Judge Starforth Hill QC for an extract from a letter to *The Times*, January 1977.

Sweet & Maxwell Ltd: K.J. Eddy, *The English Legal System* (1977).

The Times for an extract from an article by Mr Eric Heffer, 30 January 1978.

Mr Peter Webster QC for an extract from a letter to *The Times*, January 1977.

Weidenfeld (Publishers) Ltd: Sir Harold Wilson, *The Governance of Britain* (1976).

Every effort has been made to trace the owners of copyright material. The author apologizes for any omissions, and would be grateful to know of them, so that acknowledgement may be made in future editions.

Index